Cold War women

MANCHESTER
UNIVERSITY PRESS

Cold War women

The international activities
of American women's organisations

HELEN LAVILLE

MANCHESTER UNIVERSITY PRESS
Manchester and New York

distributed exclusively in the USA by Palgrave

Published by Manchester University Press
Oxford Road, Manchester M13 9NR, UK
and Room 400, 175 Fifth Avenue, New York, NY 10010, USA
www.manchesteruniversitypress.co.uk

Distributed exclusively in the USA by
Palgrave, 175 Fifth Avenue, New York,
NY 10010, USA

Distributed exclusively in Canada by
UBC Press, University of British Columbia, 2029 West Mall,
Vancouver, BC, Canada V6T 1Z2

British Library Cataloguing-in-Publication Data
A catalogue record for this book is available from the British Library

Library of Congress Cataloging-in-Publication Data applied for

ISBN 0 7190 5856 2 *hardback*

First published 2002

10 09 08 07 06 05 04 03 02   10 9 8 7 6 5 4 3 2 1

Typeset in Palatino
by Servis Filmsetting Ltd, Manchester, UK
Printed in Great Britain
by Biddles Ltd, Guildford and King's Lynn

To John and Elizabeth Laville

Contents

Acknowledgements

My father has a hatred of credits at the end of films, seeing them as an unnecessary vanity. He explains that when a copper fitting left the factory he worked at, the box was not weighed down with paper listing 'Primary Production: John Laville'. Acknowledgements in books often serve a similar purpose to film credits – there is a serious thank you to people who helped in a serious way, and then a gratuitous list of family, friends, colleagues and pets. I hope he will forgive this unnecessary vanity. Everyone I know and respect reads acknowledgements first. People who only thank librarians and funding bodies need to get out more. Besides, librarians are paid to help you. Your friends may have been putting up with your endless references to 'the book' for years, just on the chance of earning a place in the acknowledgements.

I would like to acknowledge the assistance of the librarians at the Sophia Smith Collection, Smith College, the Schlesinger Library, Radcliffe Institute, Harvard University, and the Special Collections department of Syracuse University. In particular I would like to mention what a pleasure it is to work at the Mary McLeod Bethune Memorial Museum housed in a beautiful brownstone building in Washington, DC. Since I was the only researcher there that week, the archivist closed for lunch when I was hungry, made photocopies the minute I requested them and played classical music. In the evening the museum shut and I made my way to the impersonal National Archives, where hostile librarians stared at me suspiciously, seemingly convinced I was there with the sole intention of scribbling across all their documents with a ballpoint pen I had somehow hidden about my person. I would like to thank Marlen E. Neumann for kind permission to quote from the papers of Ruth Woodsmall.

For very serious help with the book I would like to thank my supervisor Richard King and my examiners Margaret Walsh and Rhodri Jeffreys-Jones. Their criticisms were invariably constructive and to the point. Andrew Johnstone generously shared his work and thoughts on American internationalism.

In the gratuitous list I would like to thank my family, especially Steven, Jim, Dave and Jenny. Janet, Martin, Jonathan, Katy and Emma provided a welcome and much loved retreat. My necessary angels were Solange, Aengus, Adrian, Alistair, Francesca, Liam, Graeme, Matthew, Emma, Michael and Lauren. I especially want to thank Maria, with whom I have shared the writing of thesis and book, child-bearing, child care, numerous coffee-breaks, lunches, dinners, large quantities of wine, shopping, holidays and an ice-cream maker. We know how to live. My children, Ryan and Lauryn, and their partners in crime, Jake and my lovely goddaughter Lily, offered no help at all (except for the bit on transnational identities, which they explained to me over a Ribena and a rusk). Their total lack of interest was valuable beyond measure.

In the not-at-all gratuitous list I would like to thank Scott, for emotional support, intellectual inspiration, spell-checking and fact-checking. Any mistakes are, of course, his. I cannot imagine any further ways I could have abused shamelessly his good nature.

Finally, without any apology, I thank my parents, John and Elizabeth Laville, to whom I dedicate this book.

List of abbreviations

AAUW	American Association of University Women
APC	American Peace Crusade
BMD	ballistic missile defence
CAW	Congress of American Women
CCCMF	Carrie Chapman Catt Memorial Fund
CCCW	Committee on the Cause and Cure of War
CCF	Congress for Cultural Freedom
CCUNR	Citizens Committee for United Nation's Reform
CFA	Committee for Free Asia
CIA	Central Intelligence Agency
CIER	Committee for International Educational Reconstruction
CofC	Committee of Correspondence
CWWA	Committee of Women in World Affairs
DFD	Demokratische Frauenbund Deutschlands
ECOSOC	Economic and Social Council
FCDA	Federal Civil Defense Administration
FOA	Foreign Operations Administration
FOR	Fellowship of Reconciliation
GFWC	General Federation of Women's Clubs
HICOG	High Commissioner in Germany
HUAC	House on Un-American Activities Committee
IAW	International Alliance of Women
ICFTU	International Confederation of Free Trade Unions
ICW	International Council of Women
IFBPWC	International Federation of Business and Professional Women's Clubs
IFUW	International Federation of University Women
LWV	League of Women Voters

NAACP	National Association for the Advancement of Colored People
NAWSA	National American Women's Suffrage Association
NCCW	National Council of Catholic Women
NCJW	National Council of Jewish Women
NCNW	National Council of Negro Women
NCSAF	National Council for Soviet–American Friendship
NCW	National Council of Women
NFBPWC	National Federation of Business and Professional Women's Clubs
NOW	National Organisation of Women
OEF	Overseas Education Fund (of the Women Voters)
OMGUS	Office of Military Government of the United States
PSB	Psychological Strategy Board
SPD	Social Democratic Party
UN	United Nations
UNESCO	United Nations Educational, Scientific, and Cultural Organization
UNICEF	United Nations International Children's Emergency Fund
UNRRA	United Nations Relief and Rehabilitation Administration
USIA	United States Information Agency
WIDF	Women's International Democratic Federation
WILPF	Women's International League for Peace and Freedom
WOMAN	World Organization for Mothers of All Nations
WSP	Women Strike for Peace
WTUL	Women's Trade Union League
WUUN	Women United for the United Nation
YMCA	Young Men's Christian Association
YWCA	Young Women's Christian Association

Introduction

In January 1945, *Life* magazine published a special edition on 'The American Home'. The edition included blueprints for the new American home, articles on the latest developments in domestic technology and advice for couples planning the purchase of their new home. An editorial recognised that the search for domestic contentment owed much to the disorientating and dislocating effects of the Second World War, 'The trials and separations of war have made real to millions of Americans the beauties and contentment of home. As a sentimental notion, the home today is a great success'.[1] The manufacturers of white goods, anxious to secure post-war markets and a share of the accumulated savings and credit options of the new homesteaders, nurtured and encouraged a nationwide collective nesting. Maytag offered pictures of their gleaming yet to be built washing machines as a fantasy in delayed gratification, promising, 'You've waited a long, long time for a new washer. But there'll come a day when Uncle Sam will say, "Go ahead" . . . Then we can start making those handsome new "post-war" Maytags we have planned for you'.[2] The end of the war would mean fulfilment for these dreams of domesticity as Kelvinator promised, 'When you come home to stay . . . we'll live in a kingdom all our own . . . A kingdom just big enough for three . . . with a picket fence for a boundary'.[3] An advertisement from Roger Brothers cutlery expanded the theme, 'It's what every girl wants, I guess. Happiness. And somehow, that's all wrapped up with a home'.[4]

The home, as a reward for the bravery of Americans in facing the perils of the Second World War, was a cultural, social and physiological construction, fuelled by the economic needs of the post-war conversion economy and funded and subsidised through the provisions of the GI bill. As a national icon, however, the new domestic ideal owed its longevity to the emerging context of the Cold War. Americans may have spent the war dreaming of their future life of security in their suburban homes but the explosion of atomic weaponry effectively destroyed the idea of a safe home front. The physical threat to the idea of the home as a private haven was matched by political and cultural anxieties that invaded the sanctity of the home. The Rosenberg spy trial implicated domesticity in subversion, communism and treason. The home, rather than a retreat from politics, was exposed as a hidden hotbed of radicalism. Films such as *My Son John* hammered home the message that communism began at home. The idea of the home as a private retreat, which had been nurtured by the war years, seemed increasingly defenceless in the face of the encroaching physical, political and emotional public threats and demands. The vulnerability of the private realm, however, did not result in a widespread recognition of the permeability of the boundaries between private and public worlds. Instead, as Elaine Tyler May has argued, Americans responded to the destruction of the reality of a secure home front, not by abandoning the domestic ideal but by retreating further into domestic fantasies. Tyler May asserts, 'The home seemed to offer a secure private nest removed from the dangers of the outside world . . . The self-contained home held out the promise of security in an insecure world'.[5]

The image of the happy housewife, which has come to dominate our idea of American women in the 1950s, should be understood not as historical fact but as a cultural fantasy. As historians such as Susan Ware, Susan Lynn and Joanne Meyerowitz have shown, the happy housewife was not the limit of women's ambitions or activities in the post-war period. Women's public role during the war may have contributed to longing for a return to the private home, both as a personal respite and as a symbolic restoration of national order and normality. However, as Cynthia Enloe explains, 'Despite all . . . state and private attempts to restore the status quo, expectations of women and men are irrevocably changed by their war-time experiences and women do not suddenly lose their hard-won skills or their new sense of public place'.[6]

The longevity of the myth of the happy housewife, ironically, owes less to those who advocated and promoted it, and more to those who critiqued it, notably Betty Friedan. Friedan's insistence on the centrality of the domestic life to the experience of women in the post-war period, expressed in her influential book *The Feminine Mystique*, has played a large role in the perpetuation of the myth of the happy housewife. However, historians have begun to question the accuracy of Freidan's account, suggesting that her account of women's experience in what she called 'the comfortable concentration camps of suburbia' is a flawed one. Susan Ware has noted concisely: 'Friedan . . . overdrew her pictures of the 1950s. Not only was the Feminine Mystique not a phenomenon unique to the post-war world, but many women managed to lead active and interesting lives, even at its height'.[7] Ware points to Friedan's own survey of her classmates at Smith College, which showed that three-quarters of the respondents had interests outside the home and their families that they found satisfying. Ware's conclusion, based on League material, is that the mythology of the happy housewife has obscured the importance of voluntary associations, such as the League of Women Voters (LWV), as a political outlet for American women. Historian Susan Lynn concurs, arguing that the contribution of American women through 'a loose coalition of organizations committed to progressive social reform' has been overlooked, not least because of a belief in the ubiquitous nature of the limited and limiting experience of 1950s domesticity.[8] Joanne Meyerowitz concludes, 'Whilst no serious historian can deny the conservatism of the post-war era or the myriad constrains that women encountered, and unrelenting focus on subordination erases much of the history of the post-war world'.[9] Susan Ware summarised in her study of the LWV:

> Did the League members of the 1950s suffer from a terminal case of the feminine mystique? Not at all. Rarely in the volumes of survey material or in its supporting correspondence was there any manifestation of frustration, boredom, or conflict between activity outside the home and women's domestic roles. There was no hint of defensiveness about being a modern, activist woman volunteer of the 1950s. In fact the [League] survey presented strong evidence that the members were quite fulfilled by combining familial roles with participation in local and community affairs.[10]

The cultural icon of the happy housewife, then, was an advertiser's dummy, rather than a role model.[11] American women did not slavishly follow her example, seeking contentment and excitement entirely through the careful purchase and use of white goods. The work of historians such as Meyerowitz, Ware and Lynn has challenged the conventional historical wisdom on the inactivity and domestic isolation of women in 1950s America. Historians have begun to bring American women out of the kitchen.

To date, however, this re-examination has been predominately 'domestic'. The gendered configuration of the public/private division is still unchallenged in the area of international relations where the construction of the nation into the public/private and masculine/ feminine has been mirrored and, arguably, magnified. As Rebecca Grant argues, 'International Relations adopted several classic concepts of political theory without investigating the gender bias in them, therefore International Relations duplicates the pattern of them'.[12] An example of this gendered division between the international and domestic realms can be found in the work of former State Department official Louis Halle. In a description of the inevitable failure of international world government innocently entitled *The Society of Man*, Halle argued that cultural and social differences between nations should be respected since they could not be resolved. Illustrating his point, Halle argued, 'Having made our own conceptual model, however, we men cannot agree on what it should be. In some parts of the world girls are considered adult and ready for marriage at thirteen; and in others they have to be nineteen'.[13] Halle's example of the differences between states in the conduct of internal domestic affairs is described in gendered terms, as the male control of women's (or to use his term, 'girl's') lives.

A more famous example can be seen in the oft-quoted 1959 'kitchen debate' between Vice-President Nixon and Soviet Premier Nikita Khrushchev. In her narration of the event Elaine Tyler May asserted, 'Nixon insisted that American superiority in the cold war rested not on weapons, but on the secure, abundant family life of modern suburban homes', and quoted Nixon's comment, 'I think that this attitude towards women is universal. What we want is to make easier the life of our housewife'.[14] Tyler May uses the kitchen debate to illustrate the interconnection between the public sphere of Cold War politics and the private sphere of the suburban home. Contained in their sparkling well-equipped modern kitchens, American housewives served as lipsticked symbols of the superiority of American capitalism.

Within this construction, American women's role in Cold War internationalism has been restricted to the symbolic level. While they might be used to demonstrate the superiority of the American system to a global audience, their participation is passive rather than active.

However important this use of women as symbols, representing American domesticity to the world, it should not elide the actual contribution of women to international relations as active participants. In their study of the relationship between women, state and the nation, Nira Yuval-Davis and Floya Anthias have challenged accounts of women and international relations that accept the symbolic, non-active participation of women at face value. They assert, 'We find it vitally important to emphasise that the roles women play are not merely imposed upon them. Women actively participate in the process . . . reproducing and modifying their roles'.[15]

Even before the end of the Second World War, leaders of American women's organisations were making strenuous efforts to maintain and increase their participation in international relations. While this initially went through traditional channels of internationalism such as the State Department, American women quickly realised that the biggest scope for their contribution lay in the exploitation of the emerging links between the public world of government and their position as representatives of private associations. Co-operation between the government and the private sphere has long been a feature of American foreign relations. Emily Rosenberg has shown in her study of American economic and cultural expansion from 1890 to 1945 that private groups were frequently an integral part of the foreign policy of the US government.[16] Yet at no time was the importance of extra-governmental international relations more significant in the USA than the Cold War years. The US government consistently framed international relations within the Cold War framework not as a battle of national strategic, diplomatic, military and economic interests, but as a wider struggle of opposing ways of life. Within this context the traditional divisions between private organisations and public representatives became increasingly blurred. The US government sought and elicited the co-operation of private groups in the promotion of their foreign policy. By sponsoring exchanges and tours and encouraging non-governmental relationships, the US government drew private organisations into a network of state–private links. The distinction between a State Department employee and a representative of an organisation such as the LWV or the National Association for the Advancement of Colored People (NAACP) became increasingly difficult to make, both being funded by their government to travel the world as advocates for the USA.

This book explores the relationship between mainstream American women's organisations and their government in the early years of the Cold War. This relationship challenges traditional understandings of women and international relations in three ways. First, the history of the international work of American women's organisations is part of a growing body of evidence that challenges the prevailing view of the 1950s as a period of inactivity and political apathy for American women. Chapter 1 explores the importance of American women's associations in offering American women an active role outside the home, a function that had been recognised and applauded by feminist historians of the pre-suffrage era. This chapter investigates the continuing relevance of the 'separate sphere' of women-only organisations after the extension of suffrage. American women's organisations in the twentieth century continued to offer women an opportunity and a justification for a role outside the private confines of the home. Furthermore the public activism of American women's associations was not restricted to domestic issues. American women in the post-war years utilised a range of strategies in order to claim an international role that was seemingly denied them by a cultural discourse that defined them through their location in the private sphere.

American women's organisations justified and explained women's interest and responsibility in international relations, making repeated references to an international sisterhood. However, this international discourse, which implied the primacy of international relationships based on gender over claims of national loyalty, did not prevent the leaders of American women's organisations from also demanding an increased role as representatives of and participants in national government.

Second, the links between women's associations and the US government challenge conceptions of international relations that rely on traditional diplomatic history focused upon the international relations of official government bodies as representatives of the state. In their co-operation with the government, American women became

part of a complex web of links between government agencies and voluntary 'private' associations. Chapter 2 considers the traditional importance placed on voluntary associations in American life as guardians of freedom and as a medium for the activities of private citizens outside the processes of the public sphere of government. The chapter evaluates how the Cold War both relied upon the ideological value of the 'private' status of voluntary associations, and undermined this distinction as private associations co-operated with their government in international work. This new relationship is investigated in Chapter 3, through the case study of post-war West Germany, exploring how American women's associations worked with the US government to export their example of voluntary participation as a model for German women.

Finally this book seeks to challenge the idea of an international gender-based identity. During the Cold War, American women's associations may have mouthed words of sisterhood and commonality, but they sought and assumed ascendancy based on their national identity as Americans. They shared and spread the belief of Henry Luce that the end of the Second World War would usher in an 'American Century'. Chapter 3, on post-war West Germany, explores the contradictions between American women's assertions of sisterhood and equality with West German women and their assumption of a position of superiority based on national identity. Chapter 4 explains how American women's organisations moved from espousing an internationalist position, based on their gendered identity, to advocating a position more in line with the Cold War agenda of their government. Chapter 5 explores the struggle of American women's organisations to maintain their commitment to peace, upon which many of their claims to an international position were based. At the same time they repudiated and actively campaigned against international peace campaigns, which they saw as Soviet-sponsored. Chapter 6 presents the history of the World Organization for Mothers of All Nations (WOMAN), an organisation of women established by journalist Dorothy Thompson to harness women's interest in peace to a global pressure group. This effort at internationalism was thwarted by established mainstream women's organisations that sought to produce and police a coherent national position. Having discredited the efforts of a genuinely private and non-governmental organisation to forge international connections, leaders of mainstream women's organisations instead offered the chance to communicate with American women through the medium of a new organisation, the Committee of Correspondence (CofC). Chapter 7 explores how this organisation advertised itself to women across the globe as a private non-governmental international group, even though it received its financial support from the Central Intelligence Agency (CIA).

The aim of this book is to challenge women's exclusion as actors from the international dimension of the Cold War. While gender is becoming an increasingly central trope to studies of the Cold War, women as actors, rather than as symbols, metaphors and poster-girls for American democracy, remain elusive. In defining themselves as Cold War Women, leaders of American women's organisations sought an international agency that would allow them to challenge, manipulate and redefine the role of women in international relations. However it is not my intention simply to recover American women's international activities. Rather, I seek to explore the way in which American women, under the cover of an international identity, followed an explicitly national agenda.

Women's internationalism has too often been written about in heroic terms. Asserting a sisterhood with women across the globe, women have frequently invoked an idealised vision of women as internationalists. Internationalism has provided women with an unassailable position from which to preach harmony, demand action and deflect criticism. With laudable aims of peace, international understanding and unproblematic conceptions of maternal benevolence, women have insisted on their moral superiority in the international sphere. While men have supposedly represented the embattled, competitive and destructive interests of political nations, women have argued that they stand for bigger international issues.

The ideal of an international sisterhood is a problematic one, however. Indeed, the idea of sisterhood between groups of women, even those within the same nation, has come under fierce attack with a widespread refusal to accept the idea that a shared gender identity exists. Feminist theorist Donna Harraway, for example, has asserted, 'There is nothing about "being" a female that necessarily binds women'.[17] African-American feminist Audre Lorde concurs, 'There is a pretense to a homogeneity of experience covered by the word *sisterhood* that does not, in fact, exist'.[18] Differences among women that problematise the construction of sisterhood include claims of race, class, ethnicity, age, demographic status and sexuality.

'International' sisterhood is further challenged because national loyalty remains of primary concern for most women. Under historical examination, women's position as 'internationalist' generally falls apart, rarely surviving the outbreak of national tensions. Carrie Chapman Catt's assertions of international sisterhood could not prevent her belief that American women had more to gain by siding with their national brothers than with their global sisters. In the UK, Christabel Pankhurst abandoned internationalism in favour of an

almost rabid patriotism. While women such as Elizabeth Gurley
Flynn and Alice Paul stood out against the war, their motivation was
often more to do with national strategies than international loyalties.

In her excellent study of international women's organisations in
the period before the Second World War, Leila Rupp explains that the
vibrant internationalism she examines throughout her book waned in
the post-war period. This change, she suggests, was the result not just
of the tremendous disruptions of the war, but also of the new attitude
of the American members and the emerging Cold War. American
women's new approach to internationalism was based less on partnership and communication with their counterparts in other countries, and more upon taking a position in the developing Cold War.
Rupp notes, 'The cold war enveloped the world of international
women's organizations . . . The Second World War marked a turn, not
an end or beginning, for international organizing among women'.[19]

American women's associations embraced internationalism in
the wake of the Second World War, but it was an American internationalism, based on a national righteousness and the crusading zeal
of the victors in a moral war. The developing Cold War ensured that
the pro-American leanings of this internationalism hardened, becoming increasingly urgent in the face of the communist threat. That
American women's organisations should see their work as a vital part
of the Cold War effort is not surprising. President Truman explained
the Cold War to Congress as a stark choice between two ways of life:

> At the present moment in world history nearly every nation must
> choose between alternative ways of life. The choice is too often not a
> free one. One way of life is based upon the will of the majority, and
> is distinguished by free institutions, representative government, free
> elections, guarantees of individual liberty, freedom of speech and
> religion and freedom from political oppression.[20]

As one of the 'free institutions' alluded to by Truman, American
women's organisations were determined to secure victory for their
way of life. Embarking on their international mission after the Second
World War with the conviction that their way was the best way,
American women quickly concluded that, in the face of encroaching
communism, their way was the only way. The Cold War and
American women's associations' role in it left no room for the multi-
plicity of viewpoints, ideologies and beliefs encompassed within a
true internationalism.

10 *Cold War women*

Notes

1   *Life*, 22 January 1945.
2   *Life*, 15 January 1945.
3   *Life*, 22 January 1945.
4   *Life*, 26 February 1945.
5   E. T. May, *Homeward Bound: American Families in the Cold War Era* (New York: Basic Books, 1988), p. 3.
6   C. Enloe, *The Morning After: Sexual Politics at the End of the Cold War* (Berkeley, CA: University of California Press, 1993), p. 62.
7   *Ibid.*, p. 290.
8   S. Lynn, 'Gender and post World War II progressive politics: A bridge to social activism in the 1960s U.S.A.', *Gender and History*, 4:2 (1992).
9   J. Meyerowitz, 'Introduction', in J. Meyerowitz (ed.), *Not June Cleaver: Women and Gender in Post-War America 1945–1960* (Philadelphia, PA: Temple University Press, 1994), p. 4.
10 *Ibid.*, p. 290.
11 Historian Eugenia Kaledin has pointed out that the image of the 'Happy Housewife' is for the most part drawn from the imagery of advertising. Kaledin asserts, 'It may be inevitable that historians of the media age over-use advertising images to define the entire society'. However, this inevitability should not blind historians to the fact that advertisers had a heavy investment in portraying the domestic realm as a haven of contentment. Eugenia Kaledin, *American Women in the 1950s: Mothers and More* (Boston, MA: G. K. Hall and Co., 1993), p. 62.
12 R. Grant, 'The sources of gender bias in international relations theory', in R. Grant and K. Newland (eds), *Gender and International Relations* (Milton Keynes: Open University Press, 1991), p. 9.
13 L. J. Halle, *The Society of Man* (London: Chatto and Windus, 1965), p. 133.
14 May, *Homeward Bound*, pp. 16–18.
15 N. Yurval-Davis and F. Anthias (eds), *Women, Nation, State* (London: Macmillan, 1989), p. 11.
16 E. Rosenberg, *Spreading the American Dream: American Economic and Cultural Expansion 1890–1945* (New York: Hill and Wang, 1982).
17 Quoted by C. Crosby, 'Dealing with differences', in J. Butler and J. W. Scott (eds), *Feminists Theorize the Political* (New York: Routledge, 1992), p. 138.
18 A. Lorde, *Sister Outsider: Essays and Speeches* (Freedom, CA: The Crossing Press, 1984), p. 116.
19 L. J. Rupp, *Worlds of Women: The Making of an International Women's Movement*, (Princeton, NJ: Princeton University Press, 1997), p. 47.
20 As quoted in S. Lucas, *Freedom's War: The US Crusade against the Soviet Union 1945–56* (Manchester: Manchester University Press, 1999), p. 7.

1

'No limit to what I can do': American women's voluntary associations

The role of American women's voluntary associations in offering their members an opportunity to become politically active before the extension of suffrage in 1920 is well documented.[1] In her influential article 'Separatism as strategy: Female institution building and American feminism 1870–1930', Estelle Freedman recognised:

> A major strength of American Feminism prior to 1920 was the separate female community that helped sustain women's participation in both social reform and political activism . . . Most feminists did not adopt the radical demands for equal status with men that originated at the Seneca Falls Convention of 1848. Rather they preferred to retain membership in a separate female sphere and one in which women would be free to create their own forms of personal, social and political relationships.[2]

This 'separate sphere', however, lacked longevity. Freedman asserts that with the advent of suffrage and the birth of the 'New Woman' the appeal of female-only institutions waned, to be replaced by women who were eager to assimilate 'in the naive hope of becoming men's equals overnight'.[3] While it is undeniable that, following the extension of suffrage, membership in women's organisations underwent a decline, historians have begun to re-evaluate the role of 'separate female organisations and institution building' post-suffrage. Freedman has reconsidered her position, acknowledging, 'New historical research . . . has shown the ways that separatism or female institution building did in fact survive as a reform strategy after 1920'.[4]

Feminist historians have lauded the role of nineteenth-century women's organisations in fostering female activism in a period where the feminine ideal was the domesticity of 'true womanhood'.

However, their activities during the 'feminine mystique' (what Rupp and Taylor have called 'the traditional ideal dressed in fifties garb'[5]) have been less appreciated. This may in part be ascribed to a contemporary feminist dislike of voluntary associations as a method of either consciousness-raising or political activity.[6] As Susan Ellis and Katherine Noyes point out in their 1978 study, '"Volunteering" is often synonymous with acts of charitable social welfare and not connected to other voluntary involvement such as politics and policy making . . . What is recorded by most histories is a clear division of roles: we remember the men for voluntary political reform and the women for their voluntary social welfare acts'.[7] Contemporary dissatisfaction with the volunteer role was described by political theorist Irene Dubrowski as a concern that 'volunteerism . . . [constitutes a] sexist institution that robs women of their potential economic resources and delegates them to the status of second-class citizens'.[8] Identifying the women volunteer as 'the un-named political woman', Dabrowski lambasts the National Organisation of Women (NOW) for defining volunteerism as 'a sexist institution that robs women of their potential economic resources and delegates them to the status of second class citizens'.[9]

To ignore the role of post-suffrage women's organisations is to overlook an important stage in the political development of American women. Their organisations served as an important forum for activism at a time when there was little enthusiasm for any role for women outside the home. They were, to use Susan Lynn's phrase, a bridge between pre-war progressive activities of women reformers and the involvement of women civil rights, anti-war and feminist movements in the 1960s.[10] Voluntary associations, by avoiding a direct challenge to cultural tropes which placed women within the domestic and outside the political sphere, were instrumental in allowing and encouraging American women to expand their horizons. If traditional political activities were closed to women, either legally or through social and cultural restrictions, involvement in a voluntary association could be the only socially acceptable way to escape from the monotony of their domestic lives. A United States Information Agency (USIA) report, 'Profile of America', approvingly documented the involvement of a 'Homemaker and Civic Worker' in the LWV. Mrs Mancourt Downing asserted, 'I don't believe in working mothers', but recognised the value of activities outside the home, 'I do believe all women are better wives and mothers if they realize there is more to life than their home and local surroundings'.[11] Mrs Downing was frank about the escape that membership in the League offered: 'After the baby came . . . I felt as if I were in a vacuum with only diapers and bottles around me. I heard about the League of Women Voters and joined because I felt that it was a place where I could work and gain knowledge at the same time'.[12]

The reasons why American women continued to direct their energies through voluntary associations, even after they were supposedly granted access to mainstream politics, can be described in similar terms as their motivation for involvement before suffrage, 'On the one hand, the negative push of discrimination in the public, male sphere, and on the other hand the positive attraction of the female world of close personal relationships and domestic institutional structures'.[13] Both of these factors were present after the Second World War. Perhaps the most obvious reason women pursued careers in voluntary associations rather than in more mainstream political areas were the problems in entering what was still a male stronghold. Susan Hartmann explains, 'Women's eligibility for voting and office-holding had . . . left unshaken the cultural norms which defined politics as masculine'.[14] Prejudice against women as politicians was common, even among women themselves. A 1945 Gallup survey revealed that only 26 per cent of men and 37 per cent of women would vote for a woman for President, even if she were the best qualified candidate.[15] The women's magazine, *Woman's Day*, while encouraging its readers to get involved in local politics nevertheless, warned:

> Rule Three: Don't try to fly above your ceiling . . . Few women rise to the highest altitudes in politics . . . The main difficulty obviously is biology. Being a woman is almost a full time job. So is big time politics . . . So the men who run political organizations are sometimes reluctant to push a young woman ahead as rapidly as her ability merits. 'Why invest all the time and effort to build up the gal into a household name', remarked a political friend of mine about one such case, 'when she's sure to cross out of the game to have a couple of kids at just about the time we're ready to run her for mayor?' The prudent woman thus sets a realistic ceiling on her political ambitions.[16]

For many women, family obligations were the ceiling. Thus, the local nature of voluntary associations was a crucial advantage over mainstream political activities.[17] Susan Ware explained, 'Groups such as the League of Women Voters . . . created public roles for women denied access to the usual sources of power. And they made these roles available on the local level, where women could most easily make political contributions without necessitating drastic changes in their familial arrangements'. Activism in a woman's voluntary association offered the benefits of a 'pseudo-career' without causing a difficult confrontation with women's popularly-ascribed role as a 'homemaker'. Alice Leopold, Assistant Secretary of Labour for Women's Affairs, told participants in a 1957 'Girls Nation' conference about women volunteers who 'assumed their role as homemakers in their own communities – a role which we know is of the utmost importance. But they made an additional choice. They decided to become active citizens as well as homemakers . . . They have enjoyed their combination of career and homemaker'.[18]

 American women's organisations provided an acceptable face for this public activism. Emphasising the 'service' element of their work, voluntary associations constructed the activities of their members as those of concerned and supportive citizens, rather than frustrated or politically ambitious housewives. The National Federation of Business and Professional Women's Clubs (NFBPWC) in 1956 changed the name of their magazine from *Independent Woman* to *National Business Woman* because the earlier title tended 'to set us apart as a group of independent women interested only in ourselves'. Their President explained, 'We are independent, yes as far as earning our own livelihood. We are not independent as far as our interests in our families, our communities, our country are concerned'.[19] Dorothy Height, a veteran of various voluntary associations including the Young Women's Christian Association (YWCA), the National Council of Negro Women (NCNW) and civil rights organisations, illustrated this attitude through membership in her college sorority:

> When I was president of my sorority, Muriel Rahn, one of the very popular actresses said to me . . . 'Well Dorothy, you took the fun out of the sorority', . . . So I said back to her, 'Maybe I didn't understand it, but for me a sisterhood has to have a purpose and you don't just have a sisterhood for a sisterhood, and I don't see how it is that you cannot enjoy yourself and also do something to make life better'.[20]

Height, reflecting in 1991, concluded with an assertion of the service ethos: 'There has been a recent challenge coming from some elements of the women's movement, who hold that volunteering is sort of a feminine activity that displaces people who might otherwise have jobs and that, if women didn't volunteer, then a society might find a way to pay for the services that volunteers render. I happen to believe . . . that it would be a pretty sad society if it paid for everything that was done for everyone.'[21]

The service ethic might have been an important ideological, emotional or often religious element in American women's organisations, but it also had a practical function, training women in citizenship and activism in a non-threatening atmosphere. Anna Lord Strauss of the LWV explained:

> As a result of the great proliferation of a variety of organizations women . . . in the United States have developed considerable civic prowess. Some observers believe that there should not be so much emphasis on groups solely of women members but there is little doubt that feminine self-confidence has been nurtured in them and many women have gone on to broader interests.[22]

Strauss, considering arguments for and against changing the LWV's name, pointed out that 'good citizenship should not have a sex differential' and 'it has always been a weak spot for us to discriminate against men within our organization'. More practically, 'it would be easier to enlist contributions if "Women" was not in the name'. However, her paper concluded that the segregated nature of the LWV had important benefits, for, if the name were changed, 'some people fear that the men would gain control of the organization and would be the more forceful influence or turn it over to be staff run'.[23] Similarly the YWCA investigated the possibility of merging with the Young Men's Christian Associations (YMCA) but decided that the two organisations had radically different operating procedures. A 1958 report quoted an academic who argued, 'It becomes increasingly difficult to justify separate organizations and completely separate facilities on the basis of sex alone. It is doubtful whether there are now any significant reasons. Separateness is based mainly on personal preference, tradition and resistance to change'.[24] The report concluded, however, that there were important positive benefits to the continuation of separatism. The report reasoned that sex segregation:

> has provided and at present provides for women an autonomous agency where, in an atmosphere of religious commitment, they can (1) marshal resources to work for a greater measure of freedom for women (2) demonstrate the capacities of women to operate an institution indigenous to themselves and serve the community through

its program and (3) have a testing ground in a supportive climate for the newly-found freedoms wrested from the male-dominated society.[25]

The report concluded that co-operation, not consolidation, was the best way to ensure that the positive values of women-only voluntary associations were not lost.

Membership in a women-only voluntary association offered women the chance to pursue a rewarding career. Anna Lord Strauss explained in a working paper to a United Nations seminar, 'Since the wider participation of women in government calls above all else for the development of many inspired leaders and few of them can be paid, I should like to describe the evolution of voluntary public service, for the volunteer spirit, is, in my opinion, the key to success'.[26] Strauss explained the way in which the volunteer sector offered women an opportunity to make a career for themselves while gaining valuable leadership skills:

> There is no longer so sharp a differentiation between career women and homemakers as there once was. Women move back and forth from paid to voluntary work according to circumstances and with no loss of status . . . The advent of the competent volunteer and her increasing effectiveness in public affairs is perhaps the most valuable chapter in the history of the development of women as citizens.[27]

In undertaking leadership in a voluntary association, many American women described their activities as an important career choice. Lena Phillips, President of the NFBPWC and subsequently of its International Federation, was given this introduction to an audience in Lawrence: 'Dr Phillips was once a lawyer in New York. There came a time, however, when she realized she had to choose between her vocation and her advocation. She realized that the world could do without another lawyer, but women needed another woman.'[28] Anna Lord Strauss also chose between a salaried career and a voluntary career. She was asked to take the examination to become a Foreign Service officer in the State Department following her service at the US Shipping Board and at the War Trade Board during the First World War, but she refused, preferring to pursue a career in voluntary associations.[29] She recalled that a later director of the LWV made a similar choice, 'I always remember what Zelia Ruebhausen said when she was asked why she did voluntary work when she could have almost any professional job. She's a very bright intelligent person, and she said, "Because as a volunteer there's no limit to what I can do"'.[30]

While convinced of the importance of a career in voluntary service, American women's organisations were vocal in their belief that women must also increase their representation in mainstream politics. Lena Phillips ran for the office of Lieutenant-Governor of Connecticut in 1948 on Henry Wallace's Progressive Party ticket.[31] She frankly assured her friends in the New Zealand Federation, 'Please do not plan to visit me in the State Capitol as there is no chance of my being elected'.[32] Instead she was driven by the conviction that she must set an example of political involvement to other women. She explained to the nominating convention, 'It is not from desire, however, that I accept this nomination, but solely in the line of duty. I mention this in the hope that other members of our party may be encouraged to realize and to assume their political responsibilities'.[33] Volunteer organisations could be a stepping stone to activism in mainstream politics. Jeane Kirkpatrick, a US Delegate to the United Nations, defined two potential paths to mainstream politics for women, the first as a worker in party politics, the second through 'the volunteer route'. She argued, 'Volunteer community service and volunteer political work alike provide women without special professional or educational training for a legislative career an opportunity to acquire experience, skills and reputations that qualify them for public office'.[34]

Ironically, however, the very existence of voluntary associations may have distracted and contained women's political energies. Historian Susan Hartmann argues that, while women's organisations meant that American women 'became familiar with political issues, enjoyed opportunities for leadership and public visibility and gained self-confidence in a supportive environment', they also functioned to 'isolate women from mainstream party politics'.[35] Contemporary commentators recognised the danger. In an interview for the journal, *Women's Day*, Bertha Adkins, a Republican Party activist, asserted that the associations had 'drained off too much time, energy and resources'. Adkins argued, 'A good deal of this could be diverted to doing a job in politics'.[36] In this opinion she was joined by a young (or, as *Woman's Day* equivocated, 'youngish') senator from Massachusetts, John F. Kennedy, who told a Virginia women's club, 'This nation cannot rely upon the members of the male sex. Our political leaders must be drawn from the ranks of the most capable, dedicated citizens regardless of sex'.[37] Kennedy asserted that voluntary associations were, by themselves, insufficient for women's political talents.

American women's voluntary associations described their membership in terms of voters, citizens and consumers of policy, rather
than as potential producers of policy. Voluntary associations were
supposed to preserve liberty by keeping check on the government, so
their role was constructed in terms of the governed and the governors,
the citizens and the state. Even the name 'League of Women Voters'
stressed their role as citizens and voters, rather than policy-makers.
Lucille Koshland, in a speech marking her retirement as director of the
Overseas Education Fund (OEF) of the LWV, explained:

> I am proud of the OEF because it is a non-governmental organization
> which stresses the role of the volunteer. When we talk of the govern
> ment by consent of the governed, whom do we mean by 'the gov
> erned', whose consent is the sine qua non of our democracy? Who are
> the governed? They are not just the professionals and the experts.
> They are the business men, the housewives, the laborers, teachers
> and doctors – just plain citizens.[38]

However active, informed and intelligent they may be, the 'governed'
members of a voluntary association served as a foil, a watch, and a
check *on* government rather than as participants *through* government.
Because American voluntary associations explicitly defined themselves as extra-governmental, any emphasis on increasing the participation of women in mainstream politics risked a negation of the
importance of women's activities through the association. The strict
principle of 'non-partisanship' to which some organisations, such as
the League, subscribed often resulted in non-participation; officers of
the League were prohibited from involvement in partisan politics.[39]

This positioning meant that women's organisations often viewed
themselves as the government's servants, rather than as its equals.
Consequently the government frequently used women's organisations
while making little attempt to incorporate them into the policy-making
process. Truman's Secretary of State, Dean Acheson, far from being
unaware of the value of flattery, warmly told Eleanor Roosevelt of the
importance his department placed on the involvement of women. Mrs
Roosevelt reported to the member organisations of the Committee of
Women in World Affairs (CWWA) that Acheson 'said in so many words
that Bretton Woods would not have been adopted had it not been for

the work of women's organizations'.[40] Reassuring as this might have
been, the emphasis was clearly on women's organisations role in pub-
licising the decisions of the government rather participating in those
decisions. Nor did the wooing of women as voters translate into any
real effort to increase their role in policy-making. President
Eisenhower's electoral strategy vividly demonstrated this. A confidential memorandum, 'Consideration of a direct appeal to women by the
President', recognised the importance of the women's vote.[41] Mrs J.
Ramsey Harris, the Chair of the Women's Division of Citizens for
Eisenhower wrote: 'In my opinion, women, by and large, are still
fearful of actual political alliance and yet are increasingly and intensely
interested in good government. They do not necessarily vote with their
husbands.'[42] Eisenhower's campaigns therefore made a concerted
appeal to women, specifically in terms of domestic and spiritual values.
In a message to 594 leading Republican women, Eisenhower confided:

> More and more in recent days I've been laying plans for the cam-
> paign, I have turned for counsel to the women, especially with
> respect to the spiritual and moral aspects of our crusade. Women feel
> these values more deeply than men, I believe. Perhaps we men are
> too busy, are too hard-boiled, but with thoughts of their children and
> grandchildren in mind, and with real concern for the kind of world
> these youngsters will go into, women are mightily interested in these
> values.[43]

In fact the only woman on Eisenhower's campaign was Katherine
Howard, who served specifically as the 'Women's Advisor'.[44]
Republican women were included in the Eisenhower campaign in
very gender-specific ways. For example, the National Federation of
Republican Women's Clubs carried out highly specialised polls for
the party that returned the following form of data:

> Baker, grocer, veteran and next-door neighbour are for Ike. About
> half the milkmen are for Eisenhower, and the other half don't like Ike.
> The shoe-men are not enthusiastic. The next-door neighbor in the
> mid-west are more against or are not talking. In the Northeast or New
> England many of the neighbors will not get into discussions. The
> laundry-men are silent except in the Far West where most of them are
> for Eisenhower . . . Several women from the different areas said their
> hairdressers were for Eisenhower.[45]

Women were also encouraged to throw themselves into celebrations for Eisenhower's birthday in October, although a memo from

Eugene Munger, Director of the Eisenhower Birthday Celebrations, to Ivy Priest, Director of the Women's Division, warned, 'Do not sponsor cake baking contests. Experts tell us these contests create competition and complications among women – a thing we do not want'.[46] The culinary theme continued following Eisenhower's elections, as the National Federation of Republican Women's Clubs established a 'Kitchen Kabinet', which was to be comprised of; 'Republican women representing each of the presidential Cabinet Posts', whose job would be 'to clearly interpret to the Housewives of America the job that is being carried out in each of the departments under the Republican Administration' or, in the folksy words of the publicity department, 'keep the women of America informed on what's cooking in Washington'. The aim of the Kitchen Kabinet was 'to provide Republican women with nutritious political recipes to serve their friends and neighbors with a cup of coffee'.[47] This method of involving women in politics was very much resented by some, who believed in a more central role for women. India Edwards, who had served as an advisor to Truman, asserted in an interview:

> The men were perfectly willing to have the women help in the campaign in a menial way ... give teas and you know. But most of them around the country – not Roosevelt and not Truman – but most of the country acted as if women had no brains and that they weren't capable of anything more than a seven-year-old child could do – something of that sort.[48]

The leaders of American women's organisations may have regretted the lack of women in policy-making posts, either elected or appointed, but it was not something they necessarily pursued.[49] Because their own access to government was relatively high, the difficulties for these leaders to gain power through other means were ameliorated. Grant McConnell has argued that the function of the private association has been to enlist, on the behalf of the state, the support and co-operation of spokespeople of significant portions of the population in return for minimum concessions and rewards. McConnell asserts that the relationship between leaders of voluntary associations and their government is the 'means by which leadership elites have perennially been co-opted for the maintenance of at least a minimal unity'.[50] He argues:

> Through the private associations it has been possible to discover authoritative spokesmen for segments of the population which have

the capacity to disrupt common life. Through these leaders it has been possible to strike bargains permitting a reasonable degree of social peace, to obtain the disciplining of the segments of the population and guarantees of their performance.[51]

The rewards for co-operation with government were, for the leaders of sizeable organisations, plentiful. Perhaps the most important for them was the prestige that frequent consultation with the government carried. Truman's frequent meetings with Anna Lord Strauss and other members of the LWV served to convince her that she, on behalf of her organisation, played an important role in national and international affairs. Her somewhat patronising descriptions of meetings with Truman show that she regarded her input as important and valuable:

> We did a very good job of educating President Truman. We were very close to Truman, particularly in his first days. Mr Truman was a scared rabbit when he came into office as President. The Vice-President really wasn't very involved in what happened in those days. He was given rather formal responsibilities. When he became President he was ill at ease.[52]

Since President Truman was new and, according to Strauss, lacked confidence, she asserted that the League exerted a good deal of influence through her meetings with the President, 'I really got embarrassed because we went over to the White House so often to talk to him. I thought he would say, 'My goodness, here she is again', but he was really interested . . . He was truly grateful for the information we brought to him of what was happening throughout the country'.[53]

There is some evidence that the League's cosy relationship with the White House changed under Eisenhower. Mrs John Lee, then President of the League, wrote to Strauss in February 1954, soliciting her advice on the declining influence of the League. Lee complained that in April of the previous year she had asked for an appointment with Eisenhower, 'so a few members of the National Board could acquaint him personally with the League's experiences and interests', but that the request was denied. Furthermore the League was passed over for appointment on the Public Advisory Board of the Foreign Operations Administration (FOA), despite the fact that 'at least two of the three women's groups represented have less background in this field that the League'.[54] While Strauss felt that her influence with the White House waned when Eisenhower came to office, it is interesting that his letters to her are worded as respectful solicitations of her advice and help. A letter enlisting her participation in the People-to-People programme, which Strauss was initially wary of, informed her, 'There is a matter in which the President is personally interested and on which we would very much like to have your counsel and help'.[55]

Generally, the former military leader, despite his professed faith in their spiritual counsel during his election campaign, exhibited little concern for the opinions and influence of women during his terms of office. Eisenhower was more comfortable with the company of men at his 'stag dinners' than when surrounded by women. When the all-male character of these evenings was pointed out to Eisenhower at a press conference by Bell Syndicated columnist, Doris Fleeson, Eisenhower explained, 'with a belligerent air of injured innocence', that he wanted to invite women but 'the women couldn't decide who should come'. As an answer to the negative publicity generated by the all-male dinners, Bertha S. Adkins, a former head of the Women's Activities Committee of the Republican National Committee and then Under-Secretary at the Department of Health, Education and Welfare, organised a series of breakfast sessions with President Eisenhower and the leaders of women's organisations. These meetings included twenty women, each of whom were allocated two minutes to tell the President about their organisation. The breakfast sessions were more an exercise in public relations than an effort at consultation. Adkins admitted, 'The breakfasts gave him, I think, an insight into the ways in which women's organized efforts were being used. Certainly it gave a satisfaction to the heads of women's organizations to be able to have this personal association with the President of the United States'.[56]

The involvement of the leaders of American women's associations in government, albeit on an ad hoc and unofficial basis, diminished in their eyes the urgency of demands and efforts to increase the number of women in policy-making roles. In her study of American women's organisations and the Federal government, Cynthia Harrison points out that actual political appointments for women tended to be rewarded to 'party women', women active in national party organisations such as the Democratic National Committee and the Republican National Committee. Harrison argues, 'Party-women considered high-level positions for deserving qualified female candidates to be both encouragement and reward for the campaign work of thousands of loyal women in local precincts'.[57] Harrison argues

that 'party women' took pride in this manifestation of their influence
with the federal government, even at the expense of the two other
groups of women (leaders of voluntary associations, and 'militant'
feminists working for the Equal Rights Amendment): 'Although the
actual number of women named to important positions was in fact
small it satisfied political women who themselves took pride in their
access to the chief executives. Of the three groups competing for
federal attention, only the party women could claim success.'[58]

How 'success' is measured is crucial to this argument. In fact, voluntary associations counted success in terms of gaining federal attention, but not necessarily federal appointments. After all, leaders of
voluntary associations, believers in the principle of the importance of
non-governmental work, may not have valued political patronage
appointments in the same way that women who choose to channel
their efforts in electoral politics may have done. It was the appointment of their leaders to non-governmental appointments – particularly on the international sphere, where they already had contacts and
possibly some reputation – which were prized by leaders of American
women's organisations. In this area they had an important advantage
over 'party women'. As Rhodri Jeffreys-Jones points out, appointing
partisan women to important international positions was disruptive,
as a change in government led to resignations and new appointments.
For example, when the Republican President Eisenhower was elected,
the Democrat Eleanor Roosevelt had to resign from her position at the
United Nations.[59]

In their relationship with the government, leaders of women's
organisations such as Strauss or Virginia Gildersleeve of the
American Association of University Women (AAUW) served
American women in two ways. They were 'representative' in that
their presence within government circles 'represented' the inclusion
of women in American political life, though their low numbers
perhaps make the term 'tokenism' more appropriate than 'representation'. They also 'represented' in the sense that they assumed responsibility for mediating between American women and the
government. In their liaison with the US government, leaders of
American women's organisations claimed not only to represent their
specific organisation but also functioned as the representatives of the
'symbolic' group of 'women'. This 'representing' function was, to use
Daniel Bell's phrase, 'symbolic'. He explains, 'The fact that decision-
making has been centralized into the narrow cockpit of Washington,

rather than in the impersonal market, teaches groups like the National Association of Manufactures, the Farm Bureau, the American Federation of Labour et al to speak for "Business", for the "Farmers", for "Labor"'.[60]

In reality leaders of women's associations could legitimately claim to represent only a small group of American women. Susan Ware's comment that the membership of the LWV was such that 'it could more accurately have been called the League of Affluent Women Voters', could equally be applied to the other leading women's organisations.[61] Membership of a voluntary organisation was limited to those with sufficient leisure time to organise and attend meetings and events. The higher the position in the League, the greater the time commitment and, consequently, the need for uncommitted time. As a result, the leadership of women's voluntary associations could be characterised as the well-heeled leading the well-to-do.

Moreover, with the obvious exception of the NCNW the leading American women's organisations were predominately, if not exclusively, white. The YWCA served in many ways as a torch-bearer in moves towards integration, having accepted and encouraged African-American membership as a deliberate policy since 1923. Clara Payne had served as the first African-American board member in 1926.[62] At their Seventeenth National Convention in Atlantic City, March 1946, the Association, recognising that 'today racial tensions threaten not only the well-being of our communities but also the possibility of a peaceful world', adopted an Interracial Charter.[63] The Charter recognised the leading role of the YWCA, noting that in Missouri the only interracial dining room in the entire city was the YWCA cafeteria. Nevertheless, they were forced to recognise that the goal of integration could not be achieved nationwide, recommending that 'in communities where, because of rigid patterns of separation it may not now be possible for white and Negro women and girls to be members of the same groups, inter-club council processes and other inter-group activities be consciously employed to bridge the gaps between groups separated because of race.'[64] Other women's groups were slow to follow the YWCA's lead. The period between the Second World War and the Civil Rights movement saw mainstream American women's organisations struggle with the question of integration. While they recognised the need to address racial inequalities, not least because of their potential to be exploited for propaganda value by the

Soviet Union, most National Boards were unwilling to make integration of their own organisations a priority. While by-laws in the AAUW recognised the goal of integration, branches in the South continued, as a matter of custom, to be segregated. While some branches, such as New Jersey, reported a small African-American membership and one Indiana division elected an African-American as chairman, the national leadership remained white. Women's associations remained effectively segregated, with African-American women directing their efforts for the most part through associations such as the NCNW and the National Association of Colored Women's Clubs.

For middle-class African-American and white women, voluntary associations in the post-suffrage period continued to offer an opportunity to become active outside the home. Women's organisations offered a public role for women, while retaining the rhetoric of the importance of women's public role. Organisations such as the LWV or the AAUW should best be understood as quasi-private associations. They spoke the language of the private realm, while at the same time offering women a public role. Historians have begun to consider the extent to which female-only institutions framed and contained female political experience in the USA. Susan Hartmann, for example, in her work on American women during and after the Second World War has concluded, 'Their organisations afforded women autonomous and more active vehicles for engagement in the political process'.[65] Political historian Louise Tilly concurs, arguing that the involvement of women in voluntary associations created a social and political space for women which was relatively unaffected by the granting of suffrage, 'Both philanthropic organizational and civic reform activities remain characteristic of women even after they gained the suffrage . . . partly because the local community area continued to be the arena of so many of their socially-constructed, self-defined interests'.[66]

Both Tilly and Hartmann consider the continuing work of women's associations in the domestic sphere of social activism. However, records and journals of American women's associations in this period show that their leaders and members were not only interested in the traditional women's areas as social welfare and domestic politics. American women's organisations in the post-war period were determined to claim and justify an international role for themselves. American women's organisations argued forcefully that they had an interest in and understanding of women of other nations because their shared identity and experience created an 'international sisterhood'. Their argument drew upon essentialist values which defined women as pacifist and less nationalistic than men. While aspects of this construction can be seen as ahistorical, American women's organisations strengthened their claim to essentialist identity by reference to contemporary events and concerns. In particular, American women referenced the development of atomic weaponry, which had destroyed the concept of the untouchable domestic haven and thus required women's involvement in the international realm. Furthermore, the experience of the destruction and devastation of the Second World War convinced many women that their international involvement was vital to the maintenance of a peaceful world.

 In encouraging American women's involvement in international affairs, American women had to contend with an ideology of femininity that limited women's concerns not just to the domestic context of their country, but also to the domestic context of their individual homes. In September 1939 *American Home* magazine had put international affairs into perspective for its readers, telling them, 'Hitler threatens Europe, but Betty Havens' husband's boss is coming to dinner – and *that's* what *really* counts'. American women's organisations sought to combat domestic containment by advocating women's involvement in the international sphere. Countless articles and speeches asserted women's equality with, if not superiority to, men as international citizens. Yet in their construction of an international role, American women's organisations were first obliged to defend their reasons for moving outside the domestic sphere. Helen C. White of the AAUW explained:

> Sometimes I think that the chief difference between our Victorian grandmothers and ourselves is that they thought that a good woman could create her own oasis of quiet goodness in a bad world by staying within her own home and garden and making them as nearly perfect as anything could be in this imperfect world. But we know that the weeds outside the garden will blow over the wall and the germs of the unswept streets will be tracked on the cleanest floor.[67]

Much of the extension of women's roles beyond domestic boundaries was justified by reference to the vulnerability of those boundaries to an atomic threat. It has been argued powerfully by Elaine Tyler May that American women responded to the threat by retreating with renewed enthusiasm into the false haven of the home and hearth. This approach was typified in the government campaign that called upon women to become active in civil defence. Katherine Howard, the Deputy Administrator of the Federal Civil Defense Administration (FCDA), told the Ladies Auxiliary to the Veterans of Foreign Wars, 'It is in the hands on the American housewife and mother that the defense of our home front must lie in a very large part'.[68] Alice Leopold, head of the Women's Bureau of the Department of Labor, asserted:

> Civil Defense begins at home, and since time began women have protected home and hearth while men in the family go out and fell the enemy – be it wild animals on the frontier or the battlefronts of modern welfare. We women might not shoulder muskets nor protect our homes from Indians, but we have a job to do in educating the people about Civil Defense.[69]

However the inability of the individual or the community to protect the home-front from nuclear attack could not be dismissed, and thus proved an important motivation for women to assert an active political role. The vision of the retreat to the home was one of false security. As early as 1946, anthropologist Margaret Mead had recognised the possibility that paralysing fear and hopelessness would be the response of many to the threat of atomic warfare. In the journal, *Woman's Day*, she acknowledged:

> The very size of the undertaking, the great sums of money which had to be spent, the cities that had to be built to house the workers on the bomb and the size of the cities in Japan which were devastated – all makes us feel that this is something outside our power to act, something like an earthquake which will either come or not and there is nothing any individual can do about it . . . Women especially, even the women who are always on hand for the PTA meeting, or to canvass voters in the local election, even the women who worked so hard during the war, feel this problem is just to big.[70]

However, Mead urged her readers not to permit atomic power to scare them into inactivity:

> It is not true that there is nothing women can do about it. We don't have to sit quietly by while our lives and those of our children hang by a single thread – wondering when someone, some dictator, some nation, may let loose these forces which could wipe out the world . . . They can keep their families thinking – not just about the bomb alone – for that is just one little part of the whole problem, but about the whole question of our new power and what we are going to do about

it and keep doing about it . . . The day the polls show that people aren't thinking about atomic power any more, that they are either too satisfied or too frightened even to talk about it, then the men who govern the country will start to relax.[71]

In destroying the security of the home, atomic weapons contributed to the expansion of women's role beyond the national boundary. The atomic threat increased American women's claims of political obligation by making the penalty for ignoring that obligation monstrous. The threat of atomic destruction gave new urgency to the age-old wisdom that women could, if they made the effort, divert men from their aggressive ways. Susan B. Riley, President of the AAUW, instructed her members through the organisation's journal, on 'The art of survival':

> In the long evolution of society, generic Man has represented the forces of destruction, generic Woman of conservation. Women have more power than they have dreamed of. If their latent strength was once aroused and organized they could accomplish miracles. They could even stop war . . . If women cared passionately enough to consider the whole world their home and if women of all nations and races would unite and say: 'No more of this talk of World War III. Find another way to settle your differences. But we will have no more talk of war. For in this Atomic Era we must live in peace if we would live at all.'[72]

The response of women to the threat of nuclear warfare was not limited to the inactive fear and domestic retreat described by Tyler May or the lament of Erik Erikson in his essay 'Inner and outer space: Reflections on womanhood':

> Maybe if women would only gain the determination to represent as image providers and law-givers what they have always stood for privately in evolution and history (realism of householding, responsibility of upbringing, resourcefulness in peacekeeping and devotion to healing), they might well be mobilized to add an ethical restraining, because truly supranational, power to politics in the widest sense.[73]

Erikson's expression of forlorn hope ignored the substantial efforts that women's organisations had made in the previous twenty years to involve their members in international affairs. Nuclear and atomic weaponry served as a powerful symbol, raising awareness among American women of the terrible possible consequences of another failure to keep the peace. The response of some American women was to campaign for control, if not abolition, of such weaponry, but many American women's organisations argued more broadly for women's responsible involvement in international affairs as champions of peace. *Independent Woman*, the journal of the NFBPWC, urged its members to channel their energy into the promotion of the United Nations:

> Those who are asking the question 'What can I individually do for peace?' may find the answer in this account of the general disregard by the newspapers of the fundamental work of the United Nations for the establishment of World Peace. Can you not locally bring to the attention of your newspaper editors the underlying facts and the fascinating stories connected with them?[74]

In justifying and encouraging American women's internationalism, American women's organisations drew from a long-established international female identity. Leila Rupp has analysed the creation of 'the international we' among international women's organisations in the pre-Second World War period. She explains, 'The International bonds of womanhood rested upon the assumptions that all women shared certain characteristic and thus naturally would flock together in women's organizations'.[75] Rupp argues that women's international organisations drew upon an ideology of women's difference from men based upon their hatred of war, their experience of maternalism and their nurturing skills. American suffragist Alice Stone Blackwell, for example, had urged, 'Let us do our utmost to hasten the day when the wishes of mothers shall have their due weight in public affairs, knowing that by doing so we will hasten the day when wars shall be no more'.[76] A similar motivation had inspired many women to become involved in international affairs after the First World War.[77] The failure of women to secure peace in the aftermath of that conflict was not seen as proof of the futility of their efforts but rather as evidence of the need to work even harder the next time. Virginia Gildersleeve, President of the International Federation of University Women (IFUW), explained in an article entitled 'International reconstruction – the second chance',

> We should not feel discouraged by the loss of the first race. The task of educating and organizing the world for peace and human welfare is a stupendous one. University women played a good part in the first great effort. They have learned from that experience and will do far better now that mankind is given a second chance.[78]

With the Second World War demonstrating the failure of male-dominated international relations, American women argued that they must be given the opportunity to practice a better way of mediating disputes. The International Alliance of Women (IAW) asserted in 1946 that the circumstances facing women in the world demanded that they make 'a special choice': 'Either we must ape men, or use that power for peace that rests in every emancipated woman's hand.'[79] Lena Phillips, President of the International Federation of Business and Professional Women (IFBPWC), drew upon essentialist and ahistorical concepts in her keynote address to the Fourth International Congress in Paris in July 1947:

> I wish . . . that women could sit at these diplomatic tables where the fate and future of the world is being decided: women who think more in terms of human beings and less in terms of material things; women so long trained in protecting the weak and curbing the unruly; women who know the way to fight an idea is not through war. I wish that more women sat at those international conference tables because women are perhaps more socially conscious about many of the things that count for the most now. They are close to the Church and therefore have more faith in God and in good. They would be less bound by protocol; they have had much more experience in difficult situations and therefore might display more flexibility and ingenuity. They have had long experience in selflessness.[80]

While male-driven national interests were represented as dangerous temporalities, women's essential nature was represented as timeless. Julia Kristeva, in her essay 'Women's time', has argued that '[Women] are not just a linear history of cursive time but also monumental time in which they echo the universal traits of their structural place in reproduction and it representation'.[81] Thirty years earlier, the connection to the 'monumental time' of the world was used by American women's organisations to justify their increasing interest in international relations. A 1948 poem in the *Journal of American Association of Business and Professional Women*, normally wary of anything that reduced women to a celebration of their reproductive functions, expressed the concept:

> The Axis of the world is womankind
> She gives men birth and comforts them in death
> From woman back to woman makes the world
> On her, men's blessing or their curses rest
> And in her arms are cradled hemispheres![82]

This essentialist conception re-defined women's traditional exclusion from international relations. Lesser commitment to nation was now described as a positive, rather than a negative, attribute, for lack of national identity could be a vital element in building international peaceful relations.

The report of Dr Arenia Mallory of the NCNW at the Helsinki Conference of the International Council of Women in 1954, exemplified this approach, contending: 'Over these barriers between nations, races, professions and ideals, even over the walls of our small centered private lives, the women from different parts of the world came to see their common tasks and solve their common problems'.[83] Similarly, the NCNW report after the International Alliance of Women conference of October 1946 stated:

> Since the International Assembly met in a world of political tensions, of economic instability, of social unrest and of moral and spiritual deterioration, it was decided that these universal conditions be discussed within the framework of common needs. All delegates were asked to keep in the background their own controversial national political problems as they affect any other nation or region.[84]

Through their voluntary associations American women continued to make reference to the ideal of the international sisterhood described by Leila Rupp. While asserting their ability to overcome national identity in the pursuit of an international sisterhood, however, American women's organisations were also making claims to a greater degree of representation within that national identity. In referring to their increasing desire and right for greater participation in government-sponsored international relations, American women's organisations spoke not of their international loyalties and identity, but of their participation and inclusion in national politics and citizenship.

Women's limited role in traditional international relations is illustrated by a special diplomatic passport issued to Americans travelling on government business in 1935, which included a printed section blithely announcing, 'The bearer is accompanied by his wife'.[85] Behind this statement lies the confidence with which State Department officials were able to assume their employees and appointments were all men. International relations, for the State Department, were the prerogative of government officials, and those government officials would be men. If American women wished to be active in the international spheres they had to gain access to the exclusive clique of foreign policy personnel. American women's organisations made a concerted attempt to increase women's participation in international relations through the traditional medium of the nation-state system. Continuing with the strategy that had been conceived and directed by Carrie Chapman Catt and her allies in the Committee on the Cause and Cure of War (CCCW), mainstream American women's associations sought the inclusion of women in the foreign policy branches of their government. The CCCW was a coalition of nine women's organisations who demanded the increased participation of women in foreign policy.[86] The historian of the CCCW, Susan Zeiger, has argued that the Committee pursued a policy of educating women for their involvement in mainstream political circles: 'Looking ahead to the 1930s, Catt and her colleagues like AAUW president Mary Wooley would focus on an increasingly elitist strategy, trying to promote within the foreign policy establishment a small group of semi-professional women reformers'.[87]

Undaunted by the outbreak of the Second World War, the CCCW and its successors doggedly pursued this strategy. On 14 June 1944, at the instigation of the CCCW, a conference sponsored by Eleanor Roosevelt was held at the White House. Titled 'How women may share in post-war policy making', it was attended by 230 women. The outcome was the production of a 'roster of qualified women', a list of 260 women qualified to serve the US government in an international capacity. Eleanor Roosevelt commented that the value of the list was that 'now no man can ever say he could not think of a woman qualified in a particular field'.[88] The Continuation Committee of the conference continued until February 1945. A similar strategy was pursued by the Committee of Women in World Affairs (CWWA), founded by Emily Hickman and Mary Woolley in 1942 to push for female appointees to international organisations and conferences.[89]

American women's organisations argued strongly that their members were entitled to full representations as citizens of their nation. American women had by 1945 been able to exercise the vote for twenty-five years and their calls for increased representation in international affairs can be seen as an effort to develop and extend their role as fully-fledged American citizens on the same basis as men. American women's organisations strengthened their claims to full citizenship with reference to the immediate historical experience and contemporary events. The Second World War had shown women's ability and desire for a more active role, and women argued that their participation in the struggle had earned them that right and responsibility. The YWCA expressed this belief in the 'earning' of citizenship through contribution to warfare:

> Women have served gallantly in every endeavor they undertook during the war – on the home front and in the uniforms of all the armed forces. They drove trucks and they operated machines. They moved into key posts in the world of business and industry. The war proved women have earned the right to achievements, in business, industry, the professions, the arts the sciences and the government.[90]

The idea that women should be rewarded for their contribution to warfare through the extension of their role as political actors was not new. Women's contribution to the war effort in the First World War was clearly a major factor in the granting of women's suffrage in America in 1920. Leading suffragette Carrie Chapman Catt, previously active in the cause of pacifism, threw the weight of the National American Women's Suffrage Association (NAWSA) behind the war effort, noting as a matter of tactics, 'Wartime service would win more support for the woman's suffrage than pacifism'. When President Woodrow Wilson signed the Nineteenth Amendment giving American women the vote, he specifically mentioned the wartime service of American women and the efforts of NAWSA, claiming the amendment was 'vitally essential to the successful prosecution of the great war'.[91] The participation of American women in the Second World War aroused similar expectations of increased political involvement.

This ideological connection between contribution to a national effort and increased rights and responsibilities as citizens was not limited to armed conflicts. The Cold War was also framed as a total conflict from which the USA could not afford to exclude the contribution of women. American women's organisations were not above using the military imperatives of the Cold War as a platform on which to base their claim for increased rights and responsibilities. The AAUW sent a petition to President Truman in September 1950 calling for the full participation of women in policy-making on the basis that 'we cannot see ahead to the end of this struggle, but we do know that it will be a test of strength in which this nation cannot afford to waste the abilities and energies of any group of citizens'.[92] Judge Lucy Somerville Howarth, Chairman of the AAUW's National Committee

on Status of Women, connected the involvement of women in the
Second World War and the need to exploit their talents in the Cold
War:

> Preparation for such a struggle demands that all, not part, of the
> Nation's resources be mobilized. Women have demonstrated in pre-
> vious wars, both overseas and within the continental limits, that they
> can perform essential military tasks in a military manner. Their
> record in World War II is outstanding . . . From now on any war will
> mean total war and plans should be underway now for the utiliza-
> tion of women and men in case of war.[93]

Women's claims for increased rights as citizens were further bol-
stered by the emergence of an atomic threat. As Carole Pateman has
argued, there is an important connection between citizenship and the
willingness to sacrifice one's life for one's country.[94] In America before
1945, this sacrifice had been the preserve of those, overwhelmingly
men, who were willing (and permitted) to travel to foreign battle-
fields. The development of nuclear weaponry meant that the distinction between the public world of the battlefield and the private world
of women, already compromised by the total nature of the Second
World War, was lost for ever. Cynthia Enloe has noted:

> The nuclearisation of NATO and the Warsaw Pact military doctrine
> has made virtually meaningless one of the foundations of the mili-
> tary system for controlling women: the mythical dichotomy between
> 'home front' and 'battle front'. So long as women could be defined as
> inherently, naturally and intrinsically non-combatants and therefore
> as the objects of protection, their labour could be mobilized by gov-
> ernment strategists without the fear that such mobilization would
> shake the social order in which women are the symbols of the hearths
> and homes the armed forces claimed to be protecting.[95]

American women's organisations attempt to gain increased representation in international affairs through an assertion of their identity
as full citizens met with limited success. The San Francisco Conference
establishing the United Nations ominously signalled the State
Department's views on the inclusion of women and women's groups
in post-war planning. Of 159 delegates to the conference, only six were
women. Of the forty-two organisations represented, only five were
women's organisations. Adding insult to injury, government officials
denied women reporters entry into the press club unless a male col-
league accompanied them. For the State Department, appointment of

women was more a matter of public relations and domestic support than a meaningful policy. This was illustrated by a memorandum from Francis Russell, Chief of the Office of Public Affairs, to Under-Secretary of State Dean Acheson. Russell advised Acheson, 'I think it is desirable that some publicity be given to the action of the Staff Committee on the question of women in the Department and American delegations to international conferences'. Russell suggested the best way to do this would be through a letter, drafted by him but sent in the name of Mrs Roosevelt to Acheson, asserting, 'There is a general desire among women and women's groups in this country for assurance that women will receive full consideration for appointments on international delegations and to policymaking posts in connection with our foreign policy'.[96] 'Mrs Roosevelt' could then urge Acheson to clarify the policy of the State Department towards the appointment of women in the Department and on international missions. Acheson's reply, again drafted by Russell, would comment that he was 'glad of the opportunity afforded by your letter' to assert vaguely that the Department's policy was 'to provide equal opportunities, on the basis of qualifications, for employment and promotion of women in the department and in the Foreign Service, and for representation on United States delegation to international conferences'.[97] To his credit, Acheson scribbled on the top of Russell's memorandum, 'I don't like this', but the Under-Secretary was not above using women's organisations as a forum for publicity. When Acheson agreed to give an informal speech to the CWWA in January 1946, Russell noted, 'This undoubtedly will be a good spot for a few well chosen words on the British loan'.[98]

Because of the number of letters that the CWWA generated, it had some effect in overcoming State Department reluctance to appoint more women to international delegations and organisations. An update on the work of the Committee in 1947 reminded its members that about eighty women had served in international conferences since 1941: 'This record of eighty in five years – sixteen a year – contrasts with the previous five years when only one woman was appointed to an international mission'.[99] However, while these figures represented an improvement, the Committee was painfully aware that it was pitifully small. The national chairman warned that there was no time for the Committee to 'rest on their laurels':

There were no women in the United States delegation at the Paris Peace Conference; there was no American woman in the delegation at the Preparatory Conference for the International Trade Organization. There is no woman among the President's administrative assistants. There is no woman among the eight assistant secretaries of state. There is no American woman high in the Secretariat of the United Nations.[100]

The failure of American women to make any substantial progress in terms of access to the foreign policy elite was evident in a meeting of ten women in August 1961. While two were representatives of women's organisations, the remaining eight were 'government women, all in very responsible positions – all rather high in grade and pulling down good salaries (mostly over $13,000 per annum)'. They aimed to form a pressure group, as all were 'very tired of the general State Department posture of belittling the importance of women and women's activities both here and abroad, and are determined to do something about it'. The meeting was arranged for a Sunday in the apartment of one of the participants, Miss Jacobsons of the Office of Deputy Director for Program and Planning in the International Co-operation Administration, 'so that it could be completely unofficial and out of regular channels'.[101] The fact that the leading women in the State Department felt the need to form this kind of 'support group' speaks volumes to the failures of women's organisations to advance the position of women within the foreign policy elite.

While American women were frustrated in their attempts to infiltrate the higher levels of the State Department, this did not mean they did not have a role in foreign affairs. In common with voluntary associations representing labour, African-Americans, business and other 'special interest' groups, American women's organisations became partners with the government in the construction of a 'state–private network'. American's women's associations, with their international contacts and affiliation had in the pre-Second World War era offered American women access to an international sisterhood. In the postwar world they instead became partners with their government, pursuing an international role as representatives, not of their gender but of their nation. American women's associations continuing reference to the possibility, and often the imperative, of an international identity which united them with women across the world was an important strategy in overcoming the cultural and political discourse which restricted women to a domestic role. However, their constant reference to their internationalism and their sisterhood with women across the world should not obscure the fact that leaders of American women's associations were also framing their demand for an international role in national terms and entering into an increasingly close and co-operative relationship with their government. While they may have had limited success in securing entry to the foreign policy elite, leaders of American women's organisations were nevertheless building an international role with, if not exactly within, their government.

Notes

1   Historian Susan Lebsock summarised the field, asserting, 'For Nineteenth Century women the characteristic form of political activism was participation in a voluntary association. Whether women would have chosen this path had they the option of voting, we will never know . . . Most American women, if they wanted influence, had no choice but to work through non-electoral politics'. S. Lebsock, 'Women and American politics 1880–1920', in L. Tilly and P. Gurin (eds), *Women, Politics and Change* (New York: Russell Sage Foundation, 1990), p. 37. See also L. M. Young, 'Women's place in American politics: The historical perspective', *Journal of Politics*, 38 (August 1976) or K. J. Blair, *The Clubwoman as Feminist: True Womanhood Redefined 1868–1914* (New York: Holmes Meier, 1980).

2   E. Freedman, 'Separation as strategy: Female institutional building and American feminism 1870–1930', *Feminist Studies*, 5:3 (Autumn 1979).

3   *Ibid.*

4   E. Freedman, 'Separatism revisited: Women's institutions, social reform and the career of Miriam Van Waters', in L. Kerber, A. Kessler-Harris and K. K. Sklar (eds), *US History as Women's History: New Feminist Essays* (Chapel Hill, NC: University of North Carolina Press, 1995), p. 173.

5   L. J. Rupp and V. Taylor, *Survival in the Doldrums: The American Women's Rights Movement 1945 to the 1960s* (New York: Oxford University Press, 1987), p. 3.

6   See in particular Linda Christiansen-Ruffman's essay on the tendency to regard women's volunteer work as 'secondary' and somehow 'non-political', even when men's role as volunteers is described as 'political' despite being outside the realm of electoral politics. L. Christian-Ruffman, 'Participation theory and the methodological construction of invisible women: Feminism's call for an appropriate methodology', *Journal of Voluntary Action Research*, 14:3 (April–September 1985).

7   S. J. Ellis and K. H. Noyes, *By the People: A History of Americans as Volunteers* (Philadelphia, PA: Energize, 1978), p. 4.

8   I. Dabrowski, 'The un-named political woman', in F. Le Veness and J. P. Sweeny (eds), *Women Leaders in Contemporary U.S. Politics* (Boulder, CO: Lynne Rienner, 1987), p. 137.

9   *Ibid.*, Dubrowski considers this attitude to women volunteers particularly prevalent in the case of 'service orientated' volunteers. An example of the lack of historiography on volunteerism in this period is the biographical dictionary, *Notable American Women: The Modern Period*, edited by B. Sicherman and C. Hurd Greet (Cambridge, MA: The Belknap Press, 1980). It is easy to

criticise texts of this nature on the basis of who they omit, the exclusion of
leaders of voluntary associations does stand out. The editors list the criteria
for selection for inclusion as 'the individual's influence on her time or field;
the importance and significance of her achievement; the pioneering or inno-
vative quality of her work; and the relevance of her career for the history of
women'. Very few leaders of women's organisations are listed, with the
exception of African-American leaders such as Mary McLeod Bethune or
Eunice Carter of the NCNW. Prominent leaders such as Anna Lord Strauss,
Lena Phillips, Kathryn McHale and Rose Parsons are not included.

10   See S. Lynn, 'Gender and post World War II progressive politics: A bridge to
     social activism in the 1960s', *Gender and History*, 14:2 (Summer 1992).
11   Library of Congress, Washington, DC, League of Women Voters papers, box
     1787, file 'Government Agencies 1959–1967', USIA Feature, 'Profile of an
     American (Part IX)', undated, p. 5.
12   *Ibid.*, p. 3.
13   Freedman, 'Separatism revisited', p. 143.
14   S. M. Hartmann, *The Home Front and Beyond: American Women in the 1940s*
     (Boston, MA: Twayne, 1982), p. 143.
15   C. E. Harrison, Prelude to feminism: Women's organizations, the federal gov-
     ernment, and the rise of the women's movement 1942–1968, PhD dissertation,
     Columbia University, 1982, p. 204.
16   J. Fischer, 'Are you a political morning glory?', *Woman's Day* (September
     1954), p. 62.
17   S. Ware, 'American women in the 1950s: Non-partisan politics and women's
     politicization', in L. Tilly and P. Gurin (eds), *Women, Politics and Change* (New
     York: Russell Sage Foundation, 1990), p. 291.
18   Records of the Women's Bureau of the US Department of Labor 1918–65
     (Frederick: University Publications of America), Speech by Alice Leopold,
     'Girlpower', 28 July 1957.
19   'Letter from Miss Hazel Palmer', *National Business Woman*, 35:11 (November
     1956), p. 2.
20   Dorothy Height oral history, *The Black Women Oral History Project*, vol. 5
     (London: Meckler Westport, 1991), p. 85.
21   *Ibid.*, p. 222.
22   Schlesinger Library, Radcliffe Institute, Harvard University, Anna Lord
     Strauss papers, box 13, file 271, 27 Anna Lord Strauss working paper, 'The
     participation of women in the process of government', undated.
23   League of Women Voters papers, box 1198, Anna Lord Strauss, 'Arguments
     for and against changing the name of the League of Women Voters to League
     of Active Voters (or some such)', 22 April 1953.
24   Schlesinger Library, Radcliffe Institute, Harvard University, YWCA of Boston
     papers, file 420, The Dodson Report: The role of the YWCA in a changing era,
     1958, p. 10.
25   *Ibid.*, p. 11.
26   Anna Lord Strauss papers, box 13, file 271, Strauss working paper, undated.
27   *Ibid.*
28   Schlesinger Library, Radcliffe Institute, Harvard University, Lena M. Phillips
     papers, box 6, Newsletter of the BPWC, December 1944.
29   The reminiscences of Miss Anna Lord Strauss, Oral History Research Office,
     Columbia University, p. 30.

30   *Ibid.*, p. 563.
31   The members of the NFBPWC were the most active of all the women's organisations in traditional electoral politics. In 1951, for example, there were eight women in the House of Representatives and one woman in the Senate. All were members of the NFBPWC.
32   Lena M. Phillips papers, box 6, TEARA, Newsletter of the Federation of Business and Professional Women of New Zealand, 3:13 (July–September 1948).
33   Lena M. Phillips papers, box 6, Phillips speech, 26 June 1948. Wallace's campaign as a whole was unusual in the extent to which is attempted to appeal to women. In a pamphlet produced by the Women for Wallace Committee, Wallace made an insightful comment on the position of women in post-war American society. Noting the active role of women in the Second World War, Wallace asserted, 'Today, all women know that the drive to prevent their acting as full-fledged citizens and workers is as active as that against all our civil rights. Women are being told to abandon political and community work on the grounds that it is "unfeminine"'. Lena M. Phillips papers, box 6, Women for Wallace pamphlet, 'Woman: First class citizen'.
34   As quoted in Dabrowski, 'The un-named political woman', p. 140
35   Hartmann, *The Home Front and Beyond*, pp. 144–5.
36   R. Tunley, 'Are American women backward politically?', *Women's Day* (October 1958), p. 102.
37   *Ibid.*
38   Schlesinger Library, Radcliffe Institute, Harvard University, Lucille Koshland papers, box 1, file 1, Koshland speech to the Overseas Education Fund Board of Directors, 13 January, 1965.
39   This was not true of all women's organisations. The League was (and is) unusual in the extent to which it has followed the principle of non-partisanship (an important value in an organisation which sponsors televised presidential debates). The NFBPWC, who counted Senator Margaret Chase Smith and Representative Mrs Chase Going Woodhouse among its members, obviously took a different position.
40   Mary McLeod Bethune Museum, Washington, DC, National Council of Negro Women papers, series 5, box 8, file 1, letter from Eleanor Roosevelt, 7 February 1946.
41   Dwight D. Eisenhower Presidential Library, Abilene, Kansas, papers of Dwight D. Eisenhower, Central File, box 852, File DF 158, 'Women', Murphy to Roberts, 4 February 1954, 'Consideration of a direct appeal to women by the President'. The memorandum pointed out, 'There is a hidden dividend within this appeal to women voters which arises from the increasing youth factor in the American voting population'. The recent demographic shifts in the American population gave added weight to women's political importance, as 'the profound influence of mothers on the impressionable minds of teenagers will continue to be at work over the next few years establishing political predilections which will determine voting patterns for years to come'.
42   Eisenhower papers, Central File, box 852, file DF 158, 'Women' Letter, Harris to Murphy, 19 January 1954.
43   Katherine Howard oral history, Oral History Research Office Columbia University, p. 456.
44   Eisenhower's lack of commitment to appointing women to his White House staff comes through in an account by Katherine Howard of how she got her

job as deputy chief of the Federal Civil Defense Administration: '[Sherman] Adams was Chief of Staff. Much as he liked and respected me, he saw no place for a woman on the White House Staff. There was a great hue and cry from the women's organizations to have a woman on the White House staff – and to have me. I would have liked that. But Adams said he wasn't going to have an Arab for Arabs, a woman for the women, and a Negro for the Negroes on the White House Staff, but he wanted me to continue to be part of the team. Would I be interested in the Women's Bureau or the Labor Department? I didn't know too much about labor and social welfare laws. It didn't appeal. How about the Children's Bureau? The same there. We went over many possibilities and finally hit on Civil Defence.' K. G. Howard, *With My Shoes Off* (New York: Vantage Press, 1977), p. 248.

45 Eisenhower papers, White House Central Files, Official Files, box 106, 'Analysis of Replies to the 2nd Questionnaire sent out by National Federation of Women's Republican Clubs', October 1952.

46 Eisenhower papers, White House Central Files, Official Files, box 106, Letter, Munger to Priest, 28 September 1952.

47 Eisenhower papers, White House Central Files, Official Files, box 142, Press release, 15 April 1955.

48 Harry S. Truman Library, Oral History Collection, India Edwards oral history, 1975, p. 27. Edwards' exemption of Truman from such patronising attitudes is more partisan than it is accurate. In 1948 Edwards, at that time the head of the Women's Division of the Democratic National Committee, co-ordinated their efforts under the campaigning title, 'Housewives for Truman'. Harrison, 'Prelude to feminism', p. 190.

49 By 1952 women constituted only 2 per cent of all executive appointments. L. McEnaney, 'Civil defense begins at home: Domestic political culture in the making of the Cold War', PhD dissertation, University of Wisconsin, Madison, 1996, p. 278

50 G. McConnell, 'The public values of the private association', in J. R. Pennock and J. W. Chapman (eds), *Voluntary Associations* (New York: Pantheon Press, 1969), p. 156.

51 *Ibid.*

52 The reminiscences of Miss Anna Lord Strauss, pp. 311–12.

53 *Ibid.*

54 League of Women Voters papers, box 1198, letter, Mrs John Lee to Anna Lord Strauss, 11 February 1954.

55 Anna Lord Strauss papers, file 182, box 9, letter, White House to Strauss, 12 April 1956.

56 Dwight D. Eisenhower Library, Oral History Collection, Bertha S. Adkins oral history, 18 December 1967.

57 Harrison, 'Prelude to Feminism', p. 183.

58 *Ibid.*, p. 185.

59 R. Jeffreys-Jones, *Changing Differences: Women and the Shaping of American Foreign Policy 1917–1994* (New Brunswick, NJ: Rutgers University Press, 1995).

60 D. Bell, 'Interpretations of American politics', in D. Bell (ed.), *The Radical Right: The New American Right* (New York: Doubleday, 1964), p. 70.

61 S. Ware, 'American Women in the 1950s: Non-partisan politics and women's politicization', in L. Tilly and P. Gurin (eds), *Women, Politics and Change* (New York: Russell Sage Foundation, 1990), p. 287.

62 Papers of the YWCA of Boston, box 35, file 82, report, 'The beginnings of the inter-racial work in Buffalo NY YWCA', by Amy G. Bruce.

63 Papers of the YWCA of Boston, box 31, file 445, The Interracial Charter (1955), p. 6.

64 *Ibid.*, p. 10.

65 Hartmann, *The Home Front and Beyond*, p. 144.

66 L. Tilly, 'Dimensions of women's politics', in L. Tilly and P. Gurin (eds), *Women, Politics and Change* (New York: Russell Sage Foundation, 1990), p. 10.

67 H. C. White, 'Liberal education, 1944', *Journal of the AAUW*, 38:1 (Autumn 1944), p. 6.

68 Schlesinger Library, Radcliffe Institute, Harvard University, Katherine Graham Howard papers, box 1, file 3, Katherine Howard speech to the National Encampment of Ladies Auxiliary to the Veterans of Foreign Wars, Milwaukee, Wisconsin, 5 August 1953.

69 Records of the Women's Bureau of the US Department of Labor, reel 19. Leopold speech to Women's Advisory Committee to Federal Civil Defense Administration, 'Civil defense begins at home', 23 September 1958.

70 *Women's Day* (April 1946), p. 20.

71 *Ibid.*, pp. 53–6.

72 *Journal of the AAUW*, 40:2 (Winter 1947), p. 69.

73 *Ibid.*

74 *Independent Woman*, 27:1 (January 1948), p. 55.

75 Rupp, *Worlds of Women*, p. 83.

76 Quoted in N. E. McGlen and M. R. Sarkees, *Women in Foreign Policy: The Insiders* (New York: Routledge, 1993), p. 4.

77 The International Federation of University Women, for example, had been founded in 1918 in response to the disaster of the war. See E. C. Batho, *A Lamp of Friendship 1918–1968: A Short History of the International Federation of University Women*, (Eastbourne: Sunfield and Day, 1968).

78 Virginia Gildersleeve, 'International reconstruction – the second chance', *Journal of the AAUW*, 38:2 (Winter 1945), p. 67.

79 'Report on the 14th Annual Congress of the International Alliance of Women', *International Women's News*, 40:8 (May 1946).

80 Lena M. Phillips papers, box 6, Phillips speech to the Fourth International Congress of the International Federation of Business and Professional Women's Clubs, Paris, 19–25 July 1947.

81 J. Kristeva, 'Women's time' (1979), in T. Moi (ed.), *The Kristeva Reader* (Oxford: Blackwell, 1986), p. 190.

82 V. L. Harden, 'From woman unto woman', *Independent Woman*, 27:2 (February 1948), p. 55.

83 National Council of Negro Women papers, series 13, box 8, file 12, Mallory report on the Helsinki Conference of the International Council of Women, June 1954.

84 National Council of Negro Women papers, series 13, box 18, file 18, Summarised reports of the 1946 IAW Conference.

85 For an example of this passport see Schlesinger Library, Radcliffe Institute, Harvard University, Frieda Segelke Miller papers, box 8.

86 The initial members of CCCW were the American Association of University Women, the Council of Women for Home Missions, the Federation of Women's boards of Foreign Missions, the General Federation of Women's

Clubs, the National Board of the Young Women's Christian Association, the National Council of Jewish Women, the League of Women Voters, the Women's Christian Temperance Union and the Women's Trade Union League. The Federation of Business and Professional Women's Clubs and the National Women's Conference of the American Ethical Union joined later. S. Zeiger, 'Finding a cure for war', *Journal of Social History*, 24:3 (1990), p. 83.

87 *Ibid.*, p. 75.

88 'Roster of Qualified Women drawn up by the Continuation Committee of the 14 June White House Conference', *Journal of the AAUW*, 38:3 (Spring 1945), p. 179.

89 See Hartmann, *The Home Front and Beyond*, p. 148. United States women's organisations belonging to the Committee of Women in World Affairs included the Women's International League for Peace and Freedom (WILPF), the National Council for Jewish Women (NCJW), the National Council of Women (NCW), the YWCA, the NFBPWC, and the National Women's Party. Organisations that had observers at meetings but were not full members included the General Federation of Women's Clubs (GFWC), the AAUW, the Women's Trade Union League (WTUL), and the LWV.

90 YWCA of Boston papers, YWCA Reconstruction pamphlet, box 32, file 11.

91 N. A. Wynn, *From Progressivism to Prosperity: World War I and American Society* (New York: Holmes and Meier, 1986), p. 132.

92 'Mobilizing all our citizens', *Journal of the AAUW*, 44:1 (Autumn 1950), p. 32. The launching of the Sputnik satellite by the Soviet Union in 1957 was used by the NFBPWC as further evidence of the need by the USA to exploit all its potential human resources in the new 'space race': 'It is not a very comforting feeling . . . to recognize that others have gone out in front in the invasion of Space . . . Every field must be opened to women because they are greater in number than men.' H. Palmer, 'Achieve through action today', *National Business Woman*, 37:2 (February 1958), p. 23.

93 Records of the American Association of University Women, (Microfilming Corporation of America), series III, ref. 00508, press release, 5 November 1948.

94 C. Pateman, 'Equality, difference, subordination: The politics of motherhood and women's citizenship', in G. Bock and S. James (eds), *Beyond Equality and Difference* (London: Routledge, 1992).

95 C. Enloe, *Does Khaki Become You? The Militarization of Women's Lives* (London: Pandora Press, 1988), p. 217.

96 US National Archives, Washington, DC, General Records of the Department of State, RG 59, Office of the Assistant Secretary of State for Public Affairs, subject files 1945–52, box 1, letter, Russell to Acheson, 24 May 1946.

97 General Records of the Department of State, RG 59, Office of the Assistant Secretary of State for Public Affairs, subject files 1945–52, box 1, draft letter by Russell in the name of Eleanor Roosevelt, 24 May 1946.

98 General Records of the Department of State, RG 59, Office of the Assistant Secretary of State for Public Affairs, subject files 1945–52, box 1, Russell to Acheson, 25 January 1946.

99 National Council of Negro Women papers, series 5, box 8, folder 1, letter from Hickman to Committee of Women in World Affairs members, 1 March 1947.

100 *Ibid.*

101 Lucille Koshland papers, carton 1, file 12, Overseas Education Fund memorandum, 8 August 1961.

2

'The best possible showcase for freedom', American voluntary associations in the Cold War

The voluntary association has enjoyed a long history as an ideal in American society. Alexis de Tocqueville commented on 'the American penchant for turning to voluntary actions as a solution to social, political and personal problems',[1] while historian Arthur Schlesinger, Sr, famously dubbed the USA 'a Nation of Joiners'.[2] The importance of the voluntary association in creating and protecting freedom was both functional and structural, a product of the practice and methods of voluntary associations and of their position outside of the state, or public, realm. The forms and practices of voluntary associations taught good citizenship by teaching participation, democratic ideals and techniques. Apart from a useful education in citizenship skills, voluntary associations, like trade organisations and labour associations offered individuals a method of representation separate from that of traditional politics. Because of this alternative form of representation, a government with tyrannical designs would be faced with an organised opposition on behalf of its citizens.

The Cold War era saw the development of an important mythology of voluntarism, which lauded the association as a crucial component in the preservation of democracy. As a means of preserving the rights of individual from state encroachment, voluntary associations in Cold War America came to be seen as entirely positive. As Grant McConnell has pointed out, this approach had more in common with hagiography than with a school of criticism. He argues, 'for a rather long time now, at least since the end of World War II, we have seen the rise and consolidation in a position of dominance of a body of doctrine which exhaults the private association as an essential feature of American democracy, perhaps of any genuine democracy'.[3] McConnell defines this view of the role of voluntary associations as one that posits that 'liberty itself is best served where a multitude of associations exist. Not only is the individual under such conditions unthreatened by mass movements and totalitarianism, he has the positive values of fellowship and meaning in his life without which liberty is a negative and empty thing'.[4] The voluntary association offered an alternative, and at times a form of opposition to, the potentially coercive power of the state.

The promotion of voluntary associations after the Second World War was a direct response to the totalitarian regimes of fascist states and to the authoritarian states of communist powers. The genesis of this approach is in Arthur Schlesinger, Sr's, 1944 article, 'The biography of a nation of joiners', in the *American Historical Review*. Schlesinger pointed to the repression of private associations in totalitarian states as proof that they contained a germ of liberty that dictators had to eradicate. He argued, 'It was with calculated foresight that the Axis dictators insured their rise to power by repressing or abolishing political, religious, labor and other voluntary groups. They dared not tolerate those guardians of the peoples liberties . . . These joiners were among the earliest casualties of the totalitarian system'.[5] This interpretation became orthodoxy among post-war historians of voluntary associations. Historian Mary Handlin concurred with Schlesinger in a 1961 speech to the overseas branch of the LWV, 'It is significant . . . that totalitarian governments must immediately aim to wipe out voluntary activities for these are an obvious threat to absolute control by the State'.[6] In contrast to the repression of private associations in totalitarian regimes, Handlin argued that the USA embraced these associations as vital training grounds in democracy and liberty:

> Considering the central importance of the voluntary organisation in American history, there is no doubt it has provided the people with their greatest school of self-government. Rubbing minds as well as elbows, they have been trained from their youth to take common counsel, choose leaders, harmonize differences and obey the expressed will of the majority. In mastering the associative way they have mastered the democratic way.[7]

Handlin concluded her tribute with the assertion, 'It is in the very nature of voluntarism that it compounds itself and, by spreading to multitudinous activities, increases the potential for freedom'.[8] This view of the importance of voluntary associations was not confined to academic commentators. The associations themselves were self-consciously proud of their role in preserving American democracy, earnestly advertising their importance. Grace Daniels, president of the NFBPWC, asserted in 1959, 'Forty years ago at the time of our founding, volunteer organizations were not as closely woven into the fabric of our free way of life as they have now become . . . It is my firm opinion that today the volunteer organization is the one best possible show-case for freedom'.[9] In her first presidential address to the GFWC, Mrs Theodore S. Chapman told members, 'There is no clearer expression of the democratic process than in voluntary organizations. They are the free channels of communication and co-operation, and are essential safeguards in freedom'.[10] Walter White, Executive Secretary of the NAACP concurred, 'In America, organizations like the NAACP are free to criticize all that which displeases them – including the government'.[11]

In the years following the Second World War, American voluntary associations began to see a role for themselves beyond the domestic political scene. In the spirit of international idealism, the American advocates and leaders of voluntary associations offered themselves as an example to the world. If American voluntary associations were what stood valiantly between liberty and tyranny in the USA, they could surely perform a similar role in other nations. This panacea was as relevant in states such as Germany, which had suffered the experience of dictatorship, as in nations whose sudden emergence from colonial rule raised concerns about their population's lack of training in or understanding of citizenship.[12] As the Cold War intensified the potential role of voluntary associations grew. Protestations about the failure of totalitarian regimes to tolerate voluntary associations, with their implied importance in preserving liberty, resurfaced. This time, however, the repressive state power was communist and the enemy was the Soviet Union. '100 things you should know about communism', a booklet produced by the House Committee on Un-American Activities (HUAC), unequivocally reminded its readers of the status of voluntary associations in communist-control regions. HUAC answered the question, 'Could I belong to the Elks, Rotary, or the American Legion?':

> No. William Z. Foster, the head of the Communists in the United States, says: 'Under the dictatorship all capitalist parties – Republican, Democratic, Progressive, Socialist, etc. – will be liquidated, the Communist Party functioning alone as the Party of the Toiling masses. Likewise will be dissolved all other organizations

that are political props of the bourgeois rule, including chambers of
commerce, employers' associations, Rotary Clubs, American Legion,
YMCA, and such fraternal orders as the Masons, Odd Fellows, Elks,
Knights of Columbus, etc.[13]

The international role of American voluntary associations was
encouraged and facilitated through a partnership between the leaders
of voluntary associations and the US government. After the Second
World War, voluntary associations became a vital branch of the government's propaganda effort. To fight the Cold War the government
revived wartime contacts and called upon patriotic citizens and
groups to lend their talent, expertise and support. The participation
of voluntary associations in the Second World War had mainly been a
matter of organisation, resources and logistics, but now their involvement was sought on ideological grounds. The involvement of individuals through voluntary collective action demonstrated that the
American system was a co-operative, consensual one in which the
private sphere recognised the public sphere as their partners. This co-
operation projected the genuine beliefs of the individual, elicited
without coercion or pressure. Emily Rosenberg explains, 'Because the
American government did not usually generate or severely censor
information, liberal developmentalists could not perceive American
Culture as either value-laden or ideological, because it was based on
mass appeal and appeared inherently democratic'.[14] The output of
voluntary associations, unlike their government, was able to lay claim
to a higher level of authenticity as 'the truth' rather than merely 'propaganda'. The participation of private associations in expressing the
views, desires and character of the American people was a vital component of US cultural diplomacy.[15]

The World Town Hall Meeting of the Air was an important
example. Modelled upon a national radio programme in which participants debated issues in a 'typical' American format, the meeting
toured in 1949, directed by Chester Williams, on leave from the US
delegation to the United Nations. He summarised the importance of
its 'private' nature, with constituent members drawn from a cross-
section of voluntary associations: 'That is the kind of talk which
carried conviction, for it is the people themselves talking – not paid
propagandists grinding out a "line"'.[16]

While the Town Hall Meeting of the Air prided itself on not
being an official government programme, neither was it completely

independent. Clarence Decker, one of the members of the tour, asked in October 1947 if President Truman could record a brief message for audiences but was told that, due to 'considerations of protocol', this would not be possible.[17] Government involvement was indirect, such as the pressure brought upon Anna Lord Strauss to take part in the trip. Strauss told George Denny, organizer of the trip, that she was 'too tired' to make the journey.[18] She soon changed her mind: 'The State Department really brought very strong pressure on the League to have its President take part. They felt that we should be represented there, and they had been so co-operative with us in so many instances that I really couldn't stand out against them because I thought it was quid pro quo'.[19] Still, Strauss maintained the illusion of 'voluntary' participation in this public relations exercise for the USA, asserting, 'I think that our Hosts realized we were a country where individuals could speak for themselves'.[20]

Many associations did go to great lengths to preserve the 'private' nature of their programmes. After lengthy deliberations the Overseas Education Fund of the LWV decided it could accept government money only for specific projects, 'One of our main purposes is to demonstrate what voluntary non-governmental groups can do . . . The OEF should not accept Government funds for administration, headquarter expenses, or other expenses without which we could not continue'.[21] Yet such efforts should not obscure the extent to which many voluntary associations' involvement was sought and directed by the government. A State Department report listed numerous private groups, noting their potential influence on 'foreign shores': 'Americans are prodigious "joiners", and their voluntary organizations number in the thousands . . . the lowliest of land-locked sewing circles may be knitting mufflers for the Laplanders'.[22] One of the first documents of the Psychological Strategy Board (PSB), set up by President Truman in 1951 to co-ordinate all aspects of the US psychological battle with Soviet communism, suggested for future action 'that a series of projects be assigned to veteran's, youth and women's organizations, which appear to be institutionally inspired, which could permit contact with similar groups in other countries whose goals, aspirations and activities have a common aspect'.[23] As an example the report proposed that contact between American women's organisations and women's organisations in Japan be encouraged in order to 'ensure continued pro-Western orientation'.[24]

The government's promotion culminated in the 'People-to-People' programme, proposed by President Eisenhower in 1956, to increase international understanding by facilitating relationships between private groups and individuals. Enlisting Anna Lord Strauss's assistance with the establishment of the programme, President Eisenhower stressed the practical demands inherent in the struggle to export 'information' about the American way of life:

> There will never be enough diplomats and information officers at work in the world to get the job done without help from the rest of us. Indeed if our American Ideology is eventually to win out in the great struggle being waged between the two opposing ways of life, it must have the active support of thousands of independent private groups and institutions and of millions of individual Americans acting through person-to person communication in foreign lands.[25]

The government would never detach itself completely from People-to-People. In April 1957 officials offered a course, entitled uncompromisingly 'World ideological conflict', to all participants. Held at the International Conference Suite of the US Information Agency in Washington, the five-day course was 'patterned after the comprehensive course of instruction given to United States Foreign Service Officers'. It aimed to give participants 'a unique opportunity to broaden their knowledge of U.S. Foreign Relations and to consider how they and the committees with which they are working may more effectively combat international communism, further American foreign policy objectives and protect their own individual interests through positive contributions to international understanding and goodwill'.[26]

The boundary between what was and was not constituted as 'private' was thus confused. On one point, however, the government was intractable: the 'private' aspect of the People-to-People foundations must be maintained in the realm of funding. Charles E. Wilson, president of the People-to-People Foundation, wrote to the trustees in May 1958 complaining about the problems of fund-raising, 'My inquiries among the members of the financial community indicate a decided reluctance to support the Foundation until the government shows its own confidence in the project with substantial initial financial backing'.[27] This the government proved singularly unwilling to do, however, as Eisenhower explained to Wilson:

> In discovering and developing the right structure for the People-to-People project, there is no alternative to preserving efforts of the kind

you are making – *all based on the principle that this must be a truly private effort*, with governmental ties limited to liaison only, but with a constant readiness on the part of my associates and myself to help in any legitimate way we can.[28]

The goal of an effective propaganda campaign that could be launched without expense to the government had its attractions, and the potential financial resources offered by voluntary associations were substantial. In 1947 it was estimated that the collective budgets of voluntary agencies for that year totalled more than $200 million.[29] The alliance between American voluntary associations and their government can be seen as less a demonstration of the co-operative spirit, unity of purpose, and happy coincidence of intent between the two, than an exercise in government cost-cutting. The head of the Office of Policy Coordination, Frank Wisner explained, 'It is essential to secure the overt cooperation of people with conspicuous access to wealth in their own right'.[30]

The co-operation between the private and public spheres was, for some observers, unproblematic. For example, the view of Oscar and Mary Handlin was that the blurring of the distinction between private and public was not particularly important:

> Through the nineteenth and twentieth century, the line between public and private sectors of society was . . . impossible to draw . . . It was never possible clearly to define two distinct spheres: the public, reserved for the state and the private, reserved for the voluntary association. Politically useful as that distinction may have been, whether for liberal or conservative ends, it had no basis in actual historical development.[31]

The Handlins argued, 'That the voluntary association sometimes served the ends of the state was less important than the fact that it also offered society an alternative to it'.[32]

Other observers have been less complacent, contending that the co-operation of voluntary associations with the government has been deleterious to the role of the private association in protecting the interests of and representing the views of its members. Grant McConnell has asserted:

> In the United States, at least, private associations have also contributed to order and stability through a pattern of relationships with the government to a degree which is seldom acknowledged. In a multitude of ways, the distinction between what is private and what is

public has been blurred so that it is often extraordinarily difficult to
determine which is the character of a particular form of action or rule
... It has been particularly important in time of war when networks
of trade associations, commodity organizations, trade unions and
other private associations on the one hand and public agencies, representative committees or boards on the other hand, have been established to undertake a rigorous task of mobilization and regulation
required by modern war.[33]

McConnell argues that this co-operation between the public and
private spheres in American life was not limited to the duration of war:

This process has probably done more than anything else to procure
the co-operation of vitally placed elements in the population in the
ends of the nation during its most serious moments of crisis. The
process has been most visible – and most extensive – in wartime, but
it should be clear that it has continued in other time as well, albeit
more loosely and less conspicuously.[34]

He concludes, in opposition to the beliefs of the Handlins and
Schlesinger, that private associations, far from offering a source of
opposition, 'have been – and continue to be – important adjuncts of
government in the United States'.[35]

McConnell points to the distance between members and leadership as illustrative of the lack of any real representative function
within voluntary associations. This distance is apparent when study-
ing American women's organisations. While both branch and
national leadership was decided on by vote, matters of detailed policy
and co-operation between the leadership and government were not
for the involvement or, in some cases, awareness of the rank and file.
This was particularly noticeable on international matters. For
example, in 1951 a declaration entitled the Memorial Day Statement
was presented to the Honourable Warren Austin, Chairman of the
United States Mission to the United Nations, and broadcast abroad by
the Voice of America. The statement asserted, 'It is hoped that this
positive declaration may help to refute Soviet Propaganda against
American Women and their organizations'.[36] This statement, pur-
porting to represent the opinion and views of American women, was
not voted on by the membership but was signed, on their behalf, by
their presidents.

In drawing the leaders of voluntary associations into their elite,
 the US government created important spokespersons for group

identities. In the propaganda battle that distinguished the Cold War, both the USA and Soviet Union made specific appeals to interest groups based on their presumed characteristics. In these appeals, collective identity was constructed as essentialist identity, whose needs and desires demonstrably could be met and fulfilled by the USA but were thwarted and opposed by the Soviet Union. For example, Soviet and US propaganda targeted 'intellectuals' and sought to persuade them that their individual and collective interests would be best served under communism or democracy respectively. Following the 1949 'Waldorf Conference', many American intellectuals believed that the Soviet Union was launching a propaganda offensive to convince them that their 'natural' loyalty lay with the Soviet Union. In response to this threat, a group of American and European intellectuals, including Arthur Koestler, Sidney Hook and Arthur Schlesinger, Jr, with the helpful financial backing of the CIA, launched the Congress for Cultural Freedom (CCF) in Berlin in 1950. Historian Christopher Lasch describes the theme of the Berlin Congress as being 'that a moral man could not remain neutral in the face of the present crisis'.[37] One participant, Robert Montgomery, was more specific, arguing, 'No artist who has the right to bear that title can be neutral in the battles of our time . . . Today we must stand up and be counted'.[38]

Educators also constituted an important group identity, and the Committee for International Educational Reconstruction (CIER) was an example of its manipulation. Established in spring 1946, CIER included representatives of the State Department, the United States Office of Education, the United Nations Educational, Scientific, and Cultural Organization (UNESCO), the United Nations Relief and Rehabilitation Administration (UNRRA) and leading educational groups such as the Associations of American Colleges and the AAUW.[39] Initially the group aimed at world peace and understanding through education, proclaiming, 'The Youth of the world and their leaders look hopefully to America. Educational opportunity is not only the right of each individual but the basis of international understanding and world peace'.[40] By 1948, however, the organisation had assumed a patriotic and combative tone, reporting, 'UNESCO has asked CIER to estimate the total of American aid for educational, scientific and cultural reconstruction during the calendar year 1947. This report will be extremely useful in making known the world the extent of American philanthropy, but also the concern which American organizations are showing for educational and spiritual reconstruction'.[41]

Similarly, 'workers' were also targets of Cold War propaganda. Richard J. Barnet explains:

> Millions of American workers now heard much the same message [through the educational department of their unions] that was being promoted by business groups. American workers should be against Communism, not only to protect God, country, family, and the American way of life, but also to express solidarity for repressed workers, for nowhere in Stalin's domain did a free labor movement exist.[42]

The category of 'women' also constituted an international group identity. Positing an essential identity for women around the world, US propaganda explained that the American way of life was sympathetic to that identity while the Soviet system was in all ways repressive of it. A pamphlet entitled 'Women! It's your fight too!', published by the US-backed International Confederation of Free Trade Unions (ICFTU), reinforced the notion of essentialist feminine values with statements like, 'No woman would choose to work in a mine'. The ICFTU claimed that, in its insistence on 'equality of labour', the Soviet Union was repressing women's essential nature, especially that of principal caregiver in the home: 'They are called "sluggards", and "selfish" and "unproductive" if they stay at home and take care of their little children. More often they are forced by the low wages of their husbands to take jobs to supplement the family's earnings in order to make ends meet'.[43]

 The most distressing transgression of the Soviet system against essential womanhood was, the pamphlet suggested, its challenge to women's peaceful nature. The ICFTU pamphlet showed pictures of East German women holding rifles with the caption, 'In East Germany even mothers are given rifles. Have they ever thought that they might have to use them on sons of mothers like themselves?' The text elaborated:

> Women who must aim guns and targets and practice methods of destruction and also produce more and more children must feel a revulsion against it all (unless of course, the political indoctrination that goes with the military training has been successful). Even Communism can't kill the spirit of a woman! Women under communism are not different from other women. The basic desires of women are the same. If communist-controlled women had any other way of obtaining the basic necessities of life, supply their family with food, shelter and clothing, they would break away to live under freedom.[44]

The ability of the American way of life to satisfy the essentialist demands and desires of any collective identity was better supported by testimonials of members rather than government protestations. While officials could offer sincere assurances regarding their government's position on issues close to the heart of any given collectivity, witness by members of that group would carry greater authenticity. In recruiting spokespeople for group identities, the US government came to heavily rely upon the network of voluntary associations. Simply by quoting membership figures, leaders of voluntary associations could claim a representative and, therefore, authentic role. Without the backing of a large organised group following, individuals who criticised the American government could be written off as non-representative, their views being directed and informed by individual rather than collective identity.

This is demonstrated by the support of the American government for Edith Sampson, a member of the National Council of Negro Women. Sampson's international work as a representative of the NCNW led to her appointment as the first African-American delegate to the United Nations. The government's promotion of Sampson's statements on the position of African-Americans contrasted with its denunciation of the activities of singer-entertainer Paul Robeson and its refusal to issue him with a passport. Robeson's lack of group affiliation was presented as evidence of his lack of a claim to be representative of African-Americans. Edith Sampson assured an audience in Delhi, 'Unfortunately, Mr Robeson has all his training in America, and he has forgotten that he owes a great deal to our democracy. *He does not represent any organisation* – only a lunatic fringe in America'.[45] Sampson was able to assure her audience, by reference to her position within the NCNW, that she was a better representative than Robeson of African-American opinion.

The recruitment of leaders of voluntary associations into a state–private network in order to defend and promote America across the globe was an important part of the American government's Cold War effort. In their co-operation with their government, leaders of US private associations demonstrated their loyalty to and agreement with the Cold War agenda of their governments. However, it is important to recognise that these leaders were not acting as puppets or stooges, parroting the party line. Their co-operation with their government was not the result of coercion or bribery, but a reflection of these groups' own interest and enthusiasm in promoting themselves as a model for the rest of the world. American private associations were proud of the ideals and practices of their associations and their efforts to promote them internationally were none the less genuine and sincere for having been at times government sponsored, directed and even financed.

The enthusiasm with which American voluntary associations sought to promote their example across the world was particularly strong in women's associations. In 1949 the Department of Commerce estimated that there were over 100,000 women's clubs across the USA.[46] Membership of women's voluntary associations, which, as Estelle Freedman has noted, dropped dramatically following the extension of suffrage in 1920, began to climb again.[47] The AAUW's membership increased from 93,463 in 1947 to 106,593 in 1949. Membership in the LWV climbed steadily in the post-war years from 50,000 in 1944–45 to 125,000 in 1953–54.[48] Anna Lord Strauss attributed this growth entirely to the League's new emphasis on international relations and the pursuit of peace. She asserted:

> A great many of the younger women felt that they didn't want to have their husbands have to go to war again. They didn't want to have their children live under war conditions. Therefore they managed to eke out a little time to give to the LWV on the understanding that this was the best chance of developing an understanding, keeping peaceful conditions in the world.[49]

Strauss's assertion is an interesting one. First, she accounts for women's growing interest in internationalism with reference to the specific context of the post-war years. The lesson of war, for Strauss, was that women needed to become more active. However, she constructs this involvement, not through a more active approach to mainstream politics, but by participation in the LWV. Reflecting on the lessons of the war, Strauss argued that American women believed that the 'best chance' for the maintenance of peace in the world was active membership in the League. Strauss's comments reflected a very specific form of internationalism, which American women developed as an extension of their faith in voluntary association in the domestic context.

American women's associations embraced an internationalism that revolved around their membership in women-only voluntary associations. Convinced of the success of these institutions in fulfilling the political ambitions of women in America, American women embarked upon a campaign to export their model to the world. American women's organisations, while asserting the commonality between women of all nations, were in fact deeply committed to their own pattern as the model for all women's political participation. Beneath the protestations of sisterhood and equality, American women clearly saw themselves as the leaders of women of the world, and their own organisations as the ideal. American women regarded themselves as so far advanced as political actors, well versed in the skills of responsible citizenship, that their international responsibility was to educate and advise women of other nations who lacked their experience and expertise.

The political upheavals after the war resulted in women in many nations suddenly finding themselves enfranchised. In countries such as Germany and Italy, women had been enfranchised before the war, but American women argued that they had lost the habit of democracy through the repression of their political rights. The war had in part been caused by a failure of active citizenship by women as well as men. Kathryn Stone of the LWV argued that the war had demonstrated the need to attach greater importance to training in citizenship to prevent further dictatorships from threatening world peace: 'A new awareness of the importance of the individual citizen has come to this entire country from the sharp lessons of contrast between free and fascist countries'.[50] The importance of educating women as citizens was amplified by the practical fact that the war had killed far more men than women, leaving women in a majority in many countries. In the US zone of occupation in Germany there were an estimated 124 females to every 100 males.[51] The NFBPWC noted, 'Due partly to the fearful wars, women now outnumber men in many countries. They must consequentially take their responsibility for building a more peaceful world'.[52]

In countries where women had gained the franchise following the Second World War, American women displayed the superiority of those who had fought for a right rather than those who had just been granted it. American women's organisations asserted that they had experience as voters and therefore as citizens. This experience could be communicated to newly enfranchised women of the world, who might otherwise be confused by their new status. This sense of superiority was one of the experienced versus the inexperienced, and it was often combined with the usual patronage of the Western world towards the Third World. Anna Lord Strauss told the World Affairs

Council in Pittsburgh, Pennsylvania, 'Women are emerging, in many places from a tribal pattern, into the twentieth century where the U.N. [United Nations] is setting standards for equality of opportunity. It isn't an easy or necessarily a quick road to cover. But we have travelled it and have learned a lot that we should share'.[53]

American women's organisations believed they should take the lead in educating, or re-educating, women of other nations in democratic ways. The YWCA in 1946 launched a 'reconstruction' programme that aimed to extend a helping hand from American women to women of other nations. A pamphlet extolling the virtues of the programme warned:

> In many countries, however, women are unprepared for the new tasks now thrust upon them. The ways of democracy mystify young women reared under the blight of totalitarianism. Women in foreign countries will shape their own destinies. In this time of world flux, they need help and advice. It is natural for them to turn to the women of the United States, the most privileged and the most advanced in the world.[54]

The 'teaching' role of American women was illustrated by a picture of a group of young girls looking up respectfully at an American teacher. The caption informs its American audience, 'Girls learn good citizenship in the Prague YWCA. We must help them understand democracy'. Another photograph of a woman holding a baby while casting her vote is captioned, 'This young mother is casting her first ballot . . . a new privilege for Italian women. She needs YWCA guidance in democracy'.[55]

The model of democracy that American women's associations were keen to export, however, was heavily biased to their own experience. Not surprisingly, leaders of women's associations were greatly in favour of the women's association model as the medium for women's political participation. American women's preference for this model was frequently at odds with the ideas of their European counterparts, who often preferred a direct approach for women's political activism. Throughout the late 1940s the LWV had become increasingly distant from the IAW on the basis that the Alliance was simply 'too feminist' in its approach. The term 'feminist' in this context was usually used pejoratively to express the dissatisfaction of the leaders of American women's associations with those who argued for increased political representation and rights for women. After her attendance at the IAW Conference in 1946, Anna Lord Strauss confidentially reported to the League on the battle for control within the IAW:

> In general there were two trends that were evident. One came from the group, in the most instances of the older and more vocal women, who have the typically feminist point of view and who have fought hard and long for women's rights. Some of them have a chip on their shoulders and feel that the only way of obtaining the equality of which they are always talking is to continue to fight. The other group is in most instances the younger women . . . who believe that the best way of progressing is for women to do a good job.[56]

The IAW made repeated attempts to coax the League into greater involvement, complaining that 'people think our Alliance to be on the left because of the absences of our American members'.[57] Responding to a letter from Mrs Corbett Ashby of the IAW regarding the inactivity of the League within its organisation, Anna Lord Strauss responded:

> Frankly, I believe the reason we do not manage to arouse more interest [in the IAW] is because of the feminist angle of the Alliance work. Since the war the average age of the members of the League of Women Voters has dropped markedly. We have now a majority of young women to whom the feminist approach has little appeal. They think of themselves as citizens first and as women incidentally . . . We find in this country that we further the advancement of women by doing what needs to be done, rather than by spending time nursing our grievances over the slights which may have come our way.[58]

Given the high level of investment in their role as the representatives of women in their domestic political life, leaders of American women's organisations perhaps lacked motivation to improve other forms of representation for women such as electoral politics. Their reluctance to emphasize this issue was reinforced by the unpopularity amongst American women's organisations of any activity that could be construed as 'feminist'. American women in post-suffrage years often expressed the feeling that activity which focused on the issue of 'women's right's' and 'women's status' were 'outmoded'. The dismissal of feminism in these terms is a consistent thread in the discourse of American women's organisations. Margaret Hickey, President of the NFBPWC, had, in the words of historian Susan Hartmann, 'sounded the death knell on the "old selfish strident feminism"' in 1945. Hickey called for a 'new feminism' that 'emphasised women's responsibilities as citizens rather than women's rights'.[59]

Women's associations that were devoted exclusively to the issue of women's rights drew scepticism from American women. The AAUW grudgingly acknowledged that the International Council of Women 'serves a purpose, since the women's groups belonging to it are in that stage of feminine history that some groups in this country are still, but was more typical of women's groups 25 years ago'.[60] Anna Lord Strauss was particularly hostile to what she saw as the 'feminist' standpoint of some of the international women's organisations, complaining to her office staff, 'If I hear much more about women's rights, I am going to turn into a violent anti-feminist'.[61] In particular she criticised the IAW, arguing, 'It was so very feminist in its point of view and I felt that the day of the feminist approach was over and they should work from a wider base'.[62] Judge Dorothy Kenyon, an observer at the IAW's 1946 conference, concurred, 'The group was divided into those primarily interested in women (the old-line "feminists") and those primarily interested in seeing women play their part in world affairs'.[63] Rejection of the label 'feminist' was a common strategy among American women's organisations. Historian Cynthia Harrison asserts, 'No matter how devoted to the quest for women's rights and improvement in women's status, female leaders between World War II and the second half of the 1960s eschewed the label "feminist"'.[64]

The differences between the American associations and their international affiliates illustrated a serious disagreement on the question of women's political activism. After praising the organisational skills and the enthusiasm of the League members, Hannah Ryah, an observer from the IAW at the League's nineteenth annual conference in 1950, reported:

> One question is, however, burning on the visitor's lips when she leaves this convention. How can it be that these skilled American women seem not to care for using their political ability directly in the political work? Only 1 percent of the members of Congress are women. Is it that they feel they must penetrate the problems deeper and deeper before they share the responsibility of putting into effect the declaration which during many years introduced the League's Programme: 'The realization of efficient government depends upon making laws, charters and constitutions fit the needs of the people,

upon the nomination and appointment of responsible officials, upon
the acceptance by citizens of participation in government as a public
trust'?[65]

Ryah recognised the weaknesses of the approach of the American's
women's organisations. Their international identity and activity was
constructed rigidly through the medium of their voluntary associations. Their goal domestically was not just to encourage American
women to become involved in international affairs, but to direct this
activity through the voluntary associations. American women's
organisations advocated the creation of an international role for
women based on their participation in women-only voluntary organisations. Their own pride in the methods and successes of their associations drove them to advocate membership in voluntary
associations as the ideal medium for the expression of the political
interests and identity of women across the world

     Armed with their model of political participation and assuming,
in common with their countrymen, a national superiority, leaders of
American women's organisations threw themselves into an international mission to make the world more like them. Five American
women's organisations in particular were frequent participants in
government/private initiatives. They were the LWV, the AAUW, the
YWCA, the NFBPWC and the NCNW. These established, mainstream
American women's organisations were privileged and acknowledged

as the leaders and representatives of American women by the US government. Other organisations were excluded from this relationship.
The WILPF, for example, was too independent and, arguably, too
international in outlook to enter into co-operation with the American
government. The Women's Party was ostracised because of their
pursuit of 'feminist' objectives such as the Equal Rights Amendment.
In other cases, the co-operation of the government with other associations was limited. The GFWC worked with the government on
certain programmes, but its view of the functions of women's organisations was too introspective to fulfil official goals. In 1947 its handbook had asserted: 'The primary function of a Club or federation of
Clubs is education – to educate the homemaker who would like to
keep up with the trends of the day, who would like to learn something
about international relations, legislation, fine arts etc., but who cannot
leave the home to enter an educational institution'.[66] Thus the GFWC
lacked the activist outlook of the League, the AAUW or the NFBPWC.

A 1950 tour by forty members of the organisation to Europe, rejoicing in the grandiose title, 'The Ramparts of Freedom' had been briefed by the State Department on foreign policy. The report of the tour, however, was concerned with more material matters:

> Dollars spent by Americans abroad are a help to the Marshall Plan. American travelers give substantial help by the dollars they spend in Europe and they provide a stimulus to European trade and recovery. This was true in a high degree of our party of forty generous club-women. Hats, coats, capes, shoes and many other garments were eagerly purchased. Jewelry of all kinds, including cameos, 200 watches, two eterna-matic clocks and four singing birds were among the items taken back to America.[67]

The co-operation between the leaders of American women's organisations and their government was channelled mainly through the Women's Bureau of the Department of Labor. The Women's Bureau had a history of working with voluntary associations and shared with them a distaste for 'equal rights' feminism. Addressing a conference sponsored by the Women's Bureau of the Department of Labor, 'The American woman, her changing role: worker, home-maker, citizen', Frieda Miller, the head of the Bureau assured her audience, 'This conference will not yield a 1948 declaration of women's rights. Women have gone too far and achieved too much to make action of that kind either necessary or appropriate'.[68] The Bureau explicitly involved women's organisations in its programmes, hoping to use them as a model for women in other countries. Alice K. Leopold, Assistant to the Secretary of Labor for Women's Affairs, told the National Order of Women Legislators in June 1957:

> Women, I think, are helping to achieve . . . benefits through several different lines of action. One of these is through their work in women's civic organizations. Another is through their co-operation in international exchange projects, which bring to our shores women from countries the world over. Still another is through their service on international bodies – the United Nations, NATO [the North Atlantic Treaty Organization], the ILO [the International Labor Organization], the Inter-American Commission of Women. All of these activities add up to accomplishments – what we might call women's new role on the international scene.[69]

Leopold suggested that this model, in which women participated through organisations other than national governments, was becoming typical across the world. Using the example of women's political involvement in Latin America, she explained:

> Frequently . . . the first step is an organization of a woman's club. This may be a sewing group, or a committee for a hospital, or a study program on child welfare. Any such group provides experience in the conduct of meetings and the problems of organizations . . . But, and this is important, helping the official authorities are the private organizations. Here is what Miss Hahn [US Representative on the United Nations Commission on the Status of Women] said about them: 'The great international federations which sit with us as non-governmental consultants begin in local clubs. Some of them already have branches in countries where women have not yet won the vote.'[70]

The political path for which women were being trained by voluntary associations was not intended to follow that of masculine involvement. Leopold concluded her 1957 talk by referring to an 'outstanding' example of women's involvement in international relations, their co-operation in the 1955 programme 'Operation American Home'. The emphasis of the programme, which brought thirty-six women from France and thirty-one women from Italy to the USA, was 'on American homes, churches, schools, welfare – or in short, "the heart of America"'.[71] In a speech to the Catholic Federation of Women's Clubs of Greater Cleveland, Leopold again stressed how foreign exchange visitors were informed that an American women's political role proceeded from her primary loyalty:

> Mindful again that the home is woman's first obligation, we try to give each visitor the opportunity to see for herself what American women are doing, how they work through organizations and as individuals and how they raised their families and still had an articulate voice in their communities . . . It was encouraging to see how these women reacted. To see how they were always surprised at the breadth of our vision, our energy, and our community spirit. Their remarks all tended to reflect a growing sense that women all over the world share the same goals and the same objectives – peace, and the opportunity to be of constructive usefulness within our communities and to extend this usefulness to our government wherever possible.[72]

In their proposal for the first visits from leaders of women's organisations of the western and eastern hemispheres, the Women's Bureau stressed the role of American women's organisations as examples. The proposal for five women leaders to be invited to the US as 'specialists and distinguished leaders' under the International Exchange of Persons programme would, the Women's Bureau asserted, 'give the leaders opportunities to study and observe the democratic techniques of representative women's organizations in the United States. They will visit national headquarters and typical local branches of those organizations. Through personal contacts they will be able to establish avenues for future co-operation'.[73] When the women actually arrived, the Women's Bureau let no opportunity slip to bring home to their visitors the importance of American women's organizations. Mary Cannon, chief of the International Division of the Bureau, wrote to Mrs Lozano, a visitor from Monterrey, Mexico, ostensibly to tell her, 'You will be glad to know that Miss Escobar bought a new top for your pen and the shop cleaned it for you. Shall we keep it in Washington until you return?' She continued, however, 'I would like to be sure that you understand why [a visit to] the League of Women Voters was made part of your program'. Stressing the value of the League as a model for women's' participation, Cannon wrote:

> I know you do not have a League of Women Voters in Monterrey and may never have one, but no doubt some programs and methods used by the Illinois League in educating their members and the public on important issues which affect the people in their legislative action programs, can be adopted to your women's organization in your city.[74]

If the exchange of persons programmes expanded and became broader in scope, the message of the Women's Bureau did not. In 1955 eighty women were brought to the USA from France and Italy, sponsored by seventeen different women's organisations. The relentless focus on the women's organisations model convinced many visitors that they had learned the secret of American women's success. One French visitor commented:

> When we first came to the United States we were very dubious about the work of women's organizations and we kept asking ourselves – how effective are their so-called legislative programs? Now we are convinced of the place of women's organizations have in the country and we feel guilty because we haven't taken a more active part in community organizations in France.[75]

One of the Italian visitors was affected by a similar conversion, promising, 'I shall try to establish a Women's Bureau along the lines of the one in the Department of Labor'.[76] Another enthused, 'Your women's organizations are vital to the national well-being and the most important factor in the standing of the American woman today'.[77]

The co-operation between the leaders of American women's organisations and their government, channelled through the Women's Bureau, created a partnership between the private and public spheres. The public sphere of government could call upon the expertise, contacts and goodwill of the leaders of American women's organisations in their campaigns to direct and influence women across the globe. These leaders, in return for their active support and vocal pro-Americanism, were able to claim membership in a foreign policy elite, and to participate in international programmes which allowed them to direct women in other nations in their own footsteps. While this approach would be pursued across the globe, American occupation in West Germany was to be its first testing ground.

Notes

1   Quoted in C. Smith and A. Freedman, *Voluntary Associations: Perspectives on the Literature* (Cambridge, MA: Harvard University Press, 1972), p. v.
2   A. Schlesinger, Sr, 'Biography of a nation of joiners', *American Historical Review*, 50:1 (October 1944).
3   G. McConnell, 'The public values of the private association', in R. Pennock and J. W. Chapman (eds), *Voluntary Associations* (New York: Atherton Press, 1969), p. 147.
4   *Ibid.*, p. 150.
5   Schlesinger, 'Biography of a nation of joiners', p. 25.
6   Schlesinger Library, Radcliffe Inststute, Harvard University, Lucille Koshland papers, carton 1, Mary Handlin speech, 'The values of translating the voluntary association concept into other societies', Annual Meeting of the CCCMF, 23 May 1961.
7   *Ibid.*
8   *Ibid.* Mary Handlin's view of the central role of voluntary associations in the preservation of American democracy was more fully expressed in her 1961 work (co-written with Oscar Handlin), *The Dimensions of Liberty*. Taking a historical perspective, the Handlins argued, 'The emergence of a distinctive pattern of voluntary associations was inextricably bound with the history of liberty in America for it created a significant range of . . . alternatives to the use of coercive power through the state.' O. Handlin and M. Handlin, *The Dimensions of Liberty* (Cambridge, MA: The Belknap Press, 1961), p. 89.
9   G. B. Daniels, 'An anniversary message', *National Business Woman*, 38:7 (July 1959), p. 5.
10 Mary McLeod Bethune Memmorial Museum, Washington, DC, National Council of Negro Women papers, box 7, file 12, Chapman speech, Sixty-Third Annual Convention, Denver, Colorado, 4 June 1954.

11 Quoted in A. M. Rose, *Political Process in American Society* (New York: Oxford University Press, 1967), p. 240.
12 This was particularly the case in societies in which political interests were thought by Americans to be closely tied to non-democratic interests. In his 1962 study *Political Development in the New States*, Edward Shils deplored the lack of voluntary associations in states formed after the Second World World War, arguing that, in their absence, 'strong attachments to kinship, caste and local territorial groups' were allowed to exercise undue influence. Shils elaborated: 'Outside the State, the major institutions through which authority is exercised are the kinship and lineage groups and the religious and caste communities. None of these is voluntary; in many of them there is no publicly acknowledged mode of contending for positions of influence. The 'infrastructures' for collaboration in pursuit of influence and for the exercise of influence in the wider society are largely lacking.' E. Shils, *Political Developments in the New States* (The Netherlands: Mouton and Co, 1962), p. 29.
13 Library of Congress, Washington, DC, League of Women Voters papers, series IV, box 1741, Committee on Un-American Activities, US House of Representatives, '100 things you should know about communism'.
14 *Ibid.*, p. 11.
15 In his ground-breaking work *The Diplomacy of Ideas*, Frank Ninkovich outlines the importance of the role of voluntary associations for cultural diplomacy: 'A bed-rock principle underlying the cultural approach was the conviction that peoples ought to communicate directly with peoples. Although some governmental involvement seemed necessary, the voluntarist tradition dictated that the "task of institutionalizing a set of ideals" as one writer characterized it, should properly remain the preserve of the private sector.' F. A. Ninkovich, *The Diplomacy of Ideas: U.S. Foreign Policy and Cultural Relations 1938–1950* (Cambridge: Cambridge University Press, 1981), p. 87.
16 Schlesinger Library, Radcliffe Institute, Harvard University, Edith Spurlock Sampson papers, box 9, folder 194, Chester Williams, 'Adventure in understanding', in *'Good Evening Neighbors! The Story of an American Institution'*.
17 Harry S. Truman Presidential Library, Independence, Missouri, Clarence Decker papers, file 1, letter, Decker to Truman, 3 October 1947.
18 The reminiscences of Miss Anna Lord Strauss, Oral History Research Office, p. 323.
19 *Ibid.*, p. 324.
20 *Ibid.*, p. 333.
21 Lucille Koshland papers, file 12, OEF board minutes, 7 February 1963.
22 State Department Survey of Agencies and Private Groups, undated, US Declassified Documents Reference System, 1990, Document 1545.
23 US Declassified Documents Reference System, 1992, Document 945, Psychological Strategy Board report, 11 October 1951.
24 *Ibid.*
25 Schlesinger Library, Radcliffe Inststute, Harvard University, Anna Lord Strauss papers, box 9, file 182, letter, Eisenhower to Strauss, 29 May 1956.
26 Anna Lord Strauss papers, box 9, file 182, pamphlet, 'World ideological conflict', April 1957.
27 Anna Lord Strauss papers, box 9, file 182, letter from Charles E. Wilson to Trustees, 12 May 1958.
28 *Ibid.* The financial position of the People-to-People programme was never

very secure. In the first five months of its existence, it had secured, as a gesture of good faith, $25,000 from the government, and a paltry $1,000 from private foundations.

29 Harry S. Truman Presidential Library, Independence, Missouri, Harry S. Truman papers, White House official files, file 426-G 'Statement by the President to delegates of American Council of Voluntary Associations for Foreign Service', 20 February 1947.

30 T. Powers, *The Man Who Kept the Secrets: Richard Helms and the CIA* (London, Knopf, 1979).

31 Handlin and Handlin, *The Dimensions of Liberty*, p. 103.

32 *Ibid.*, p. 112.

33 McConnell, 'The public values of the private association', p. 155.

34 *Ibid.*, p. 156.

35 *Ibid.*

36 'Winning the peace: A statement from women's organizations', *Journal of the AAUW*, 44:4 (Summer 1951), p. 253.

37 C. Lasch, 'The cultural Cold War: A short history of the Congress for Cultural Freedom', in B. J. Bernstein (ed.), *Towards a New Past* (New York: Pantheon Books, 1968), p. 325.

38 *Ibid.*

39 American Association of University Women Archives 1881–1976, series VIII, 'AAUW relations with other organizations', reel 144, 'The Bulletin of the Commission for International Education Reconstruction', 1:1 (30 October 1946). By March 1948 the membership of CIER included; the Department of the Army, National Educational Association, Department of Elementary School Principals, National Council of Christians and Jews, National Red Cross, American Association of Colleges for Teacher Education, Institute of International Education, State Department Division of International Exchange of Persons, Association of Childhood Education, American Association of University Women, the Department of Classroom Teachers of the National Education Association, American Junior Red Cross, Girl Scouts International Division and the American Friends Service Committee.

40 *Ibid.*

41 Records of the AAUW, series VIII, reel 144, CIER letter to its member organisations, 10 February 1948.

42 R. J. Barnet, *The Rockets' Red Glare: War, Politics and the American Presidency* (New York: Simon and Schuster, 1990), p. 299.

43 Schlesinger Library, Radcliffe Institute, Harvard University, Esther Peterson papers, box 9, file 254, International Confederation of Free Trade Unions pamphlet, 'Women! It's your fight too!', 1956.

44 *Ibid.*

45 Edith Spurlock Sampson papers, box 9, folder 192, transcript, Town Hall Meeting of the Air, 'What are democracy's best answers to communism'.

46 D. Bell, 'Interpretations of American politics', in D. Bell (ed.), *The Radical Right: The New American Right* (New York: Doubleday, 1964), p. 55.

47 Estelle Freedman, 'Separation as strategy: Female institution building and American feminism', *Feminist Studies*, 5:3 (Autumn 1979), pp. 512–19.

48 League of Women Voters papers, series IV, box 1725, file 1, 'League growth, April 1954'.

49 The reminiscences of Miss Anna Lord Strauss, p. 153. Strauss further

speculated that the input of these younger, focused and motivated women was an important factor in the professionalisation of the League. She argued, 'I think any organization or institution that grows can start off with just an informal understanding between the people because they have a common objective and are apt to have had similar experiences. Then it grows and it has to become more professionalized, and it did during my period'.

50   League of Women Voters papers, box 1725, pamphlet by Kathryn H. Stone, '25 years of a Great Idea' (1946), p. 33.

51   Frieda Segelke Miller papers, box 13, file 271, memo by Frieda Miller, 'What about women in post war Germany?', p. 7.

52   *Independent Woman*, journal of the National Federation of Business and Professional Women, 27:2 (February 1948), p. 64.

53   Anna Lord Strauss papers, box 3, file 47. Speech by Anna Lord Strauss to The World Affairs Council, Pittsburgh, Pennsylvania, 1 May 1959.

54   YWCA of Boston papers, box 32, file 11, Pamphlet on the Reconstruction Fund.

55   *Ibid.*

56   League of Women Voters papers, box 1787, Report on IAW Conference, 18 October 1949.

57   League of Women Voters papers, box 745, letter from Mme Vischer Alioth to Anna Lord Strauss, June 1948.

58   League of Women Voters papers, box 745, letter, Anna Lord Strauss to Mrs Corbett Ashby, IAW, 8 March 1949.

59   S. M. Hartmann, *The Home Front and Beyond: American Women in the 1940s* (Boston, MA: Twayne, 1982), p. 152.

60   Records of the AAUW, series VIII, reel 145, ref 00585, letter from McHale to Heinman, 17 March 1948.

61   Quoted in L. J. Rupp, 'The survival of American feminism: The women's movement in the post-war period', in R. H. Brenner and G. W. Reichard (eds), *Reshaping America: Society and Institutions 1945–60* (Columbus, OH: Ohio State University Press, 1982), p. 42.

62   The reminiscences of Miss Anna Lord Strauss, p. 378.

63   League of Women Voters papers, box 1882, file 'International Alliance of Women', Kenyon report on the IAW Conference, 18 October 1946.

64   C. E. Harrison, Prelude to feminism: Women's organizations, the federal government, and the rise of the women's movement 1942–1968, PhD dissertation, Columbia University, 1982, p. i.

65   H. Ryah, 'League of Women Voters of the U.S. invites board members of the IAW to its 19th Conference, April 1950, Atlantic City', *International Women's News*, 44:8 (June 1950).

66   S. A. Whitehurst, *The Twentieth Century Clubwoman: A Handbook for Organization Leaders* (Washington, DC: General Federation of Women's Clubs, 1947), p. 5.

67   Schlesinger Library, Radcliffe Institute, Harvard University, Records of the General Federation of Women's Clubs 1950–1959, pamphlet 'General Federation of Women's Clubs world co-operation tour, "To help build the ramparts of freedom", 28 August–3 October 1950'.

68   Records of the Women's Bureau of the US Department of Labor 1918–65, part one, reel 10, Frieda Miller speech to Women's Bureau Conference, 'The American Woman, her changing role: Worker, homemaker, citizen', 17–19 February 1948.

69 Records of the Women's Bureau of the US Department of Labor 1918–65, part one, reel 19, Leopold speech before the National Order of Women Legislators, 7 June 1957.

70 *Ibid.*

71 *Ibid.*

72 Records of the Women's Bureau of the US Department of Labor 1918–65, part one, reel 19, Leopold address to the Catholic Federation of Women's Clubs of Greater Cleveland, 'Spotlight on women', 13 March 1958.

73 League of Women Voters papers, series III, box 751. 'Proposed program in the United States for leaders of women's organizations of the western and eastern hemispheres' (1949).

74 League of Women Voters papers, series III, box 751, letter, Mary Cannon to Mrs Aurelia Lozano, 6 May 1949.

75 AAUW Archives, 1884–1976, series VIII, reel 144, ref 00708, 'Women community leaders from France and Italy – report of a special project, 1955', p. 24.

76 *Ibid.*, p. 26.

77 *Ibid.*, p. 27.

3

'The recipe for American democracy': American women's associations in Germany

American occupation in post-war Germany was not just a military, economic or political project. The USA, in common with its allies, also approached occupation as an ideological mission. Germany who, from the Allied perspective at least, had plunged the world into two global wars in the space of thirty years, seemed to be curiously prone to totalitarian, undemocratic and dangerous governance. Assistant Secretary of State, Archibald MacLeish, argued to Secretary of State Byrnes that US occupation policy must 'encourage the self-government of people on the grounds that tyrannies have been demonstrated to be dangerous to the security of the world and that nations in which the people govern themselves are more likely to keep the peace and to promote the common interests of mankind'.[1]

The effort to establish successful democracy in West Germany took many forms. Educational policy, youth and the re-establishment of a German press, run on American principles of free speech, were obvious areas. Similarly, it was soon clear that the role of voluntary associations in preserving democracy, which had become something of a mantra in the USA, would be a vital part of the effort to re-educate Germany in democracy and to transform its hitherto totalitarian-minded population into active citizens.[2] A group of eleven prominent members of the American educational establishment toured the US zone in Germany in 1946 under the chairmanship of George F. Zook, President of the American Council on Education. In its recommendations to General Clay, the US Military Governor, and the Departments of State and War, the group asserted the importance of private input into re-education programmes, insisting that 'the combined resources of the United States Government, of voluntary agencies and of private individuals must be utilized and co-ordinated'.[3]

The input of voluntary associations was particularly important in reaching German women, many of whom would have no exposure to re-education through labour, professional or political channels. Moreover, the importance of women to the success of the re-education programme was, on demographic grounds, obvious. Because of wartime losses, women made up a disproportionate amount of the German population, outnumbering men by 7.5 million. In a report for the Women's Affairs Bureau, Director Ruth Woodsmall wrote, 'There has been an alteration of a normal population structure to an abnormal one as a result of the war losses. There has been no corresponding change in the social mores within the German community'.[4]

Moreover, Americans believed that German women would be more receptive to the democratisation project since they had, according to US conventional wisdom, been less involved and therefore less culpable in National Socialism than had German men. Americans often accepted at face value the Nazi approach to women as 'Kinder, Kueche and Kirche'. This statement, used by contemporary analysts and subsequently by historians, often operates as convenient shorthand for the lack of real knowledge about women's activities in Nazi Germany. In his 1939 study on German women, Clifford Kirkpatrick documented the involvement of women in National Socialism. Recognising the stereotypes Americans had of German women, Kirkpatrick prefaced his remarks with the complaint, 'The average American newspaper reader conceives of German women driven out of offices by storm troopers and herded back into the home and enforced motherhood . . . The women of Germany are dimly perceived through a fog of headlines, slogans, atrocity stories and selected anecdotes'.[5] Historian Claudia Koonz concurred, arguing that after the war attitudes to German women were shaped by their exclusion from the national life: 'Because Nazi contempt for women was so blatant from the beginning, it . . . [was] easy to assume that women ought not to share in the question of German Guilt'.[6] Koonz argues that American beliefs about the non-participation of German women had less to do with a calm knowledge and consideration of the evidence and more to do with a refusal to contemplate the complicity of women in a regime that was responsible for death camps. The refusal of many Americans to ascribe guilt and blame to German women was a direct contradiction to American occupation policy that forbade fraternisation between Americans and Germans, regardless of their sex, by reminding US servicemen of the widespread popularity of National Socialism. An article in the military newspaper, *The*

Stars and Stripes, warned, 'In heart, body and spirit . . . Every German is Hitler! If in a German town you bow to a pretty girl or pat a blond child . . . You bow to Hitler and his reign of Blood'. Historian Petra Goedde has explained that the policy of non-fraternisation was based on the premise that every German was guilty of war crimes. However, US occupation troops recognised differences between the German population that were constructed mainly by age and gender. Goedde writes:

> Despite the fact that women had contributed to the war effort, GIs adhered to the traditional notion that warfare was a male domain and that women and children were largely passive bystanders. Except for a few highly popularized cases – such as Ilse Koch, the so-called bitch of Buchenwald – few Americans blamed women for Germany's wartime atrocities.[7]

German women's ability to escape a share in 'national guilt' illustrated a belief in the primacy of women's gender identity over national identity. Sociologists Alice Eagly and Mary Kite have shown that national stereotypes are usually thought to be more applicable to men than to women, resulting in a situation whereby 'women are perceived more in terms of their gender stereotype than their nationality stereotype'.[8] In their study of American attitudes to other nationalities, Eagly and Kite found that the distancing of women from the national identity is especially strong when the inhabitants of the country in question were particularly disliked:

> The inhabitants of these disliked countries were perceived as relatively unfriendly and unkind. However, the women of these countries largely escaped this characterization, presumably because they were not responsible for the problems these countries were thought to have created for the United States. As shown by the relatively low agency ascribed to the women of these disliked countries, women's powerlessness becomes much more evident for these countries than for more likeable countries.[9]

American attitudes to German women, therefore, were not over-laden with war-generated hostility. American women's organisations were initially nervous that it might prove difficult to gather up the threads of communication with European counterparts as if the war had been merely an unpleasant interruption. The first post-war meeting of the Fellowship Award Committee of the IFUW debated the problem. While acknowledging the 'intense and determined desire among University women to co-operate with each other', the Committee recognised the 'appalling difficulty and complexity of the business'. Unsure of what attitude to take towards conquered nations, the Committee agonised, 'How are we to make complete understanding among them all? Between neutrals and belligerents, between occupied and unoccupied countries, between those who resisted strongly and those who are suspected of collaborating or even merely of acquiescence?'[10]

It was the lack of involvement (or 'innocence') of German women in National Socialism that enabled American women to sidestep the potentially embarrassing question of war guilt. Eagly and Kite explain that women's powerlessness in a national political system allows them to escape responsibility for the events which may have caused outside disapproval of their countries.[11] As Elizabeth Heineman has persuasively argued, this escape from national responsibility also allows women to be at the forefront of reconstruction in the aftermath of a war. Although 'German women were not, collectively, simply passive victims of a ruthless regime', their narratives emphasised 'the sufferings and losses and downplayed their contribution to and rewards from the Nazi regime'.[12] Heineman argues that 'Women of the Rubble', or *Trummerfrau*, became symbolic of German women's new role in reconstruction, concluding, 'The Women of the Rubble quickly came to suggest a story that began with the bombing of German cities, focused on terrible hardships and promised renewal by the co-operative efforts of ordinary Germans'.[13]

In most cases American references to German women's activities under National Socialism amounted to little more than mild chastisement. For example, Eleanor Roosevelt told German women, 'We are shocked to find that the women in many cases did not stand out as firmly as they should against the encroachment of totalitarian power in Germany'. She quickly recovered from her shock, however, to express the hope that 'the realization will come to all women the world over that they themselves have as individuals a responsibility within every nation to act as citizens to prevent anything which may bring suffering and deprivation again to the people of the world'.[14] This approach was echoed in a letter from Mrs Heming, the President of the Carrie Chapman Catt Memorial Fund (CCCMF), thanking Eleanor Roosevelt for her help in arranging the educational programme for seven German visitors to the USA. Heming asserted, 'We want to emphasize our belief that in a democracy every single person counts and that none of us can evade the responsibility for what happens in our country. This seems to me a more constructive approach than it would be to talk of "guilt". Don't you agree?'[15] The refusal to consider German women as culpable in National Socialism allowed American observers to place German women at the forefront of German reconstruction. US Congresswoman Mrs Chase Going Woodhouse announced during a tour of West Germany:

> It is not only a question of numbers; psychologically women are better orientated to reconstruction on a democratic basis than are the men. They have no 'face to save'. Since 1933 they have had no status. In fact their post World War I spurt to a better position flickered out by 1928. They were not a part of policy-making Nazi Germany. They have everything to gain, nothing to lose in democratic reorganization.[16]

The Women's Affairs Division of the Office of Military Government of the United States (OMGUS) saw it as their responsibility to educate previously politically innocent German women about their civic responsibilities. This education was a two-stage process. First, Germany women must be awakened from the political apathy with which Americans were convinced they approached life. Once German women were aroused from apathy, they could be 're-educated' in the ways of democracy. Lorena Hahn, the original Chief of the Women's Affairs Division, informed Dr Alexander, the Chief of the Educational and Religious Affairs Branch:

> National Socialism isolated German women from public life, restricted them from women in other countries and indoctrinated many women with Nazi ideals. There are German women who are keenly aware of these facts and are eager to re-establish the social, political and economic structure of their lives. On the other hand a large number of German women are indifferent to this reconstruction. We are therefore confronted with a stimulus program as well as one of guidance and education.[17]

In their insistence on channelling the political activities of German women through voluntary associations, American women betrayed a serious misunderstanding of the role of Germany women under National Socialism. They assumed that women's organisations, for Americans synonymous with freedom and liberty, could not coexist with totalitarianism. Ruth Woodsmall, chief of the Women's Affairs Section, told representatives of American women's organisations, 'Women's organisations that were disbanded by Hitler are being re-organised'.[18] The CCCMF of the League of Women Voters told its members, 'Although women in Germany had the vote for many years before the rise of Nazism, they suffered the set-back of being relegated to subservient domesticity . . . Many were so intimidated that they are still terrified of putting their names on any list'.[19]

Indeed the independent women's organisations that had existed in Germany before National Socialism were consolidated under *Frauenwerk*, where all independence and autonomy was denied. However, the concept of women's organisations as a medium for the activities of women was not abolished in the 1930s. Claudia Koonz's study, *Mothers in the Fatherland*, shows that many women were wholehearted supporters of Hitler. Nazi women leaders created an empire of organisations that, while advocating traditional sex-roles and subservient femininity, also held great power. Koonz argues, 'Without encouragement from Party leaders, several women Nazis independently organized in what one women leader called "a sort of parallel movement", separate from the Nazi party and yet supportive of it . . . At the local and national level, women leaders emerged, each with her own style, objectives and class of followers'.[20]

In his study of women under National Socialism, Kirkpatrick documented the organisation of German women into voluntary associations. Nazi women believed that their role was vital to the future both of their political cause and their country. While using rhetoric that celebrated their role as mother and homemaker, they enjoyed a sense of crisis that necessitated their involvement in the public world. Claudia Koonz recounts the story of a Nazi housewife, canvassing passers-by, who was confronted by an irate businessman telling her that good Nazi women ought to stay at home and serve dinner to her family. 'The nation is in peril!', she responded, 'I cannot remain happy and carefree at the supper table when Mother Germany weeps and her children die. Germany must live on, even if we sacrifice our lives!'[21]

This picture of women's lives in Nazi Germany is vital to understanding the reaction of German women to the efforts of American women's organisations. The attitudes of US women towards German counterparts were based on two assumptions. First, they believed that the model of political participation through voluntary women's organisations would appeal to women who had previously been isolated in the home. A report by Mrs Bartlett B. Heard, a member of the

LWV and the YWCA sent to Germany by the State Department, confirmed this attitude:

> In Germany, where for centuries women have been relegated to a status below that of man and psychologically conditioned to interpret the role of homemaker in its narrowest terms, very special effort will have to be made over periods of years before women and men understand that while home is the centre of a woman's life, it cannot be the boundary.[22]

Second, American women believed that the post-war world was the crisis situation that would inspire women to become politically active. These assumptions were deeply flawed. For German women, the Second World War had been the 'crisis situation', which had left many drained and apathetic to anyone offering political solutions. This apathy is illustrated in a meeting organised by an army adviser on 'Women and youth affairs' between twenty German women from Bad Homberg and several American women: 'Due to German reticence, the dialogue got off to a creaky start. Urged to speak up, they did, but to vent their anger over the food policies of the American army, not to air abstract hopes for democracy'.[23] A panel of American women representing national women's organisations were told by German women, 'because of the shattered illusion of the Hitler era, women in Germany were hesitant to join new organisations and many were apathetic

towards policies and their civic responsibilities'.[24] The practical priorities of German women were illustrated in the despairing comment of Mrs Melle, Vice-President of the German women's group, Notgemeinshaft, on a visit to the USA, 'The difficulties of attracting the women are enhanced by the fact that in the Russian Zone, when the Communist women meet, a heated hall is provided, plus a dinner, both of which have an undeniable appeal to people who are cold and hungry'.[25] Mary Decker, a member of the 'Town Hall Meeting of the Air', observed the lack of enthusiasm among German women for joining anything. At the seminar entitled, 'What problems are women facing in Germany today?', Decker complained:

> These women leaders are disturbed because the mass of German women are not coming into organizations. They are not active in political and social welfare work. They are too burdened with poverty, home cares, too fearful – recalling what happened to Nazi women – too man-dominated to respond to the democratic organizations struggling to help them.[26]

This notable lack of enthusiasm among German women in response to attempts to push them into voluntary associations did nothing to check American zeal. The importance placed by Americans upon the role of voluntary associations was clearly illustrated in the Exchange of Persons programme. While it eventually became a genuine exchange in the sense of being reciprocal, with West Germany as an active partner, the programme was initially conceived as 'a unilateral American-initiated, American-funded and American-directed implementation of United States policy, serving primarily United States' interests'.[27] Under the offices of OMGUS and the High Commissioner in Germany (HICOG), a total of 14,000 people participated in exchanges between the USA and Germany, the largest government-sponsored programme with another country.[28] Henry Kellerman, the State Department historian of the programme, asserted that its purpose was 'to help assist Germans in creating a new society modelled on Western democratic concepts'.[29] Kellerman explains that each proposal from private organisations to send representatives to Germany subsequently 'had to be submitted to the Reorientation Branch of C.A.D. [the Civil Affairs Division] by responsible institutions or organizations with full responsibility assumed by sponsor, sources of funds, name of person to be sent, description of type of service, length of time'.[30] The proposal was then forwarded to the Department of State before finally going to the theatre commander for approval. William K. Hitchcock, Assistant Secretary for Educational and Cultural Affairs at the US Department of State, emphasised the importance of the contribution of voluntary associations, acknowledging, 'The Department-sponsored program has been dependent from the outset on a solid and enthusiastic partnership with a large body of private organizations and citizens to numerous to count'.[31]

Women's place in the exchange programme was not made formal until 1947, following the appointment of Herman Wells, the President of Indiana University, as Educational and Cultural Advisor to the Military Government. 'Women' became a category in its own right, alongside others like 'agriculture', 'education', 'youth' and 'religion' in the programme. A women's affairs section was established within OMGUS in 1948. Lucille Koshland credited General Clay, the Military Governor in the US zone, with some assistance from Anna Lord Strauss, with the idea of women's participation. Koshland wrote to Strauss:

Didn't you sit next to General Clay at a dinner when he mentioned his idea, as Military Governor of Post-war Germany, to bring some Germans to the U.S.A. to observe democracy in action at the grass roots? And didn't you ask him innocently how many women would be included? Apparently a new idea to him, which led to him asking whether the League of Women Voters would assist in programming such a group.[32]

In 1946, even before the official policy on the exchange of persons had been announced, General Clay made an urgent request that Mrs Gabrielle Strecker, an employee of OMGUS, be sponsored by the US government to attend the convention of the International Assembly of Women. Mrs Strecker thus became the first German visitor to the USA under government auspices.

The re-education of West German women was the first post-war programme in which women's voluntary associations and the US government co-operated at a high level. In November 1948 the Civil Administration Division of OMGUS requested that the CCCMF sponsor an orientation project for a group of German women. The US government paid travel and living expenses for a visit to the USA while the CCCMF financed and organised an education programme for the women. This initiative accorded with the founding principle of the Women's Affairs Section, established in May 1948 within the Educational and Cultural Relations Division of OMGUS.[33] Chief of the Section was Ruth Woodsmall, who had served as the General Secretary of the World YWCA from 1934 to 1947.[34] The Section operated on the principle that its role was to 'observe, supervise and assist' German women through the agency of women's voluntary associations, 'It is the policy of this section to further the attempts of the above mentioned groups [German voluntary associations of women] to exercise a constructive role in the re-establishment of democratic procedures in community life'.[35]

Initial public statements of the Section often described its activities as 'demand-driven' by the spontaneous requests of German women:

Literally hundreds of women's organizations are beginning to spring up throughout the zone. German women leaders are eagerly seeking advice and help in the formation and development of these organizations along democratic lines. It is therefore the duty of the Chief of Women's Affairs to assist in setting up these new organizations and to keep in touch with them until firm democratic patterns are attained.[36]

The terms of reference for the Section stated its intention to encourage this process: 'It is the policy of this office to serve as a liaison agency and a clearing centre for information between German voluntary women's organisations and other countries'.[37] With German women unwilling to enter political life, the Section encouraged voluntary associations to work to overcome this hesitancy.

The private–state co-operation in Germany was mediated, not only by the Women's Affairs Section, but by the Women's Bureau of the Department of Labor in the US. The Bureau announced the Women Leaders Program in April 1949 as 'a project which is designed to foster better international understanding through the channels of women's organisations'.[38] This programme was not limited to German exchanges but was worldwide in its scope: the first five women leaders to visit the USA were from Mexico and Latin America. The head of the Women's Bureau, Frieda Miller, praised the nine women's organisations involved in the programme, arguing 'their actions undoubtedly will establish the avenues for future co-operation between women of this and other countries and serve to help women everywhere to meet certain of their problems through strengthening the work of their democratic women's organizations'.[39]

Both the Women's Affairs Section and the Women's Bureau were eager to avoid any hint that their activities could be seen as an encouragement of what they saw as 'old school' or 'equal right-style' feminism. In 1949 the Section co-operated with several German leaders on a project to raise the status of German women through a version of the Civil Code (Buergerliches Gestetzbuch). The Section stressed:

> In giving assistance to German women in their effort to revise the Civil Code with special reference to the inequalities affecting women, the representatives of women's affairs are in no sense promoting a 'feministic' movement in the traditional concept of the word ... There will be need for a careful interpretation of the basic necessity for the revision of the Civil Code in order to avoid the misinterpretation in the press.[40]

Despite this care, the US military newspaper, *The Stars and Stripes*, published an account of the programme under the headline 'Suffragette movement revived to help women in the U.S. Zone'. The story reported, 'The equal-suffragette movement is being stimulated by Women's Affairs officers in Hesse, Bavaria and Wuettemberg-Baden'.[41] The next day *The Stars and Stripes* published a correction,

'HICOG officials pointed out that a story in *The Stars and Stripes* erred Friday in reporting that German women, "encouraged" by HICOG women's affairs officers, were reviving a "suffragette" movement in the U.S. Zone'.[42] Mrs Bartlett B. Heard's report to the Women's Affairs Section in 1950 assured, 'Any apprehension that programs for women will bring about a feminist movement seem to be unfounded. In my opinion it would be impossible to revive feminism or create a feminist movement in Germany'.[43]

The model of democracy advocated for German women by American women's organisations was not focused on claiming rights but on embracing responsibility. One of the first experts in women's affairs to visit occupied Germany, Congresswoman Mrs Chase Going Woodhouse, had asserted that German women needed coaxing to enter political life. She explained that her strategy of involving more German women in public affairs after the Second World War was one of connecting the timeless concerns of women as mothers with the specific problems facing German women under reconstruction:

> The good mother tradition can be used in an appeal for more partic-
> ipation in public affairs. The good mother today must be a good
> citizen for only she can help assure the right community environ-
> ment for her children. Many of the acute problems, touch the family
> – juvenile delinquency, returning POWs, refugees, housing, school
> reform, for example. Women can see when it is pointed out to them
> how their families are affected by the solution, or lack of a solution to
> community problems.[44]

Direct participation in the political process was not a focus of the programmes of either the Women's Bureau or the Women's Affairs Section of OMGUS. A tour of ten American women at the request of the State Department and OMGUS typified this approach. The national news release of the AAUW related:

> In a discussion over tea with the Lord Mayor of Wiesbaden and with
> leaders of the local women's organisations, the Americans learned
> that many problems that are the concern of private organisations in
> the United States are handled by government agencies in Germany.
> The group gained the impression that the paternalistic strain which
> persists in the German Government discourages initiative and frus-
> trates the political influence of women's organisations. At the same
> time, the American groups observed that there are a number of social
> problems confronting German women which need the crusading
> efforts of their organisations to correct them.[45]

Between the start of the programme in 1946 and 1953, an estimated 4,000 German leaders visited America; at least 800 of them
women.[46] The importance of educating German women about the role
of voluntary associations was stressed by the Bureau in its
'Suggestions to sponsors' note to American women's organisations:

> These women are brought to the United States in order that they may
> have a broad and sympathetic understanding of American life,
> culture and ideals, that they may learn about non-governmental
> organisations and how to adopt the knowledge and experience
> gained here to their important task of contributing to the develop-
> ment of Germany as a democratic state.[47]

All twelve members of this tour were members or leaders of German
women's organisations. The description of each of them concluded,
'She is here to study Women's Organizations in Reference to Civic
Participation'.[48]

While it is not extraordinary that a group visiting women's organisations should profess to have such an interest, it is significant that
the model dominated German women's experience of the US to the
exclusion of other aspects of American life. The segregation of women
into a 'category' of exchange visitor, alongside such groups as 'labor',
'youth' or 'religion', meant that their trips were specifically organised
on the basis of assumed gender interests. Not infrequently, the
German visitors resented this approach and disliked the bias of the
exchange programme towards women's associations. Mary Cannon,
Chief of the International Division at the Women's Bureau, passed
Mrs Anna Maire Heiler's complaints to the State Department, 'Her
primary interest was in government rather than in women's organizations. She resented being sponsored by women's groups rather than
by political scientists'.[49] Since twenty-eight of the first fifty women
who came to the USA under the HICOG programme were members
of the Bundestag, rather than members of women's organisations, it
is likely that this complaint was widespread.

Yet the Women's Bureau, directing the proposed programme of
German women visitors, remained dedicated solely to the need to
encourage volunteer women's groups in Germany. Doing so, they followed American women's use of 'social feminism' through voluntary
associations as a 'pathway to power'. Even when the Bureau envisaged a role for German women outside voluntary associations, it was
as officials involved in the 'feminine' field of welfare:[50]

The Woman's Bureau is also aware of the fact that there is an increasing need for volunteer leaders who, with the help of their organizations, can supplement the work of the women who are professional social welfare workers or government officials in related fields, active in carrying out social welfare in their countries.[51]

Issues of national pride further hindered understanding between German visitors and their American hosts. American women expected to be in a superior position to German women and were not receptive to any criticism of their own system by the Germans. Indicative of this is the nature of the exchanges. Rather than an exchange between equals, eager to learn about the other, the German women were to come to the US to learn valuable lessons about the American way of life. American women visiting Germany were there to spread the message about American values to German women not fortunate enough to make the trip for themselves. In other words, German women travelled to the USA to learn, while American women travelled to Germany to teach or perhaps to reinforce their pre-existing prejudices about the status of German women relative to their own. Ten US women visiting Germany in 1951 under the auspices of the State Department explained that they had 'discovered' how far German women were behind American counterparts in the establishment of women's organisations. One report noted, 'The American delegation . . . was told that their counterpart German organizations have a long way to go before they can achieve the active role and effective influence in community affairs which is second nature to American women's groups'.[52] A group of American women leaders touring Bavaria stated their superiority over German women through the metaphor of the 'helping hand', 'If American women residing in Germany will extend a helping hand to German women in their fledgling efforts to find a way to democratic living . . . they will hasten the day when Germany will assume full status among other countries'.[53]

Any observations that German women made about the USA which were less than overwhelmingly positive were often met with indignation. The AAUW collated the opinions of its members in Montana who played host to a German exchange visitor, Dr Hildegaad Wolle-Egenolf, in a programme intended to 'give German women a working knowledge of the American way of life and the part women played in it'.[54] Reaction was mixed. The chair of the Havre branch described Wolle-Egenolf as 'a very brilliant and aggressive seeker of the truth of the facts about the place American women have taken in society'. The chair concluded, 'If her visit fails to be one of constructive value, I should feel inclined to blame the American women with whom she comes into contact. She has the involuntary resentment of the conquered for the conqueror . . . Perhaps due to this she seemed at times more impressed with our failures than with our successes'.[55] The Great Falls branch was also sympathetic, reporting, '[Wolle-Egenolf] has been a good tonic for us her in Great Falls. We had an informal open house for her, and she had all the women at her feet while she told them what is wrong with American women'.[56]

Not all branches were quite so understanding of Wolle-Egenolf's candour. A representative of the Helena branch reported:

> I had expected an amount of misunderstanding but was not prepared for the constant vigilance that had to be exercised. Nor was I prepared to cope with her apparent suspicion that I was trying to cover up . . . Her own personality and nature are such than she made more confusion for herself . . . I have greater respect than ever for the tremendous efforts of the State Department.[57]

The Bozeman branch reported on Wolle-Egenolf's 'habit of outspoken criticism and belligerent cross-questioning', concluding, 'She had definite pre-conceived ideas which she may have brought with her from Germany or acquired during her stay in this country. At any rate her mind was pretty much closed to anything we had to tell her'. The chair of Bozeman reported unfavourably how Wolle-Egenolf insisted on petting the bears in Yellowstone Park, despite warnings from the driver, and proclaimed, 'See, they don't hurt me. They are so friendly'. All groups commented on Wolle-Egenolf's legal approach to women's position and her lack of interest in the 'women's association' approach. The Harve branch commented, 'Her attitude is almost one of our old-time feminists'.[58] Many correspondents complained to the Women's Bureau that on some days Wolle-Egenolf insisted on speaking only German. Most American women were unwilling to make this level of effort to understand their visitor.

Other German visits were not so negative. Mrs Margitta Richstadt, brought to America by the LWV, professed herself eager to learn 'the American recipe for democracy so that I can make it a part of all phases of German life'.[59] The Women's Bureau chose in its speeches and statements to emphasise the positive aspects of exchanges and the sense of shared female identity for which they were designed, asserting, '[The] remarks [of German women visitors to the USA] all tended to reflect a growing sense that women all over the world share the same goals and the same objectives . . . peace and the opportunity to be of constructive usefulness within our communities and to extend this usefulness to our government wherever possible'.[60]

Clearly, American women's efforts at the political re-education of their European sisters were not designed to encourage introspection and self-analysis. It was disheartening for US women to find, when lecturing about the advantages of American life, that their audience often seemed more interested in focusing upon negative aspects of what they had heard about America. The issue of racism vividly illustrated this. American women's organisations had often admitted to themselves that it would be necessary to solve the problem of racial discrimination if the USA were to represent itself to the rest of the world as the bastion of freedom. Zelia Ruebhausen, the observer for the LWV at the United Nations (UN), reported that while the USA had had considerable success in condemning the Soviet Union for putting down the Hungarian uprising in 1956, the issue had been clouded by the trouble over integration of schools in Arkansas. The Soviet delegate told the Ambassador from Ceylon in the UN General Assembly that 'he would be safer in the streets of Budapest than he would in Little Rock'. Mrs Ruebhausen concluded, 'If the United States is to exert leadership, it cannot do it by dollars alone. We must also live up to our beliefs in the dignity of man and the rights of all citizens to equal opportunities'.[61]

American women were often unwilling to be this frank with critics from other nations. Perhaps they displayed the 'restless vanity' that de Tocqueville had observed over a century earlier, making Americans in their dealings with strangers, 'impatient of the slightest censure and insatiable of praise'.[62] The primary argument Americans used were that reports of discrimination had been widely exaggerated and that the situation was improving all the time. This attitude was typified in a 1955 report of the *San Francisco News*: 'Better view of Americans – East Bay woman corrects some of Britain's distorted ideas'. Mrs Harry Kingman, of the Berkeley LWV, had visited Britain under the sponsorship of the CCCMF and was shocked to find 'that even schoolchildren knew the name of Emmett Till and details of his Mississippi murder and the subsequent trial and acquittal of the accused white man'. The article described this version of events as a 'distorted idea', although it made no attempt to explain exactly in what respect this account was 'distorted'.[63]

The eagerness to correct the appearance of discrimination was echoed by American women in the treatment of visitors to America. Lucille Koshland of the OEF complained, 'Unfortunately we find that so many exchanges arrive here with very unfavourable pictures of us in their minds (Communist Propaganda? Maybe.) They all seem to have heard about Little Rock and Lynching'.[64] Mrs Robert Lambkin, a member of the Arlington, Virginia, branch of the AAUW, wrote to headquarters about her concern that German women voters not get the 'wrong' picture of the conditions in which African-Americans were living:

> Mrs Meyer-Spreckels [a German visitor] unburdened her soul about the Negro situation. She had had a rather disillusioning experience that afternoon – had been taken by a Negro group to a fine housing development for Negroes, but had then been taken to the back alleys and into the homes of the poorest Negroes. She was left feeling that Americans were doing little for the poor Negro. Mrs Goode [Meyer-Spreckels's confidante] thought felt that whoever had been her guide had not done too good a job. Although it was important to see conditions as they are, it might be well in future trips to reverse the process and watch the guide in charge.[65]

American women's organisations were not alone in their concern that German visitors received what they saw as the 'correct' picture of American life and women's place in it. Sponsoring government agencies also kept a watchful eye on the reports of the exchanges. One German visitor, Suse Windisch, reported on her visit: 'I don't think any of the housewives whom we met has prepared fresh vegetables for lunch or dinner (with the exception of salad) but they always used canned vegetables. This fact as well as some others seem to explain to me why American women can spend much more time for club activities'.[66] Betsy Knapp, the Cultural Attaché in Frankfurt, commented:

> I am just a little bit concerned about Miss Windisch's conclusion that the participation of American Women in the community is primarily related to household conveniences . . . I think it important for our foreign visitors to know that there was a tradition of participation in the community long before gadgets and time-saving devices became so plentiful. It is all too easy for people to jump to the conclusion that our behaviour pattern is completely the product of the conveniences of life.[67]

The increasing anxiety about the impression German women received about American society was part of a shift in US policy towards Germany. While initial American attitudes towards Germany may have been shaped by a concern for their de-nazification and re-education in democracy, the wider context of the Cold War quickly ensured that it was of equal, if not greater, importance that the loyalty of the West German people towards the USA be assured. This change manifested itself through an increasing concern over perceived Soviet attempts to target West German women for propaganda. As early as spring 1945, a proposal for International Study Grants from the AAUW for 'Women of the Liberated Countries' noted, 'Our enemies have been diabolically clever in sowing seeds of suspicion and hatred. We need to get about the business of sowing our own seeds of understanding and friendship with all speed'.[68] In a 1948 report, 'The forgotten women may decide the German battle', journalist Anne O'Hare McCormick explained to readers, 'The Russians have worked to make women feel important; first in comparison with the position under Hitler, who started by shooing them back into the home and ended by pulling them out to work in the factories; and second, in contrast with the indifference manifested toward them by the other occupying Powers'.[69]

Mrs Elizabeth Holt, a women's activities specialist stationed in Berlin, also voiced concern: 'There is a great danger of communism in the women's groups. As I'm fond of telling . . . the communists have said, "Take the women and the youth and the Americans can have the men"'.[70] The Women's Affairs Section made repeated illusions to the Soviet targeting of women's groups as justification for an increased importance for their role. Their report for July to December 1949 warned:

> In this formative period of the new Germany, women's organizations merit careful consideration as they are of important political potential. They may be developed as a democratic force or used as an effective instrument for propaganda. There is evidence of systematic efforts from the Eastern Zone to undermine the Western German state by appealing to certain women's organizations through slogans of peace and unity and condemning the division of Western Germany.[71]

The report concluded, 'The great majority of women's organizations are orientated towards Western Ideology and are developing as an affirmation of democratic ideals. The support of these organizations is a sound investment towards German Democracy'.[72]

To ensure the support of these groups, the Women's Affairs Section co-operated in the organisation of the Congress of Women at Bad Pyrmont. Attended by more than 600 German women, the Congress led to the foundation of Deutsche Frauenring, a federation of women's organisations that immediately affiliated to the International Council of Women (ICW). The Section asserted, 'The founding of the Deutsche Frauenring and its affiliation to the ICW has definite significance as a countercheck to the claims of the over-all women's organization in the Eastern Zone, Demokratischer Frauenbund, which is affiliated to the Women's International Democratic Federation (WIDF), the Soviet propaganda organization on a world scale', and linked this to the broader American policy of uniting West Germany as a viable and strong national power. [73] The Section concluded:

> The founding of a Federation of Women's Organizations of Western Germany has considerable significance. An overall organization uniting the three zones is indicative of growth toward the cultural unity of Western Germany. It may also have wide political influence as the channel for expression of opinion of women on public issues throughout Western Germany. It is one of the salient evidences of the de facto end of the period of trizonal division of Western Germany, even though the zonal boundaries still exist.[74]

This strategy was evident in the 'Tripartio Project', organised by the Women's Affairs Section in February 1951 for citizenship training with the specific purpose of countering the communist threat. The Section asserted, 'Such a joint training project for all three zones will greatly strengthen the solidarity of German women from different *Länder* and give them a stronger sense of their total responsibility as citizens, as well as a clearer understanding of the integral relationship of Germany to Western Europe'.[75]

Despite the best efforts of the Section to counter Soviet propaganda, concern grew that a full response to Soviet efforts was beyond the scope of its meagre resources. The Section fretted about the Women's International Day celebrations held in Berlin in March 1950:

> Although the Soviet movement has not succeeded in its appeal in Berlin, there is apprehension of the effect of such large-scale campaigns which appeal to masses of women under the perverted

slogans of peace and unity. The lack of help from the U.S.A. in Berlin, since the Women's Affairs position in Berlin was eliminated last summer, has been difficult for Berlin women to understand and has been a cause for alarm. The mass effort campaign in Berlin is considered by some as more dangerous than the youth rally because of the degree of unemployment among women, who constitute more than half the breadwinners in Berlin.[76]

A parallel report, 'Communist propaganda and influence in relation to women's organizations and the Women's Affairs Program', by Women's Affairs Advisor Betsy Knapp connected the issue of 'defence' against communist propaganda to the earlier concern to educate German women in democracy: 'The problem of meeting the present pressure on the part of the Communists against the women is the same problem that the United States Government has been endeavouring to meet through the Women's Affairs Program'.[77] Knapp concluded with regret:

> The pressure from the Communists only indicates that the work was started late, that sufficient top level political importance has not yet been attached to the factor of women, that there have been inadequate facilities for tackling the problem on an all out basis. The size of the task of overcoming the basic political apathy of the German women, of doing something about their political ignorance and of bringing about basic changes in behaviour patterns which will make it possible for the women's organizations to be effective instruments of education and activity, has been consistently underestimated, or perhaps the importance of tackling it on a large scale has been underappreciated.[78]

While she sympathised with the problems the Women's Affairs Section faced, Knapp's report specifically criticised their concentration on the 'voluntary association' approach, asserting, 'There is some tendency to simplify the problem of women's affairs by thinking of it as "women's organization" rather than as a business of bringing women into all types of activity: Boards, Committees, forums, offices – all the agencies where community and public problems are involved'.[79]

The exchange programme with America continued to stress the model of women's associations, perhaps due to the reliance of the programme upon such organisations, but the Section within Germany was increasingly aware of the need for a more diverse approach. The Section's report on women's conferences in Bad Pyrmont and Furth in 1949–50 made an interesting comparison between the conference in Furth of the Social Democratic Party (SPD) and the non-party (or, to use their terms, 'above-party') conference of women in Bad Pyrmont. The report pointed out the advantages of an emphasis on party gatherings, particularly the fact that 'there was a welcome lack of any vague resolutions on world peace, so characteristic of above-party conferences, as sincere as they are unconstructive'.[80]

Still, this was not to say the 'above-party approach' was useless, since it could attract the mass of German women who were 'totally unenlightened politically'.[81] The founding of the Deutsche Frauenring at Bad Pyrmont was recognised as an important alternative to the Communist Demokratische Frauenbund Deutschlands (DFD), since 'women who would not join a political party but are looking around for some sort of activity with a wider scope might well have joined the DFD in the sincere belief that they were becoming members of a genuine non-party organization'.[82] Moreover, the report noted that the affiliation of Deutsche Frauenring to the ICW would serve a useful purpose in connecting German women with women of other countries, a benefit the 'party' approach lacked.

The effect of American women's organisations in the re-education of German women is difficult to gauge. The efforts of the Section to gain the support and loyalty of German women had some tangible results. The German women who were picked to take part in the exchange programme were carefully selected in order to have the maximum effect on their return to Germany, contrary to historian Harold Zink's claim that 'in certain cases . . . American officials took advantage of an excellent opportunity to send their German mistresses on an excursion to the United States'.[83] Many of the German women chosen to visit America became formidable allies of the Americans. Gabrielle Strecker, an employee of OMGUS and a founder of the Christian Democratic Union, had been sent to the USA in 1946 to attend the International Assembly of Women in New York.[84] A later memorandum on psychological warfare from the Women's Affairs Bureau suggested the possibility of financial support for German women's groups who were making counter-communist efforts on their own initiative. An example was the work of Strecker, who had established a group of women in Frankfurt to educate women on the 'real meaning of Communist Propaganda'. Strecker subsequently wrote a book, *Propaganda Tactics*, on the strategies of the Soviets, published under German auspices with a US subsidy.[85]

In an application to the Ford Foundation for a grant to fund further international exchanges, the CCCMF, perhaps none too surprisingly, waxed lyrical about the positive effect a visit to American women's organisations had on European women:

> Our visitors have commented over and over again on the warm friendliness of their hosts, on the fact that government officials here are regarded as public 'servants' not 'masters', that it is the 'spirit of co-operation' rather than wealth and gadgets in the home that makes it possible for more women here to take part in community activities, that Negroes and members of other minorities have many opportunities for public service and are not at all oppressed, that American Democracy has a 'spiritual side'.[86]

Beyond producing a positive feeling about America and American values, the international exchange of women leaders had an important role to play in strengthening the Free World against communist encroachment, claimed the CCCMF. In carefully selecting women who 'have standing and prestige in their own communities', the CCCMF argued, 'The results of their stay . . . [will] in turn influence large numbers'.[87] The AAUW was similarly confident of the effect of the exchange programmes, asserting, 'Exchange of persons has been a major part in the democratic re-orientation of the cultural rehabilitation of the occupied countries'.[88]

 German women's organisations certainly developed a 'special relationship' with American women's organisations through the post-war American programmes. At the Conference of the International Council of Women in Helsinki in June 1954, Dr Ulrich-Beil, head of the German delegation, was fulsome in her praise of American women's leadership:

> America is the home of the world because she has spiritual integrity and high moral virtue. Surely the United States is the logical country to lead the world and the women of the National Council of Women of the United States and its affiliates are the logical ones to spearhead the movement for a great spiritual revival. As earlier American women led in the movement for the International Council of Women, let today's American women lead in the movement for spiritual regeneration of the world.[89]

In her article on German women's 'consciousness and activity' in Frankfurt, Donna Harsch points to the conservative political outlook of German women as an outcome of the model of participation impressed upon them by Americans: 'In the Federal Republic, women voted at a higher rate than men for the Christian Democrats, a party that implemented a conservative family policy, promoted the housewife, resisted the enactment of egalitarian family law, opposed the legalization of abortion and tightened the divorce law'. More specifically, Harsch points out that German women's organisations which emerged from post war Germany were 'by and large, very moderate', Harsch argued, 'By concentrating on issues that arose out of women's experience in the family, they revived the "organized motherliness" and what Ann Taylor Allen has called the "maternal metaphor" of pre-1914 bourgeois women's associations'.[90] The export of the model of voluntary associations as a medium for women's political activity was not restricted to Germany but was applied to other countries. United States representatives displayed the same disregard for, and impatience with, any 'native' conditions that were at odds with the voluntary association model. As late as 1957 Anna Lord Strauss was assuring the readers of *Bangkok World* that the model of women's associations was appropriate for Asian women:

> The outstanding single factor of the just conducted Asian Women's Seminar is the emphasis laid on individual and voluntary initiative. Government activity will never be enough to arouse the Asian woman and to free her from her many bonds . . . She herself must be educated in her rights and her duties and dignities . . . And this can best be done by women's organizations.[91]

The Overseas Education Fund of the LWV gradually came to see the error of applying American models to overseas development. In their 1961 annual report, it recognised:

> The voluntary association, especially as directed towards citizenship education, has achieved its highest degree of effectiveness in the United States. This is a concept that individuals and groups in many countries request in increasing numbers that we share with them. But it cannot be transported intact – it needs to be adopted and translated into terms appropriate to the culture and level of functioning of the society in which it is to take place.[92]

Recognising this, the new full-time field worker of the OEF in Latin America was described as a 'transformer', that is, one who 'enables the Fund to convert U.S. Patterns and ideas into a frame of reference that is meaningful and valuable in Latin America'.[93]

Nevertheless old ideas died hard, and the OEF was unusual in its

change of policy. In 1967 Elizabeth Greenfield, a visitor to Korea and
Japan on an American Specialist Grant, concurred with Anna Lord
Strauss on the importance of the wholesale export of women's organ-
isations:

> The women of Japan and Korea can learn much about democracy by
> its introduction into their own organizations. Democracy in the
> United States is constantly being re-enforced by the demands of the
> electorate reflected in voluntary group action. I think we can import
> some of our know-how and experience in the field of voluntary com-
> munity organization.[94]

The model of co-operation between American women's voluntary associations and the US government as applied in Germany produced a template for US involvement with women in other nations.
This template dictated that women's political participation be directed
through voluntary associations. The claim of American women to
share an identity with German women was the basis for their assertion that they were the most suitable 'teachers' in the re-education of
German women. Such a role was not always easy, often being marred
by misunderstandings and resentment. But American women's belief
and confidence in their mission was part of a national pride in the per-
fection of American political institutions. Richard L. Merrit, in his
study of American efforts to re-educate West Germany explains,
'Democratizing Germany was a particularly bewitching notion in the
United States. Americans had long viewed their constitutional system
as a model for other countries to emulate'.[95] However, this altruistic if
deeply chauvinistic aim became embroiled in the emerging Cold War.

Instead of focusing on creating a new democratic Germany, American
policy-makers became increasingly concerned with the need to mould
Germany as a bulwark against encroaching communism.

The efforts of American women's organisations were part of this
shift in priorities. While initially they sought to establish German
women's organisations along democratic lines, as Cold War imperatives became apparent they became increasingly concerned with
directing these organisations along pro-American and anti-commu-

nist lines. Rather than a task of 're-education', their aims became more
focused on propaganda, aimed at refuting the allegations of the Soviet
Union and winning the loyalty of the women of Germany and else-
where to the American cause. The rhetoric of American women's
organisations, which had in the immediate aftermath of the Second

World War proclaimed them internationalists and women, became increasingly focused on their role as Cold War warriors and Americans.

Notes

1 J. F. Tent, *Mission on the Rhine: Reeductaion and Denazification in American-Occupied Germany* (Chicago: University of Chicago Press, 1982), p. 1.
2 I use the term 're-education' here in a broad sense to refer to the many methods which the USA employed with the aim of fostering German democracy and citizenship. James F Tent explains that '"reeducation" became the conquerors' catchword to describe their efforts to democratize Germany'. While the term was most often used to describe the US reformations of the educational system in West Germany, it is also used to refer more broadly to efforts to encourage citizenship among the wider population.
3 *Ibid.*, p. 23.
4 Sophia Smith Library, Smith College, Northampton, Massachusetts, Ruth Woodsmall papers, box 50, file 4, Women's Affairs report, undated.
5 C. Kirkpatrick, *Women in Nazi Germany* (London: Jarrods, 1939), pp. 33–4.
6 C. Koonz, *Mothers in the Fatherland: Women, the Family and Nazi Politics* (London: Methuen, 1988), p. 3.
7 P. Goedde, 'From villains to victims: Fraternization and the feminization of Germany 1945–1947', *Diplomatic History*, 23:1 (Winter 1999), p. 6.
8 A. H. Eagly and M. E. Kite, 'Are stereotypes of nationalities applied to both women and men?', *Journal of Personality and Social Psychology*, 53:3 (1987).
9 *Ibid.*, p. 461.
10 E. Batho (President of the British Federation of University Women), 'Journey to Switzerland', *International Women's News*, 40:9 (June 1946), p. 98.
11 Eagly and Kite, 'Are stereotypes of nationalities applied to both women and men?', p. 464.
12 E. Heineman, 'The hour of the woman: memories of Germany's "Crisis Years" and West German national identity', *American Historical Review*, 101:2 (April 1996), p. 359.
13 *Ibid.*, p. 375.
14 Ruth Woodsmall papers, box 50, file 4, Eleanor Roosevelt speech, undated.
15 Franklin D. Roosevelt Presidential Library, Hyde Park, New York Eleanor Roosevelt papers, box 3395, letter from Heming to Roosevelt, 18 February 1949.
16 Ruth Woodsmall papers, box 51, file 5, news release, Women's Affairs Section, 5 September 1948.
17 Ruth Woodsmall papers, box 50, file 4, Hahn to Alexander, 'General observations on women's affairs', 23 January 1948.
18 Records of the AAUW, series VIII, reel 47, 'Summary of a talk given by Miss Ruth Woodsmall to representatives of national women's organisations', 19 April 1950.
19 Anna Lord Strauss papers, file 15, CCCMF request for Ford Foundation Grant, June 1952.
20 Koonz, *Mothers in the Fatherland*, p. 71.
21 *Ibid.*, p. 78.

22 Ruth Woodsmall papers, box 51, file 5, Heard report, 27 May–28 August 1950.
23 D. Harsch, 'Public continuity and private change? Women's consciousness and activity in Frankfurt 1945–55', *Journal of Social History*, 27:1 (Autumn 1993), p. 29.
24 Records of the AAUW, Series VIII, Reel 47, 'U.S. women's panel launches Bavarian tour'.
25 'Visiting group will seek to arouse citizenship interest among German women', *Christian Science Monitor*, 14 March 1949.
26 M. B. Decker, *The World We Saw with Town Hall* (New York: Richard R. Smith, 1950), p. 63.
27 H. J. Kellerman, *Cultural Relations Programs of the United States Department of State: The Educational Exchange Program between the United States and Germany, 1945–1954* (Washington, DC: Bureau of Educational and Cultural Affairs, US Department of State, 1978), p. 4.
28 *Ibid.*, p. 1.
29 *Ibid.*, p. 4.
30 *Ibid.*, p. 44.
31 Quoted in Kellerman, *Cultural Relations Programs of the United States Department of State*, p. 1.
32 Anna Lord Strauss papers, box 13, file 288, letter, Koshland to Strauss, 8 November 1971.
33 Previously women's affairs had been co-ordinated through the Office of Personal Adviser to the Deputy Military Government for Fostering German Women's Affairs, established 1 November 1947. On 2 December 1949 the Women's Affairs Section was restructured as the Women's Affairs Branch within the Educational and Cultural Relations Division of HICOG.
34 Woodsmall was appointed after a meeting between her and Eleanor Roosevelt prompted Roosevelt to write about Woodsmall to Chester Bowles at the State Department, 'I thought possibly there might be some position for which you would like to consider her'. Eleanor Roosevelt papers, Box 3395, Roosevelt to Bowles, 20 May 1948.
35 Schlesinger Library, Radcliffe Institute, Harvard University, Lucille Koshland papers, box 2, file 38, Report of OMGUS – Educational and Cultural Relations Division, Group Activities Branch, Women's Affairs, 8 March–18 August 1948.
36 Ruth Woodsmall papers, box 50, file 4, 'Specific activities for the Chief of Women's Affairs', 14 June 1948.
37 *Ibid.*
38 Records of the AAUW, series VIII, reel 47, Bulletin of the US Department of Labor, Women's Bureau, 7 April 1949.
39 *Ibid.* The organisations involved were the AAUW, the GFWC, the National League of Women Voters, the NCJW, the National Board of the YWCA, the NFBPWC, the NCNW, the National Council of Catholic Women (NCCW), and the National Council of Church Women.
40 Ruth Woodsmall papers, box 51, file 5, Women's Affairs Branch, Semi-Annual Report, 1 July–31 December 1949.
41 *The Stars and Stripes*, 9 December 1949.
42 *The Stars and Stripes*, 10 December 1949.
43 Ruth Woodsmall papers, box 51, file 5, Heard report, 27 May–28 August 1950.
44 Ruth Woodsmall papers, box 51, file 5, news release, 5 September 1948.

45 Records of the AAUW, series VIII, reel 47, national news release, 15 May 1951.
46 Ruth Woodsmall papers, box 55, file 2, Letter, Imrie to Woodsmall, 6 March 1953. This figure does not include any women who came to Germany in the categories 'teenagers and students'.
47 Ruth Woodsmall papers, box 55, file 2, memo, 'Suggestions to sponsors of German women leaders'.
48 Records of the AAUW, series VIII, reel 43, 'German women leaders: description used by US Women's Bureau, Department of Labor'.
49 Ruth Woodsmall papers, box 55, file 2, letter, Cannon to Batson, 23 August 1951.
50 This restriction was not limited to German women. The CCCMF reported a telling incident in which the Fund had been asked to put on an educational tour for some Japanese women who were dieticians. 'The LWV of DC gals arranged a spectacular tour through the Department of Agriculture's Home Economic Division, including a research center at Beltsville Md. Then the Pentagon called again to say that the Japanese Ladies were not dieticians, but members of the DIET! [the Japanese legislative body]' Lucille Koshland papers, box 1, file 2, Heming speech to State Conference of the League of Women Voters, 1951.
51 Records of the AAUW, series VIII, reel 147, 'Proposed program in the United States for leaders of women's organizations of the western hemisphere', Women's Bureau, Department of Labor.
52 Records of the AAUW, series VIII, reel 43, national news release, 'Rocky Mountain Area AAUW leader on official tour of West Germany', 15 May 1951.
53 Records of the AAUW, series VIII, reel 47, Dyke memorandum, 'Report of US women's panel Bavarian tour', undated.
54 Records of the AAUW, series VIII, reel 47, 'A brief account of AAUW participation in the program for German women', 12 May 1950.
55 Records of the AAUW, series VIII, reel 47, 'Report from the Montana Division of AAUW on the visit to Montana of Dr Hilegard Wolle-Egenolf', 13–27 August 1950, p. 7.
56 *Ibid.*, p. 3.
57 *Ibid.*
58 *Ibid.*, p. 4.
59 Lucille Koshland papers, box 1, file 9, 'Statement of activities of the CCCMF, 1952'.
60 Records of the Women's Bureau of the US Department of Labor 1918–65, part 1, reel 19, Leopold address, 'Spotlight on women'.
61 *The National Voter*, January 1958, p. 12.
62 Quoted in D. Bell, *The End of Ideology: On the Exhaustion of Political Ideas in the Fifties* (New York: The Free Press, 1960), p. 13.
63 *San Francisco News*, 15 December 1955.
64 Lucille Koshland papers, box 1, file 32, letter, Koshland to Hoag, 12 October 1960.
65 Records of the AAUW, series VIII, reel 47, letter, Lambkin to Koshland, undated. The 'Negro group' concerned was probably the NCNW who cooperated with the Women's Bureau in the exchange programmes.
66 Library of Congress, Washington, DC, League of Women Voters papers, box 757, file 'Germany', Extract from Windisch letter, 19 December 1951, quoted in Knapp to Cannon, 3 January 1952.

67   League of Women Voters papers, box 757, file 'Germany', letter, Knapp to
       Cannon, 3 January 1952. An acknowledgement of the practical fact that
       household labour-saving devices left increased time and energy for political
       activities came from Dr Moffat, the NFBPWC's representative on a State
       Department tour of Germany. Moffat reported to her organisation, 'German
       housewives . . . are incorrigible scrubbers. Mostly they know nothing of the
       labor-saving devices that American Housewives take so much for granted. It
       is their tradition that every floor must be scrubbed by hand every day. It is
       also in their tradition that if they discharge . . . properly their duties of house-
       wives, they will have no time for keeping up with public affairs through the
       reading of newspapers, newspaper reading being the special prerogative of
       men . . . It would be better if German housewives would leave one floor
       unscrubbed each day and read one newspaper'. *Independent Woman*, 30:8
       (August 1951), p. 246.
68   'A proposal for international study grants: Our fellowship committee's plan
       for women of the liberated countries', *Journal of the AAUW*, 38:3 (Spring 1945),
       p. 176.
69   A. O. McCormick, 'The forgotten women may decide the German battle', *New
       York Times* (13 September 1948).
70   Ruth Woodsmall papers, box 50, file 5, speech, Elizabeth Holt, 'The Women's
       Affairs Section', 20 January 1949.
71   Ruth Woodsmall papers, box 51, file 2, Women's Affairs Section, Semi-Annual
       Report, 1 July–31 December 1949.
72   *Ibid*.
73   *Ibid*.
74   *Ibid*.
75   Ruth Woodsmall papers, box 56, file 1, 'Tripartio Project Report', 3 February
       1951.
76   Ruth Woodsmall papers, box 52, file 1, Women's Affairs Section, Semi-Annual
       Report, 1 January–1 April 1950.
77   *Ibid*.
78   Ruth Woodsmall papers, box 52, file 6, Betsy Knapp Memo, 'Communist pro-
       paganda and influence in relation to women's organizations and the
       Women's Affairs program', 1950. Intelligence reports seem to confirm
       Knapp's assessment that US officials were underestimating the issue of
       women as a target of communist propaganda. A report from the Intelligence
       Division of HICOG in Bremen in 1950 asserted: 'Communist endeavors to
       influence West German women encounter great difficulties insofar as West
       German women in their majority are very little interested in politics. This fact
       which worries all political parties – from SPD (the Social Democratic Party)
       to DP (Democratic Party) – constitutes a certain advantage as far as commu-
       nist activities are concerned . . . It can be said in conclusion that the overall
       success of communist influence is insignificant and not worth the efforts put
       into it.' This suggests that American intelligence underestimated Soviet pro-
       paganda targeted at women because of a misguided idea of what constituted
       'political' activity. Official intelligence, lacking access to women's organisa-
       tions, chose to ignore them. Ruth Woodsmall papers, box 52, file 6, Report of
       the Intelligence division, Bremen, 'Communist influence on West German
       women', 11 October 1950.
79   Ruth Woodsmall papers, box 52, file 6, Betsy Knapp memo, 'Communist pro-

paganda and influence in relation to women's organizations and the Women's Affairs program', 1950.

80   Ruth Woodsmall papers, box 56, file 2, 'Report of recent women's conferences at Bad Pyrmont and Furth'.

81   *Ibid.*

82   *Ibid.*

83   H. Zink, *The United States in Germany 1944–1955* (Westport, CT: Greenwood Press, 1957), p. 225.

84   Quoted in Kellerman, *Cultural Relations Programs of the United States Department of State*, p. 40. The exchange programme at that time had yet to be formally announced, but the US government gave its approval and support for Mrs Strecker's trip, following the urgent request of General Clay.

85   Ruth Woodsmall papers, box 59, file 4, Secret memorandum, 'Communist peace aggression', (undated).

86   Lucille Koshland papers, box 1, file 15, CCCMF request for Ford Foundation Grant, June 1952, p. 1.

87   *Ibid.*, p. 3. In their programme in Italy, the CCCMF claimed they had been effective in helping to prevent a communist takeover: 'It is only by helping Italian women to solve their community problems democratically that they can be saved from resorting to the extremes, the regimentation, the loss of freedom involved in accepting communist or fascist solutions.'

88   Records of the AAUW, series VIII, reel 43, 'German leaders: Suggestions to sponsors'.

89   Mary McLeod Bethane Memorial Museum, Washington, DC, National Council of Negro Women papers, box 8, file 12, Mallory report, June 1954.

90   Harsch, 'Public continuity and private change?', p. 32.

91   Schlesinger Library, Radcliffe Institute, Harvard University, Anna Lord Strauss papers, box 13, file 271, *Bangkok World*, 18 August 1957.

92   Lucille Koshland papers, box 1, file 10, Annual Report of the Overseas Education Fund of the League of Women Voters, 1961.

93   *Ibid.*

94   Schlesinger Library, Radcliffe Institute, Harvard University, Louise Backus papers, box 1, file 1967, Greenfield report, May–June 1967.

95   R. L. Merritt, *Democracy Imposed. U.S. Occupation Policy and the German Public 1945–1949* (New Haven, CT: Yale University Press, 1995), p. 4.

4

From international activists to Cold War warriors

The entry of American women's organisations into the Cold War was a long and, for some, difficult process. In 1945 most were optimistic that the United Nations could establish and preserve global peace and prosperity. A poll conducted in that year found that 85 per cent favoured an organisation that would 'marshal the forces for understanding among the peoples of the world'.[1] This popularity of the United Nations ideal was a reaction to the destructive potential of atomic power and the global destruction of traditional war. As William Preston has noted:

> Historians studying the wartime statements that U.S. political leaders made about the significance of and the necessity for international education and cultural exchange must surely believe they are witnessing an assembly of faith healers selling ideological nostrums to an audience of true believers . . . The deluge of slaughter and the menace of its total and final climax under the atom's bright sun only confirmed the authenticity of everyone's incredible paroxysms of hope.[2]

American women's organisations believed they had a special role in promoting international understanding through the UN. In an article for *Independent Woman*, Mildred Burgess praised the UN as the 'Tree of life'. Burgess asserted, 'We have learned that the roots of war are economic and social . . . By the some token, too, we have learned that the roots of peace are in the soil of humanitarianism, in human adjustments'. The United Nations could help guarantee peace, since 'it is by sitting down together to discuss the ways and means for bettering man's economic and social conditions everywhere that brotherhood and co-operation are engendered'.[3] John Sloan Dickey, the Director of the Office of Public Affairs in the State Department, collaborated with Helen Dwight Reid, President of the AAUW, to write an article for the *Journal of the AAUW*, exploring 'Some implications of international co-operation'. The article announced, 'For many years, the AAUW has endorsed "international co-operation" as the basic principle of our foreign policy. Now for the first time in world history there is a chance of putting that principle into effective operation'.[4] The AAUW asserted in an editorial in its journal, 'The only sound policy for the USA, especially in the light of our past history, is to take the lead in strengthening the United Nations'.[5] Announcing that 'there has never been a time when the international programme of the AAUW was of more vital significance', the AAUW urged its members to support actively the resolutions of the 1945 convention. Resolution Two committed the AAUW to 'foster a world society in which individuals and nations may live in security, dignity and peace. We must emphasise international co-operation as a practical test of domestic and foreign policies and we must effectively work at the continuing task of establishing and maintaining international organization'.[6] The *Journal of the AAUW* listed ten specific things that branches could do to show support of this resolution, including, 'Discuss these issues with your friends and neighbors', 'Ask your local editor to start a question and answer column on United Nations questions' and 'Ask your church, library, or school to arrange a series of public showings of documentary films of the United Nations'.[7]

American women's organisations worked hard to educate and inform people in the US about the aims and activities of the UN. Often this educational programme was directed to the more 'feminine' aspect of the UN's work, particularly the efforts of the UN in the area of human rights. A press release from the Women's National News Service in October 1949 explained, 'Women are serving as the right arm of the United Nations on one measure that has strong feminine appeal – Declaration of Human Rights'. In an interesting choice of words, the press release elaborated on the 'feminine' credentials of the document:

> The Declaration was mothered, through the necessary stages to its adoption by the UN, by a loved and respected woman, Mrs Franklin D. Roosevelt, Chairman of the UN Commission on Human Rights. And with the Declaration now adopted as the formal principles of human rights and freedom for all peoples, leaders in women's organizations think it especially appropriate that the women of this country get behind it and push.[8]

Work by women's organisations included encouragement by national boards to branches to produce educational programmes, numerous publications and a choral drama, sponsored by the YWCA and based on the UN Charter and the Declaration.

The commitment of American women's organisations to internationalism contrasted with the increasingly ambivalent attitude of their government to the effectiveness of the UN and to the value of channelling international efforts through its mediation. In 1947 the LWV displayed its support of the UN in a letter to President Truman criticising the Marshall Plan. The letter, written by Anna Lord Strauss, informed Truman, 'Although we are in general agreement with Secretary Marshall's proposals we are very much disturbed that no mention has been made of the role of the United Nations in this project, either in the speech itself or in any subsequent statement by our government'.[9] The League chastised Truman:

> We know that in by-passing the United Nations, in failing to take advantage of its existing machinery, our government is not doing its part in firmly establishing that international co-operation on which, ultimately, our own security and that of other nations depends. We know that the United Nations will never be stronger and hence able to fill the role we wish it could unless in the conduct of our foreign relations day by day we take steps to strengthen it.[10]

This hope for a peaceful world ruled through the aegis of the United Nations proved misplaced. The obvious cause was growing tension between the Soviet Union and the US. Daniel Yergin sees the early months of 1946 as pivotal in the development of the Cold War, as 'American officialdom became coherent and consistent in their hostility to an suspicion of Soviet intentions'.[11] Yergin argues that the 'Long Telegram' by George Kennan, which described the 'no compromise' attitude of the Soviet Union 'became the bible for American Policy Makers'.[12] Yet the wider American public did not at this point share this antagonism towards the Soviet Union. Yergin explains, 'The post-war anti-Communist consensus existed first in the centre, in the policy elite, before it spread out to the nation'.[13]

The Truman Doctrine of March 1947 should be understood, not merely as the expression of the Truman Administration's move towards an aggressive policy towards the Soviet Union but also as a public relations event for that policy. Gary W. Reichard explains, 'Emotional anti-communism of the post-war years was shaped by

Truman's depiction of Soviet motives and U.S. policy options, his portrayal of U.S. actions as wholly altruistic and his preference for military power over accommodation'.[14] Truman's speech to Congress, ostensibly an appeal for funds to withstand the spread of communism in Turkey and Greece, drew upon an apocalyptic vision of a world divided between democracy and communism, good and evil, light and darkness. Presenting the USSR as a threat to freedom and democracy across the globe, US policy was firmly set upon the road of an active opposition to communism, outside the mediating body of the UN. A repudiation of the tactics of accommodation, Truman's speech was quickly followed by a flood of pronouncements from his administration all underlying its central theme: the impossibility of negotiation with the Soviet Union. On 1 April 1947, Undersecretary of State Dean Acheson informed the executive hearing of the Senate Foreign Relations Committee, 'I think it is a mistake to believe that you can, at any time, sit down with the Russians and solve questions. I do not think that is the way that are problems are going to be worked out with the Russians'.[15]

The Truman Doctrine, together with American unilateral economic aid to Europe through the Marshall Plan, contributed significantly to a policy whereby, in the words of historian Harold Josephson, the USA 'undermined the world organization by committing the United States to a policy of unilateralism and globalism rather than internationalism'.[16] Josephson argues:

At the moment of [internationalism's] greatest triumph – the establishment of the United Nations Organizations with American participation – internationalism began to lose ground. As the Cold War emerged out of the turbulence of World War II, the United States backed away from adopting internationalism as the operational basis for its foreign policy. By 1950 the nation was committed to a policy of unilateralism and intervention.[17]

Within this Cold War context, American women's organisations sought to define their internationalism in terms that did bring them into dispute with the agenda of their national government. Anna Lord Strauss's message to Truman questioning the US intervention in Greece and Turkey was typical of this manoeuvring. Strauss again emphasised the League's commitment to the UN: 'The fact that the President is asking Congress to take responsibility for a problem which ideally would be handled by the United Nations emphasizes again the necessity for strengthening the United Nations'.[18] However, Strauss acknowledged that failure to act through the UN was not necessarily misguided given the demands of the situation:

> We must keep in mind that, of the methods for carrying on international relations at the present time, the United Nations is not the only one. It is only a year old and it is still in the process of organization. Every effort should be made to expand the scope of the United Nations' competence and to strengthen the collective security system. Until the organization is stronger, it is reasonable to question the wisdom of giving it problems which it is clearly not equipped to deal with.[19]

The AAUW's approach to the Marshall Plan was similarly constructed to reconcile a commitment to internationalism with an acceptance of the Cold War realities perceived by the US government. The AAUW was wary of over-stressing the anti-communist dimension of economic programme. Mabel Newcomber, a Professor of Economics at Vassar and a former chairman of the AAUW's Social Studies Committee, explained the value of the Marshall Plan in the *Journal of the AAUW* by directing her readers to Marshall's original assertion, 'Our policy is directed, not against any country or doctrine but against hunger, poverty, desperation and chaos. Its purpose should be the revival of a working economy in the world so as to permit the emergence of political and social conditions in which free institutions can exist'.[20] Regretting that 'in the US the discussion has turned more and more to the virtues of the program as a device for undermining Communist influence', Newcomber argued that this consequence should be seen as a side effect of the programme, rather than its *raison d'être*. While she accepted that some measure of control over the political institutions that administered the Marshall Plan was inevitable, Newcomber also argued against inflexibility and intolerance, specifically in restricting popular socialism:

> Our aim is to foster democracy and not to stop it when we don't like the outcome ... We will have a good chance of preventing the spread of communist dictatorships in consequence of our aid. We haven't a chance in the world of preventing some measure of socialization by the will of the majority. There is a limit to what we can buy, even with sixteen billion dollars.[21]

Like many Americans in the aftermath of the Second World War, American women's organisations had been hopeful that wartime alliance with the Soviet Union could lead to peaceful co-operation between the superpowers in the post-war world. Janette S. Murray, President of the Cedar Rapids, Iowa branch of the AAUW, wrote to President Truman in April 1945, urging that the government 'at least use good diplomacy' and 'extend just consideration to Russia'. She wondered 'if our United States officials at the San Francisco Conference [establishing the UN] treated the Russians with proper diplomatic courtesy'.[22] The *Journal of the AAUW* ran an article in summer 1947 by Vera Micheles Dean, known for her work with the Foreign Policy Association. In an even-handed discussion of the rising tensions, Dean explained:

> There are all over the world places which have been left as vacuums by the defeat of Germany and Japan and by the weakening of Britain. Into these vacuums the U.S. and Russia are both pressing in an effort to establish their influence, whether it be territorial, economic or ideological. The question is where both the U.S. and Russia will stop.[23]

Dean pointed out that the question of 'blame' and the view which many Americans had of the Soviet Union as 'intransigent' were misplaced, explaining while 'it is true that the American representative at Lake Success has been much more agreeable in his relations with the U.N. than Mr Gromyko . . . if we look behind the facade of diplomatic language, we may find that on some major points the United States is not quite as different from Russia as we think'.[24]

The AAUW's stance was that the US should attempt to understand and, where possible, accommodate the Soviet Union and avoid the appearance of implacable enmity and hostility. Even when the AAUW acknowledged the difficulty of this approach and the reality of US–Soviet Union rivalry, they were anxious that this confrontation not be 'talked up' into a world conflict. Helen Dwight Reid, an AAUW fellow in International Education and later AAUW President, expressed particular concern that American prejudice and hostility to the Soviet Union would be interpreted in neutral countries as US 'war-mongering'. Reid explained:

> One of the Canadian press representatives at the Toronto International Federation of University Women Conference commented on the fact that many of the European University women had been shocked to see the shadow of a new war behind the headlines in American and Canadian newspapers, for they thought of Russia still as an ally and good neighbor. Today more than ever we must

beware of letting our prejudices masquerade as intelligent judg-
ments.[25]

Where the AAUW recognised global conflict, they advised that
the US lead by example by improving and strengthening the practice
of democracy at home. For example, the extension of civil rights
should be encouraged, since 'democracy as a symbol and slogan is
weak unless democracy as operated in reality is strong'.[26] Sarah
Blanding, a member of the AAUW and the president of Vassar, wrote
in the *Journal of the AAUW*:

> It is apparent that the future of this nation, and perhaps the future
> of the world, rests upon the character of the decisions that we make
> at the present time in extending the democratic process. Only by
> seizing the opportunity to achieve greater unity by removing barri-
> ers of discrimination that separate group from group within our
> country, can we maintain and advance our position at home and our
> leadership among the world.[27]

As the Cold War tightened its grip, the AAUW struggled desper-
ately to maintain some sense of proportion and clung to the hope that
tensions could be defused through the UN and world co-operation.
The *Journal* argued in spring 1950:

> Although we do not, at present, enjoy the friendship of Russia, this
> fact in itself constitutes no actual hindrance to the maintenance of
> world stability. We must discard the idea that it is necessary to choose
> between a close alliance or a bitter enmity with other nations. It is a
> terrible mistake to look on war as the inevitable end of our present
> mistrusts and divided opinions.[28]

This edition of the *Journal* explored the issues behind world organisation, including an article by Cord Meyer, Jr, explaining the position of
the United World Federalists.[29]

An article by Senator William Benton in the *Journal* illustrated the
extent to which this position of accommodation was out of step with
the views of the US government in summer 1950. Benton argued, 'We
are in the crucial moments of a struggle for the minds and loyalties of
mankind. The US is in a world political campaign'.[30] The position of
liberal women's organisations would be an increasingly harried one.
Historian Susan Lynn explains:

> Women who endorsed internationalist goals faced a major dilemma.
> On the one hand, they shared the concern of U.S. political leaders that

the Soviet Union posed a real threat and thus they remained wedded to the fundamental assumption of US foreign policy: that military preparedness was essential for national security. On the other hand, women in the coalition deplored the excessive emphasis on militarism of US foreign policy and urged the government to put more energy and resources into constructive activities that could ease international tensions and create greater economic security throughout the world.[31]

This position was compromised by participation in programmes such as civil defence. Through involvement in measures for military preparedness, the organisations arguably contributed to the state of insecurity and tension that fostered and encouraged a tougher US policy in the Cold War. This position was further complicated as women consciously used civil defence as an issue upon which to mount a campaign for great responsibilities and rights as citizens. As Laura McEnaney has pointed out in her study of the FCDA, 'Club women adopted civil defense to enhance their professional and political status'.[32] American women's organisations willing participation in the Civil Defense programme was part of wider claims to greater responsibility and power in the context of a military situation. McEnaney points to the way in which involvement in civil defence, even as a tactical move to give women increased influence within the 'macho environment of the National security planning', tied American women's organisations to a Cold War agenda. Developing a more complex reading of the relationships between 'the Cold War, the feminine mystique and women's political activism', McEnaney asserts, 'Cold War anti-communism and militarism channeled the liberal maternalist and feminist impulses of the [women's organisations] network into conservative ones'.[33]

The relationship of American women's organisations to Cold War politics was further complicated by the context of domestic anti-communism. The AAUW had been subjected to repeated attempts to tag them and their leaders as subversive. Dorothy Kenyon, the Vice-President of the AAUW and the US delegate to the UN Sub-Commission on the Status of Women, was the subject of a loyalty investigation in 1950 following accusations from Senator McCarthy that she was a 'fellow-traveller'. Kenyon strenuously denied that she was disloyal, a communist, or a fellow traveller. However, she admitted that she had lent her name to 'a number of liberal anti-fascist organizations'. Kenyon received widespread support from the liberal, and not so liberal, press: *Life* acknowledged her to be a 'convincing witness [with] a look of deadly and impressive seriousness'. However, her career in government service was at an end. 'Literally overnight', she complained, 'Whatever personal and professional reputation . . . I may have acquired has been seriously jeopardized, if not destroyed, by the widespread dissemination of charges of communist leanings that are utterly false'.[34] Kenyon was accused, in McCarthy's inimitable style, of being a member of a fluctuating number of communist-front organisations. One of the more serious charges linked her to the National Council for Soviet–American Friendship (NCSAF), an organisation designated 'subversive' by the Attorney General's List. However, as historian David Oshinsky notes, '[Kenyon] was in good company'. The membership of NCSAF included four US senators and the scientist Albert Einstein. Other women affiliated to the NCSAF included not only Mrs Elinor S. Gimbel, who went on to found the Congress of American Women (CAW), the US branch of the Soviet-sponsored WIDF, but also Mary McLeod Bethune and Charlotte Hawkins Brown of the NCNW, Mary Anderson, who had served as the director of the Women's Bureau, and journalist Dorothy Thompson.[35] In an article in the *Journal* entitled 'The image of the things we hate', Kenyon attacked the loyalty investigation as a threat to American democracy, arguing that if it was allowed to continue:

> something precious will have gone out of America and we will all of us be defeated in our battle of ideas with Russia. For if there is one thing that is wholly American and Non-Russian it is our freedom to think, to express those thoughts and to hear the thoughts of others freely given without fear or intimidation of any sort. America is built on adventuring minds, ranging freely over the entire world of ideas. When the shadow of fear falls over those minds it will be the beginning of the end.[36]

Confirmation of the appointment of Kathryn McHale, the President of the AAUW, to the Subversives Activities Control Board was held up in the Senate because of charges of disloyalty. One of these charges was that she had defended Kenyon from the charges of which she had been found innocent.[37]

The AAUW's challenge to anti-communist hysteria should not be underestimated. Unlike other organisations which either collapsed in the face of accusations of subversion, such as the CAW,[38] or participated in the witch-hunt by rooting out suspected 'subversives' from their own ranks, such as the NAACP,[39] the AAUW maintained a strong critique of the dangers of the security inquisition. Mabel Newcomer in particular challenged such Cold War absolutes as the prohibition on communist texts in colleges. With education a central interest of the AAUW, the growing conformity and censorship on college campuses was noted with concern. In an article 'Citizens and scholars', Newcomer argued:

> Many people confuse teaching about communism with indoctrination . . . In the list of self-confessed Communists in recent years, the number who specialized in social sciences during their college course is conspicuously small. Are not those who are so fearful under-rating the intelligence of our youth? And the virtues of our social institutions? What have we to fear from comparison with Russia?[40]

The AAUW was not the only American women's organisation concerned with the outcome of anti-Communist witch-hunts. The LWV, as one of the most visible mainstream women's organisations, received special attention as a potential site of communist sympathies or infiltration. Anna Lord Strauss recalled that, immediately following the Second World War, the League had had 'some trouble with Communists in our ranks, not a good deal, but when there were any it too often made the newspaper and this was no help in recruiting members from the conservative element in the United States who were looking for Communists under the beds anyway'.[41]

The League learned the hard way that the accusation of communism was often enough to damage the reputation of an organisation. Anna Lord Strauss complained bitterly that she was often confused with or, she suspected, deliberately 'misidentified' as Anna Louise Strong, a woman active in communist circles on the West Coast.[42] Similar confusion was caused by Walt Disney's dramatic revelation to the House Committee on Un-American Activities that he had obtained information that the LWV was nothing less than a communist front. A few days later, Disney looked up his correspondence on the matter and apologised, saying that the organisation he had meant to refer to was the League of Women Shoppers.[43] The level of rumour and unsubstantiated accusation that followed witch-hunts was illustrated when a concerned member of the League, Mrs Sam Becker, sent the Head Office a letter she received from Charles M. Burgess, presumably an interested friend. Burgess warned Mrs Becker:

> I believe that you and other members of the Local and County League of Women Voters in all instances are not aware of the ways

and means found to utilize your efforts and your standing in the community by the National organization for purposes that I believe to be inimical to the interests of the United States . . . I obtained from the Congressional files in Washington a synopsis of a report on the National President of your organization and on one of its Board Members. This report would indicate that your President, Anna Lord Strauss, was either consciously or unconsciously an indirect supporter of the Communist party from 1937 through 1944 . . . This report also indicates that Mabel Newcomber, one of your National Directors, was even more involved, and perhaps not unconsciously, with the Communist Party activities.[44]

The League was justifiably nervous about the extent to which their sponsorship of civil liberties awareness could bring them into disrepute. In August 1949, for example, Mrs Harold A. Stone, the Vice-President of the League, wrote to Secretary of Defense Louis Johnson, 'From time to time we receive in this office rumors to the effect that the League of Women Voters is on an unidentified Army 'List' as being a Communist-front organization'. Mrs Stone asked for and received confirmation that the League was not listed by any Department of Defense agency.[45] The League moved carefully to challenge any innuendo regarding their anti-communist credentials. A draft memorandum from the League to Professor Austin Clifford, a conservative Republican lawyer and a professor at the Indiana Law School, detailed the League's concern with the current threat to civil liberties:

> The new weapons of the Cold War make us more concerned that ever before to preserve our own institutions and form of government. We have seen nation after nation brought under totalitarian control largely through well-organized minorities operating from within . . . It would be folly for us to ignore these developments and neglect to take such steps as are necessary to safeguard the national security . . . In attempting to do so, however, some of our governmental bodies are using methods which implicate the innocent with the guilty. They do not always make the distinction between actual threats to the state and unconventional economic, political and social views.[46]

Professor Clifford advised that, as discretion was the better part of valour, the League should not publish any material on civil liberties at that time:

> The United States is in a Cold War with the USSR. One of the main objectives of the USSR agents is to make America lose faith in their democratic government by proving that it isn't democratic anymore

. . . The danger to American Civil Liberties is not from the misuse of power by government agencies. The danger to Civil Liberties now is from the activities of communist groups . . . [The memorandum] repeats so many legally untenable left-wing arguments that it would subject the League to suspicion of being a tool.[47]

Perhaps because of this 'suspicion', the League's efforts to fight the threat to civil liberties was launched and run through the CCCMF, the overseas division of the League. The 'Freedom Agenda', as it was known, strove to inform the public about the danger of obsessive 'security' programmes. 'Freedom Agenda' (telephone number 1776) sought a low-profile, community-based campaign to counter the rumour and suspicion of the witch-hunts, enabling 'citizens to explore the problem of how to preserve our national security without sacrificing individual liberties'.[48] Anna Lord Strauss explained:

We wanted these organizations that had acceptance in their communities to do it on their own . . . Its potential and effectiveness was really very large because people did handle the situation themselves from their hometowns. In a way that squelched the misinformation, the innuendoes and the other things, unfortunately the gossipy kind of thing that people love to pick up and repeat.[49]

Strauss recognised that the work of the Freedom Agenda had been overlooked, due to their policy of not seeking any kind of publicity. Nevertheless, she argued, 'I think Freedom Agenda did a much more important job than is generally recognized'.[50]

However discreet the League was about the Freedom Agenda, it inevitably attracted some measure of censure. In 1955, the Un-American Committee of the American Legion in Westchester County, New York, attacked six pamphlets produced by Freedom Agenda and distributed through the League on the grounds that they were 'designed to delude the public into believing that communism is a red herring'. The National Executive Committee of the American Legion called upon the LWV to disown the pamphlets. The League was unrepentant, however, as Strauss boldly declared, 'We are proud of the Freedom Agenda program. It is as American as the Town Meeting. Communities all over the country are organizing Freedom Agenda groups to discuss the fundamental principles of American Liberty'.[51]

A sympathetic article by Malvina Lindsay, 'Defending the right to discuss freedom', in the *Washington Post* pointed out that, in the American Legion's anti-communist crusade, 'Mrs Catt, Jane Addams and Julia Lanthrop have been exhumed and accused of having "Communist front records"'.[52] Freedom Agenda, which by this time had enlisted the support of organisations such as the AAUW, the Anti-Defamation League, the NCJW and the YWCA, was undamaged by the accusations.

Under pressure from anti-communist forces at home, American women's organisations sought to shore up their position by taking a strong position in the face communism abroad. This balancing strategy was similar to that adopted by Senator Margaret Chase Smith, the first Republican 'of any standing' to speak out against McCarthy. Rhodri Jeffreys-Jones has pointed out that as a result of her position she faced attacks in the Maine press, following which she 'went to some lengths to show that she really did detest the Communists'.[53] Jeffreys-Jones suggests that Chase Smith's hawkish hardline position on communism abroad was the price for the defence against anti-communism at home. In choosing to fight anti-communism at home, American women's organisations forfeited a certain degree of freedom in the matter of anti-communism abroad. Distancing themselves from their previous endorsements of internationalism and compromise with the Soviet Union, organisations such as the AAUW and the LWV hardened their international anticommunist position. In 1951 the AAUW moved towards a more anti-communist stance, recognising the reality of global conflict with the Soviet Union. In an article written for the *Journal* by Ina Corinne Brown, Chairman of the AAUW Social Studies Committee, the division of the world into two hostile opposing ideologies, which President Truman had described, was reiterated, 'The world is rapidly being divided not merely between two political systems, but between two philosophies of life. Not only is our political and economic freedom as a people at stake, but our freedom as individuals to think, speak and worship is threatened'.[54]

The AAUW sought to maintain a precarious balance, continuing their opposition to anti-communist witch-hunts at home and asserting their opposition to communism abroad. Brown sought to link the protection of freedom from the encroachment of the Soviet Union with the defence of freedom at home from the threat of witch-hunts. Brown asserted, 'We have been shocked by the subversive activities of disloyal individuals and further shocked by irresponsible and unfounded accusations against loyal citizens and by the cropping up of such strange doctrines as "guilt by association"'. Brown refused to separate the two issues, insisting:

We are not confronted with two problems but with a single problem having two aspects. We must mobilize for physical survival but that survival will have little meaning if our basic values are lost in a disorganized and disintegrating world. Our goal is survival in a free world which has in it enough decency, trust and integrity in the relations of men and nations to make survival worthwhile.[55]

This position was formally established in the *Journal* of summer 1951. A special Convention Edition commenced with the address of Althea Hottel, President of the AAUW. Hottel affirmed the AAUW's dual strategy:

There is the external threat of the Soviet Union and there are some of our citizens who endeavor to sap the strength of our nation through subversive activities. We must have loyal Americans in our government, our schools and our industries. The third danger is found in evidence that we might be losing the right to differ and in some instances the right to a free trial. We are justifiably concerned with security, but personal freedom and responsibility for years has been the basis of our national security and thinking men and women must be equally concerned with a preservation of individual liberty.[56]

Another article by Ina Corinne Brown further explored the 'liberal dilemma' of the Cold War:

One particularly insidious aspect of this two-edged threat to our freedom is the way in which it lends itself to the false dilemma. Those who use totalitarian methods to fight communism make it appear that persons who oppose these methods are thereby revealing communist sympathies. Both the witch-hunting demagogue and the communists are threats to our freedom. We do not have to keep one of them in order to get rid of the other. Both of them are totalitarian in their methods, both of them must be repudiated if we are not to become like the thing we profess to hate.[57]

The concern of the AAUW to protect civil liberties manifested itself in campaigns to raise awareness, at branch levels, of the threat of anti-communist hysteria. The *Journal* reported in January 1952 on the activities of the Wellsville, New York branch, in an article entitled 'Security and civil rights: how one branch approached a controversial topic'. Wellsville branch members were asked to define such words and phrases as 'Communist, Fellow-traveller, liberal, subversive, seditious, clear and present danger, civil liberty and guilty by association'. Members were then asked to study topics such as Presidential

Order 9835 (which established the Federal Employee Loyalty Programme), the Civil Service Loyalty Review Program, the McCarran Act, the Subversive Activities Control Board, the Smith Act, Congressional immunity, the activities of the FBI and the Justice Department, and loyalty oaths in state education.[58]

The position outlined in the *Journal* was established as policy through the announcement of the Board of Directors of the AAUW in January 1953 that 'the time has come for a bold, positive and frontal attack on the communist threat to freedom and democracy'. The Board explained why they had delayed so long in making this decision:

> For the most part we and like-minded groups have been put on the defensive. If we attacked communism and the communists, we found ourselves in the same camp with self-seeking or fascist-minded individuals who by their methods of attack were undermining the freedom and democracy they professed to defend. If we defended our liberties as a free people, we ran the risk of being called communist sympathizers, fellow-travellers and even communists. So we have sat back, more or less paralyzed, and have allowed other people to take the initiative and create a dilemma for the honest and loyal liberal.[59]

The Board announced that the threat both from communists and from anti-communist groups challenged the essentials of American freedom and democracy: 'The direct threat comes from communists and communist sympathizers. The indirect threat lies in what fear of communism may lead us to do to ourselves'.[60] The Board committed itself to a fight against both communism and the tactics of McCarthyism:

> We believe that to attempt to fight communism by using totalitarian techniques is not only ineffectual but actually aids the communist enemies of democracy by undermining our free institutions. We do not have to choose between communist infiltration and methods of witch-hunting, character assassination and demagoguery. Both are evil; both are threats to freedom and democracy. We repudiate them both.[61]

The response to the statement was enthusiastic, and the May 1953 issue of the *Journal* reported that, 'The statement on "The Communist Threat to Freedom and Democracy" . . . has become the most-publicized, most quoted, most-praised statement ever issued in the name of the association'.[62]

By linking international anti-communism to concern about the effects of anti-communism at home, the AAUW and the LWV were hesitant Cold War warriors. Their rhetoric of internationalism did not fall silent but sat uneasily alongside pursuit of a global crusade against the Soviet Union. Nevertheless, Cold War pressures ensured that this was not an issue about which women's groups could maintain silence or equivocate. In 1953 the YWCA found it necessary to state its policy on Communism, announcing, 'The YWCA is unalterably opposed to communism and any other ideology which denies dignity and fundamental human rights to the individual. Its Christian Purpose commits the Association to fight totalitarianism in any form and to work actively to safeguard and support democratic principle'.[63]

Other American women's organisations escaped this dilemma by embracing the Cold War wholeheartedly at home and abroad. In May 1947, following the lead of the Truman Doctrine, the NCW produced and distributed a pamphlet which addressed the Cold War menace in no uncertain terms:

> It becomes increasingly clear that we are at the crossroads and that in this most crucial period of our civilization the United States is the last great rampart of freedom and democracy. The National Council of Women of the United States, realizing the importance of this crisis proposes to accelerate its program so that through the millions of women in this nation, it can help to protect human rights and fundamental freedoms . . . Through its membership in the International Council of Women it will intensify the promotion of the principles of democracy and freedom throughout the world.[64]

This militancy of the NCW was furthered after the war by its president, Mrs William Barclay Parsons, who had served as a regional director of the American Red Cross during the Second World War. Even in 1940 the NCW had been on the alert, warning 'against the insidiousness of foreign propaganda and agents who would attempt to spread their doctrines through speakers supplied for Women's Clubs'.[65] Parsons told the NCW Board of Directors in June 1948:

> There is a real need for a clearing-house in this country. She regretted the fact that a number of large organizations are not members of the United States Council and said that she felt there must be some effective way of working together with them . . . National Council of Women in other countries are looking for us for leadership and

constructive planning, as a balance to the enormous amount of pressure being put on them by communist countries.[66]

The militancy of the NCW was a result of their suspicion of the encroachment of pro-soviet international women's groups. In November 1945 Union des Femmes Francais, a subsidiary of the French Communist Party, called a conference for women from all nations in Paris. The Soviet contingent at the conference was conspicuous in their participation. The *Christian Science Monitor* noted, 'The largest and certainly the most representative delegation was that of Soviet Russia. Numbering 42 it included a woman general, a famous surgeon, wearing the uniform of lieutenant colonel, a captain who carried out night bomber flights, a Russian Film Star, architects, women industrial workers, writers and mothers of large families'.[67]

The Paris conference led to the founding of the WIDF and its US affiliate, the CAW. A press release of 27 February 1946 described the CAW as 'the first mass political organisation of American women since suffrage'.[68] There was some support for the initiative. The NCNW's report on the WIDF resolved 'that the National Council of Negro women affiliate with the WIDF for the promotion of peace and freedom'.[69] The CAW's members included Dr Charlotte Hawkins Brown, Susan B. Anthony (Jr), and aviator Jacqueline Cochran.

Initially CAW attempted to enlist the co-operation of established women activists and women's organisations. Mary Mcleod Bethune of the NCNW informed Eleanor Roosevelt in March 1946:

> Our delegates were impressed with the earnestness, the clarity of thinking and the spiritual unity which characterized the deliberations. Mrs Elinor Gimbel . . . Chairman of this committee, is very anxious for you to make a statement encouraging American women to participate in socially progressive movements in this country and to co-operate with women of other countries in the task of establishing a better world and enduring peace.[70]

CAW was short-lived and unsuccessful, however. Attacked in 1948 by HUAC, labelled as a communist-front organisation, and forced to register as 'subversive', the group folded in 1950.[71]

The WIDF became the focus of American fears about the Soviet campaign to influence women overseas. Their pro-Soviet position was obvious. At their Paris conference in 1945, a keynote speech by Isola Drago of Bulgaria explained that the government that had 'come into power' in Bulgaria on 9 September was 'a coalition of the peoples' parties', and that 'the Anglo press gave a distorted version of what had happened'. The anti-American stance of the organisation was clearly illustrated in their journal, *Women of the Whole World*. A typical article lambasted the state of childcare in the USA. In another article, 'My big family', mother of ten Anastasia Goriuchkina observed:

> Obviously it is no easy matter to care for and bring up ten children. But in our country, the Soviet Union, mothers and children are surrounded with the great many maternity clinics, dispensaries, kindergartens and crèches [which] have been set up in town and country to help parents raise their children . . . None of us has to worry about tomorrow, about the future. For us and our children the future is joyous, magnificent and cloudless.[72]

An article by R. Shahirova, the mother of a Soviet soldier, continued the theme of the US as more concerned with military issues that the welfare of children, 'We mothers of soldiers of our army feel particularly strongly the menace in the reported threats of the U.S. government to start another war. We do not want war! . . . The Soviet army has never threatened anybody, is not threatening and will never threaten!'[73] The NCW of the US noted with anxiety the tactics of the WIDF, asserting that the organisation 'directs its appeal to women by championing child welfare, peace and women's rights. The implication is that the USSR and other communist countries are the originators and sole supporters of these causes, which in fact have long been the active concern of the free world'.[74]

The activities of communist women's groups such as the WIDF gave American women's organisations cause for alarm. The communist 'offensive' targeted women not just through international organisational links and gatherings but also through the UN Commission on the Status of Women as an important battleground. Disagreements between communist and non-communist women at the Commission set the agenda for much of its early work. The conflict began with the process of nomination of commission members. The USA and the UK made advance plans to secure the nomination of Miss Sutherland of the UK as the chair, with Mrs Ledon of Mexico as the vice-chair. However, the Soviet delegates were able to secure the nomination of Mrs Begtrap of Denmark as chair and Mrs Street of Australia as vice-chair. While these candidates may have appeared as 'neutral', Rachel Nason, the Women's Bureau adviser to US

Representatives complained, 'Mrs Begtrap remained under obligation to the Russians and she presided with a vagueness and confusion that seem frequently to favor U.S.S.R. tactics'.[75] Once the nomination process for members was completed, the Soviet group sought the recognition of the WIDF, a move opposed by the US delegation. The business of deciding on suitable recognition status for competing women's groups took an inordinate amount of the commission's time, a useless exercise it was eventually ruled that consultative status was decided by a special committee set up by the UN's Economic and Social Council (ECOSOC). The Commission proposed that the debates over consultative status be eliminated from the final reports, over the complaints of the Soviet Representative, Mrs Popova, who candidly explained, 'she had "acted under instruction" and needed a record to show her Government what she had done' towards recognition of the WIDF.[76]

This frank admission confirmed the suspicions of the US delegates and observers that the Commission had become a Cold War battlefield. Frieda Miller wrote to Mr Kaiser at the Office of International Labor Affairs about her concerns:

> Any realistic consideration of the work of this commission needs to keep in mind that, whatever may have been the intention of those who got the Commission created, it has now become a very lively and prize-worthy propaganda vehicle – of first class interest in the East–West contest . . . The use of an organ of the U.N. as a propaganda vehicle is not restricted to any one field. However 'Human Rights' as a subject does lend itself peculiarly to formulations, claims and charges which may create confusion and misconceptions regarding national programs and purposes . . . the work of the Status Commission has in fact become in an important sense a testing group of the respective programs and achievements of eastern and western attitudes with respect to this particular set of human rights.[77]

Miller concluded that the Cold War division significantly reduced the opportunities of the Commission to effect positive change. The Commission was simply not strong enough to withstand political pressures. Miller complained, 'Among its members there appear to have been a high proportion of persons without solid experience in public service such as would furnish an adequate basis for operating commission meetings, guiding debate, selecting and formulating program areas'. As a result, the Commission was given more to rhetoric than action:

To be at one and the same time a vehicle for sober exploration of the nature and course of specific discriminations and of means for over-coming them – and also the source of ringing declarations of noble objectives that bear no internal evidence of how they are to move towards realization is likely to create a bad case of split personality.[78]

Miller concluded that the role of the USA in the Commission had been reduced to countering Soviet claims, since 'to do less would leave the whole field to be spread with those ringing pronouncements which are full of invidious implications of western failure and give plausible grounds for the charge that they are not interested in advancing women's status'.[79] Her views were shared by those in the State Department. When Mr Kotschnig wrote to the United Nations Association, asking for their co-operation during the Commission on the Status of Women's meeting in 1949, he warned, 'We feel some concern that the meeting of the United National Commission on the Status of Women to be held in Beirut next March may be used by the USSR to agitate against the United States in the Middle East'. Echoing the concern of Frieda Miller, he continued:

> To many it comes as a surprise that the status of women in this country has become a Cold War issue. However, the debate in ECOSOC last summer made it clear that the USSR intends to use women's rights, along with other human rights, as a basis for agitation. The USSR's claim is that under communism women have equality and that only under communism can they be assured of this equality.[80]

Through the medium of the UN, the Soviet Union and the USA became involved in a battle over which political system best assured the 'status of women'. A meeting between representatives of the Department of Labor, the Federal Security Agency, Department of State and the Department of Justice, attempted to develop some kind of strategic response to the Soviet use of the Commission on the Status of Women. The meeting noted:

> Each and every item on the Status of Women, as on Human Rights in general, must be conceived as part of a hard fought program which can be used by the eastern bloc for any audience to point up possible weaknesses in other nations, attract support from disaffected groups, create confusion . . . and, because other sources of information are lacking, influence people behind the iron curtain and those elsewhere likely to respond to USSR leadership.[81]

The meeting recognised that there was a fundamental problem for the USA in advocating the gradual improvement in the Status of Women in countries suffering from a 'time-lag' such as Beirut. In contrast to the gradualism recommended by the USA, the Soviet Union was sure to offer instant emancipation through communism. United States strategy was to emphasise educational advance, leading to political rights. However, their commitment to securing political rights through women through the medium of international agreement was, at best, weak. The Women's Bureau domestically were committed to protective legislation for women, which they felt would be destroyed by any adaptation of concept of 'Equal Rights' such as the Equal Rights Amendment. This attitude was also prevalent in their approach to international work. In their review of the references to women in the Declaration Articles of the Bill of Rights, the Committee on International Social Policy stated:

> A strong comment in support of equality for women should be made early in the Commission meeting. In this we should reiterate our interest in equal rights for women, and our belief that equality for women does not mean identity of treatment with men but rather identity where appropriate (for eg as to the vote and holding public office.) and differential treatment as needed (maternity legislation, family support legislation, protection from industrial hazards to which women are especially liable etc).[82]

The USA went to great lengths to produce a careful and considered picture of the status of American women. Discussion of the production of a picture book to illustrate the status of women in the USA, to be distributed during the 1949 Commission meeting in Lebanon, noted:

> There was some discussion as to whether women's role in American life is to be emphasized in case there should be misinterpretation of the aggressive dominance of women in American life. However, this could be neutralized if the pictures selected for the fields of home life (both rural and urban, educational advantages, employment, community service) were to include men.[83]

The Women's Bureau further planned a monthly fact sheet to be distributed during the meetings, but noted in recognition of the role of the Commission as a catalyst for wider campaigns, 'In the event that the WIDF conducts a propaganda battle on many geographical fronts simultaneously, the Fact Sheet will be equally valuable for presenting the status of women in the United States to other areas besides the Near East'.[84] Diplomatic and consular offices in Lebanon, Syria, Egypt, Transjordan, Turkey, Yeman, Iran, Iraq, Pakistan, India, Greece and Ethiopia were instructed to inform the State Department of and efforts to recruit women for the WIDF. This effort was clearly taking place, as is evidenced in Mrs Fares Ibrahin's (Chairman of the Federation of Lebanese Women) statement during that third session of the meeting, that she would like to thank the Republic of the Soviet Union and the WIDF for the encouragement that they had given her federation.[85]

The positions of the opposing sides were clearly drawn. The USA and its allies pointed to the freedom and respect associated with the status of women under democracy. A position paper by the Women's Bureau in October 1948 worried that the report of the Secretary General on the political rights of women 'may be the occasion of debate'. The paper advised, 'If the limited number of women actually holding public office is actively discussed, comment favourably on the importance of placing qualified persons in public office "without distinction as to . . . sex"'.[86]

The Soviet Union countered with accusations of domestic slavery and the denial of political rights. When the UK representative brought up the refusal of the Soviet Union to recognise the right of Soviet women to take the nationality of their British husbands, Mrs Popova countered, 'Soviet Women in England . . . were deprived of political rights, were slaves to the household and could do nothing but look after the children and cook meals'.[87] Soviet women pointed to the lack of women in political office in the West as evidence of the low status of women in these countries. At the Ninth Session of the ECOSOC the Soviet and Polish representatives made a number of criticisms regarding women's status in the USA. The Women's Bureau responded by defending the low levels of women's political participation, 'This is the result of free choice on the part of most women, who evidently prefer the comfort and privacy of their homes to the grilling experiences of political campaigns and responsibility of major public office'. The memo explained the lack of African-American women in Congress in a condescending manner, asserting, 'In due time we shall have negro women, when some of them have developed to the point where they can serve effectively, with credit to themselves and their constituents'.[88]

Inevitably, American women's organisations became part of the battle over the Commission on the Status of Women. Mrs Miller insisted upon their contribution in a memo to the US delegate to the special committee of the ECOSOC in relationships with non-governmental agencies:

> One provision that I feel must be carefully safeguarded in whatever arrangement we make for the work in the coming year is that of channelling to and from the government committees on Human Rights and the Status of Women, the interest, thinking and recommendations of the United States Women's organizations. The reason for this is that these organizations have experience in promoting at the domestic level the program these commissions deal with internationally. They are also in a position to further these programs substantively if kept informed and in a co-operative relationship.[89]

In co-operating with their government on international programmes such as the UN Commission on the Status of Women, American women's organisations inevitably jeopardised their independence of action. Their international activities became an expression, not of their sisterhood with women across the world, but of their commitment to the American Cold War agenda. Whatever hopes American women's organisations may have had of working for a new international order, Cold War imperatives pushed them towards co-operation with their government. As the world became increasingly gripped by the Cold War, American women began to see the international network of women, not as a potential force for peace and internationalism, but as a battlefield for national interests. Women's peaceable tendencies that had once been embraced by American women, as representative of the untapped potential for a new world order, quickly became dangerous vulnerabilities in the Cold War struggle.

Notes

1   W. Preston Jr., 'The history of US–UNESCO relations', in W. Preston, Jr., E. S. Herman and H. I. Shiller, *Hope and Folly: The United States and UNESCO 1945–1985* (Minneapolis, MN: University of Minnesota Press, 1985), p. 33.
2   *Ibid.*, p. 32.
3   Mildred Burgess, 'United Nations, tree of life', *Independent Woman*, 27:2 (February 1948), p. 32.
4   J. S. Dickey and H. D. Reid, 'Some implications of international co-operation', *Journal of the AAUW*, 38:3 (Spring 1945), p. 140.
5   'Let's make the U.N. Work', *Journal of the AAUW*, 39:2 (Winter 1946), p. 87.
6   'Resolutions of the 1945 Convention', *Journal of the AAUW*, 38:4 (Summer 1945), p. 202.

7   *Ibid.*, pp. 213–15.
8   Franklin D. Roosevelt Presidential Library, Hyde park, New York, Eleanor Roosevelt papers, box 3612, press release from the Women's National News Service, 31 October 1949.
9   *International Women's News*, 42:2 (November 1947), p. 27.
10 *Ibid.*
11 D. Yergin, *Shattered Peace: The Origins of the Cold War and the National Security State* (Boston, MA: Houghton Mifflin, 1977), p. 163.
12 *Ibid.*, p. 168.
13 *Ibid.*, p. 171.
14 G. W. Reichard, *Politics as Usual: The Age of Truman and Eisenhower* (Arlington Heights, IL: Harlen Davidson, 1988), p. 201.
15 Quoted in Yergin, *Shattered Peace*, p. 275.
16 H. Josephson, 'The search for lasting peace: Internationalism and foreign policy, 1920–1950', in C. Chatfield and P. Van Den Dungen (eds), *Peace Movements and Political Cultures* (Knoxville, TN: University of Tennessee Press, 1988), p. 213.
17 *Ibid.*, p. 205.
18 Library of Congress, Washington, DC, League of Women Voters papers, box 1775, file 3, Strauss memorandum to Local and State League Presidents, undated.
19 *Ibid.*
20 Quoted by M. Newcomber, 'America's share in ERP – profit or loss?' *Journal of the AAUW*, 41:4 (Summer 1948), p. 202.
21 *Ibid.* p. 203. Newcomber concluded her article with the familiar plea that America must 'set its own house in order'. She argued, 'There is one more closely related problem that we have to tackle – the problem of civil rights. If we are going to preach democracy, as we are doing, to the nations of Western Europe, we are going to have to practice democracy at home as our own Declaration of Independence and our own Constitution have defined it. This, too, is something that the Communists have taken pains to point out to our European friends. The success of our European aid program, then, depends on this, too'.
22 Harry S. Truman Presidential Library, Independence, Missouri, Harry S. Truman papers, White House central file, letter, Murray to Truman, 5 April 1945.
23 V. M. Dean, 'US Relations with Russia', *Journal of the AAUW*, 40:4 (Summer 1947), p. 204.
24 *Ibid.*, p. 205. Dean even suggested that the US resign its privilege of veto at the UN Security Council in the hope that the Soviet Union would follow their example. Referring to specific issues such as US support for the Greek anti-Communist regime, Dean warned, 'While we stand rightly opposed to political dictatorship of the communist type, we must not let ourselves become known as a country which supports reactionary governments solely because they happen also to oppose Russia and communism' (p. 205).
25 H. D. Reid, 'The US in world affairs – Russia: challenge to understanding', *Journal of the AAUW*, 41:1 (Autumn 1947), p. 49.
26 A. K. Hottel, 'Town meetings around the world', *Journal of the AAUW*, 43:2 (January 1950), p. 81.

27   S. Blanding, 'States Presidents consider program, policy, problems', *Journal of the AAUW*, 42:1 (Autumn 1948), p. 23.

28   A. G. Dannell, 'AAUW's position: continue building', *Journal of the AAUW*, 43:3 (Spring 1950), p. 141.

29   'From UN to World Federation', *Journal of the AAUW*, 43:3 (Spring 1950), p. 135. Cord Meyer, Jr, later became the CIA official responsible for links with private organisations.

30   Senator W. Benton, 'A Marshall Plan of ideas', *Journal of the AAUW*, 43:4 (Summer 1950), p. 204.

31   S. Lynn, *Progressive Women in Conservative Times: Radical Justice, Peace and Feminism 1945 to the 1960s* (New Brunswick, NJ: Rutgers University Press, 1992), p. 104.

32   L. McEnaney, *Civil Defense Begins at Home: Militarization Meets Everyday Life in the Fifties*, (Princeton, NJ, and Oxford: Princeton University Press, 2000), p. 153.

33   *Ibid.*, p. 122.

34   D. M. Oshinsky, *A Conspiracy So Immense: The World of Joe McCarthy* (New York: The Free Press, 1983), pp. 120–2. For a biography of Kenyon, see B. Sicherman and C. H. Green (eds), *Notable American Women: The Modern Period* (Cambridge, MA: The Belknap Press, 1980). For a discussion of the loyalty investigation of Kenyon, see S. M. Hartmann, *The Home Front and Beyond: American Women in the 1940s* (Boston, MA: Twayne, 1982).

35   Mary McLeod Bethune Memorial Museum, Washington, DC, National Council of Negro Women papers, box 24, pamphlet on The Council of American-Soviet Friendship, 1943.

36   D. Kenyon, 'The image of the thing we hate', *Journal of the AAUW*, 43:4 (Summer 1950), p. 220.

37   Hartmann, *The Home Front and Beyond*, p. 156. Leila Rupp has pointed out the extent to which 'Red-tagging' of women in the McCarthy era was accompanied by accusations of lesbianism. Following McHale's nomination to the Board, Senator Pat McCarran advised Truman that her name should be withdrawn, threatening that if this was not done, he would hold public hearings in which 'information would be brought out that she was a lesbian'. L. J. Rupp, '"Imagine my surprise": Women's relationships in mid-twentieth century America', in M. B. Duberman, M. Vicinus and G. Chauncey, Jr (eds), *Hidden from History: Reclaiming the Gay and Lesbian Past* (New York: Penguin Books, 1989), p. 407.

38   For a meticulous account of the effect of the anti-communist witch-hunt against the CAW, see A. Swerdlow, 'The Congress of American Women's left: Feminist peace politics in the Cold War', in L. Kerber, A.Kessler-Harris and K. K. Sklar (eds), *U.S. History as Women's History: New Feminist Essays* (Chapel Hill, NC: University of North Carolina Press, 1995).

39   For an account of the way in which the NAACP dealt with anti-communist pressures see G. Horne, *Black and Red: W.E.B. Du Bois and the African-American Response to the Cold War 1944–1963* (New York: State University of New York Press, 1986). Horne has remarked on the fact that the effect of the Cold War consensus on African-American leftists has been an unexplored area of African-American history. He argues, 'In a nation where the Cold War and the Red Scare have been the defining post-war paradigms, the attacks on the civil liberties of black leftists – which were taking place as civil rights for blacks generally were being expanded – are not part of either myth. It is as if W.E.B.

DuBois, Paul Robeson, Ben Davis, Claudia Jones and William Patterson did not exist'. Horne argues that W. E. B. DuBois' expulsion from the leadership of the NAACP was due to his 'refusal to go along with accommodation to the gathering Cold War consensus'. G. Horne, '"Myth" and the making of "Malcolm X"', *American Historical Review*, 98:2 (April 1993).

40 M. Newcomber, 'Citizens and scholars', *Journal of the AAUW*, 47:1 (October 1953), p. 17.
41 The reminiscences of Miss Anna Lord Strauss, interview by Mrs Walter Gelhorn, Oral History Research Office, Columbia University, p. 302.
42 *Ibid.*, p. 417.
43 *Action*, journal of the National League of Women Voters (January 1948), p. 12.
44 League of Women Voters papers, box 1741, file 5, letter, Burgess to Becker, 12 January 1949.
45 League of Women Voters papers, box 1741, file 5, letter, Stone to Johnson, 18 August 1949, and Johnson to Stone, 19 September 1949.
46 League of Women Voters papers, box 1734, file 4, Mitchell to Strauss, 5 January 1949.
47 *Ibid.*
48 Schlesinger Library, Radcliffe Institute, Harvard University, Lucille Koshland papers, box 1, file 9, 'CCCMF statement of activities, 1955'.
49 The reminiscences of Miss Anna Lord Strauss, p. 392.
50 *Ibid.*
51 Lucille Koshland papers, box 1, file 21, pamphlet, 'Freedom Agenda'.
52 M. Lindsay, 'Defending the right to discuss freedom', *Washington Post*, 21 November 1955.
53 R. Jeffreys-Jones, *Changing Differences: Women and the Shaping of American Foreign Policy 1917–1994* (New Brunswick, NJ: Rutgers University Press, 1995), p. 115.
54 I. C. Brown, 'We can make history', *Journal of the AAUW*, 44:3 (Spring 1951), p. 131.
55 *Ibid.*
56 A. K. Hottel, 'Making freedom a reality', *Journal of the AAUW*, 44:4 (Summer 1951), p. 196.
57 I. C. Brown, 'The things we can do', *Journal of the AAUW*, 44:4 (Summer 1951), p. 69.
58 'Security and civil rights', *Journal of the AAUW*, 43:3 (March 1952), p. 155.
59 'The communist threat to freedom and democracy', *Journal of the AAUW*, 46:2 (January 1953), pp. 67–9.
60 *Ibid.*
61 *Ibid.*
62 Editorial, *Journal of the AAUW*, 46:4 (May 1953), p. 239.
63 Schlesinger Library, Radcliffe Institute, Harvard University, Mary S. Ingraham papers, box 1, file 30, 'Policy with respect to communism', 28 September 1953.
64 Records of the AAUW, series VIII, reel 145, pamphlet of the National Council of Women, May 1947.
65 'Women urged to be guardians of democracy', *New York Times*, 6 October 1940.
66 National Council of Negro Women papers, box 24, file 11, National Council of Women of the United States, minutes, Board of Directors meeting, 14 June 1948.

67 'World Conference of Women', *Christian Science Monitor*, 6 December 1945.
68 National Council of Negro Women papers, box 8, file 11, Congress of American Women press release, 27 February 1946.
69 National Council of Negro Women papers, box 39, file 1, Report of WIDF Paris Meeting, 26–30 November 1945.
70 National Council of Negro Women papers, box 8, file 11, letter, Mary McLeod Bethune to Eleanor Roosevelt, 2 March 1946. In fact this letter was drafted by Vivian Carter Mason, the Executive Director of the NCNW, at the instigation of Elinor Gimbel. Mason wrote to Gimbel, 'I talked with Mrs Bethune and she instructed me . . . to write a letter to Mrs Roosevelt asking her for the statement which you desire'. Mason to Gimbel, 2 March 1946, National Council of Negro Women Papers, box 8, file 11.
71 For an account of the work of the CAW, see Swerdlow 'The Congress of American Women's left'.
72 'My big family', *Women of the Whole World*, 7 (July 1955).
73 'We protest', *Women of the Whole World*, 5 (May 1955).
74 Records of the National Council of Women of the United States inc. 1888 – ca 1970, complied by L. K. O'Reefe (UMI, Ann Arbor, MI, 1988), fiche 695, 'Information on the communist-dominated WIDF' Besides its publications the WIDF organised conferences such as those to celebrate International Women's Day on 8 March. Exchanges and visits to the Soviet Union were organized, with an estimated 649 exchanges between women's delegations in the Communist bloc and the West in 1956. Fiche 696, Records of a meeting with Henry Loomis, Director of the Office of Research and Intelligence, USIA, 3 April 1957.
75 Papers of the Women's Bureau, Department of Labor, National Archives, Washington, DC, General Records 1918–62, box 10, memo, Rachel Conrad Nason, Advisor to US Representatives, to Mr Hyde, US Delegation to United Nations, 24 March 1947.
76 *Ibid.*
77 Papers of the Women's Bureau, Department of Labor, General Records 1918–62, box 10, letter, Frieda Miller to Mr Kaiser, Office of International Labor Affairs (not dated).
78 *Ibid.*
79 *Ibid.*
80 Papers of the Women's Bureau, Department of Labor, General Records 1918–62, box 12, memo, Mr Kotsching, UNE, to Mr Sanders, UNA (not dated).
81 Papers of the Women's Bureau, Department of Labor, General Records 1918–62, box 12, report, meeting of subcommittee of Human Rights and Status of Women, 4 October 1948.
82 Papers of the Women's Bureau, Department of Labor, International Divisions, International work file 1945–56, box 7, Committee on International Social Policy, overall comment of specific references to women in Declaration Articles of Bill of Rights.
83 Papers of the Women's Bureau, Department of Labor, General Records 1918–62, box 12, preparatory discussion on picture book to illustrate status of women in the USA, 2 December 1948.
84 Papers of the Women's Bureau, Department of Labor, General Records 1918–62, box 12, memo, Frieda Miller to Mr Kotschnig, UNE, State Department (not dated).

85 Papers of the Women's Bureau, Department of Labor, General Records 1918–62, box 13, Summary Record of the fifty-ninth meeting at Beirut, Lebanon, 1 April 1949.

86 Papers of the Women's Bureau, Department of Labor, International Division, International work file 1945–56, box 1, position paper, 'Report on the Political Rights of Women', 2 September 1948.

87 Papers of the Women's Bureau, Department of Labor, General Records 1918–62, box 13, summary of the fifty-fourth meeting of the third session of the Commission on the Status of Women, 30 March 1949.

88 Papers of the Women's Bureau, Department of Labor, International Division, International work file 1945–56, box 3, office memo to Mrs Miller from Sara Buchanan, 29 September 1949.

89 Papers of the Women's Bureau, Department of Labor, General Records 1918–62, box 12, memo, Frieda Miller to Mr Kotschnig, Department of State (not dated).

5

'Positive peace': American women's response to the 'peace offensive'

Women's interest in peace has constituted an important, if vague, component of constructions of the feminine identity. Historian Denise Riley, illustrating the problem of 'constant historical loops which depart or return from the convictions of women's natural dispositions', chose women's interest in peace as a paradigm.[1] Jean Bethke Elshtain has argued that identifications around issues of peace and violence (what she refers to as 'Just Warriors' and 'Beautiful Souls') are crucial tropes in the construction of gendered identities:

> Man construed as violent, whether eagerly and inevitably or reluctantly and tragically; women as non-violent, offering succor and compassion; these tropes on the social identities of men and women, past and present, do not denote what men and women really are in time of war, but function instead to re-create and secure women's location as non-combatants and men's as warriors.[2]

Elshtain argues that 'the times have outstripped beautiful souls and just warriors' since 'the beautiful soul can no longer be protected in her virtuous privacy. Her world, and her children, are vulnerable in the face of nuclear reality'. Nevertheless, these identities have such force and continuing appeal that Elshtain sees their resonance in 'contemporary feminist statements [which] involve celebrations of a "female Principle" as ontologically given and superior to its dark "other" masculinism'.[3]

The link between women and peace could be described as tenuous as it is tenacious. Despite the investigations of sociologists, biologists, psychologists, historians and anthropologists, the connection has been explained and explored, admired and deplored, but has remained unproved.[4] Concurrent to debates on the existence and extent of women's connection to peace, there has been division within feminism as to the advisability of acknowledging and encouraging the link. Sara Ruddick, an influential proponent of what she calls 'maternal thinking', has claimed that women as mothers have a special role in the struggle for peace and in the assertion of the values of 'preservative love' over military destruction.[5] Ruddick advocates the proclamation of women's maternal role in peace-led politics: 'Were I a leader and a persuader, I would attempt to rally mothers and other women to a mother-identified politics of protest'.[6]

However, without absolute evidence to reinforce women's claim to a greater commitment to peace, the connection is arguably one which could and/or should be broken. French feminist Simone De Beauvoir famously challenged the validity of women's interest in peace, describing it as proceeding from the same gendered divisions which for centuries have been used to underpin and justify patriarchal constructions of women's inferiority.[7] De Beauvoir argued that such thinking would inevitably reinforce the idea of difference between women and men, 'Women should desire peace as human beings, not as women. And if they are being encouraged to be pacifists in the name of motherhood, that's just a ruse by men who are trying to lead women back to the womb. Women should absolutely let go of that baggage!'[8] Berenice A. Carroll has questioned what she refers to as 'the "gut feeling" there is some fundamental bond between feminism and pacifism, some inherent and inevitable logic that binds them ultimately together'.[9] Other feminist theorists have shared her unease, questioning whether there are valid and positive aspects to the assertion of a female identity which is closely allied with the cause of 'peace' or whether, in fact, such an identification risks perpetuating the same notions of femininity which have been used to explain women's 'difference' and to thereby justify their separate and unequal treatment. The historian of the Women's International League for Peace and Freedom, Jo Vellacott, has termed this anxiety the 'fear of feminists that any form of women's pacifism may be positively subversive of feminist purpose'.[10]

Even when women's link to peace is associated with political, rather than biological factors, it remains problematic. A commitment to peace for women can mean that they are deemed unsuitable to take leading roles within the national framework. Myrian Miedzan has argued, 'Being compassionate and concerned about human life can cause a man to lose his job. It can cause a woman not to get a job to begin with. Women's reputed empathy and compassion are viewed by many as rendering them unqualified for high offices that involve 'tough' international decision-making'.[11] Moreover, if the connection between women and pacifism can be detrimental to the status of women in reinforcing the idea of 'difference' between men and women, the connection between femininity and peace has also been unhelpful to the peace movement. To paraphrase a popular logic of the time, the peace movement may have become 'feminine by association'. International relations theorist J. Ann Tickner has argued that the association of female essentialist identities with the peace movement has had a troubling effect both for women and for peace movements:

> At best, images of peace appear uninteresting, at worse they invoke identities that are problematic and unpatriotic, identities that are associated with women and feminine characteristics . . . While peace movements more generally disturb the image of a unified national purpose embodied in states' national security policies, the association of feminine characteristics with peace has contributed to the disempowerment and delegitimation of peace projects undertaken by both men and women.[12]

Finally, feminists have critiqued the presumption of a connection between women and peace on the basis that it articulates, at best, a vague emotive agenda which might lead women down some unfortunate paths. Mary Deitz argues in her critique of the work of Jean Bethke Elshtain that 'a movement or a political consciousness committed simply to caring for "vulnerable human existence" . . . offers no standards . . . when it comes to judging between political alternatives or establishing political values'.[13]

American women's organisations drew heavily upon the assumed connection between women and peace in asserting their claim for a more active role in the post-war world. However, while this identification may have motivated and justified the *fact* of their international activities, it became increasingly problematic as the Cold War intensified and the claims of national identity grew ever more pressing. If women were indeed less influenced by national loyalties than by a commitment to the cause of peace, they could be defined as a kind of international 'floating voter' whose loyalty and support did not automatically follow national allegiance. Aloof from the details and wider considerations of national and international geopolitics, they were vulnerable to any government persuasive enough to present themselves as the defenders of peace.

After the Second World War, American women's organisations were quick to recognise that the vague desire for peace expressed by many of their members, not to mention their leaders, was in need of a more stringent definition. Behind the concern to define 'peace' carefully lay the fear that unless the term was tied to concrete and achievable aims, it would remain a lofty ideal, impossible to work for in a practical sense. The *Journal of the AAUW* worried, 'The peace, too, has to be won; and this is more difficult because there is no longer the singleness of purpose and the obvious goal that we have in time of war'.[14] To rally people and organisations to activity in the cause of peace, it had to be defined in an assertive, active and specific way. Margaret Hyndman, President of the Canadian Federation of Business and Professional Women's' Clubs, explained, 'It is not enough for us merely to yearn for peace. It is not enough to talk about peace, or to make speeches about peace – although all these things have some value. We must be ready to work for peace and even to fight for peace. By fighting I don't mean using bombs, atomic or otherwise; I mean fighting with words and with ideas'.[15]

By May 1947, American women's organisations were questioning the relationship between an abstract commitment to peace and the reality of Cold War tensions. An editorial entitled 'Wanted: adult citizens' in *Action*, the journal of the LWV, explained that women needed a sophisticated understanding of world affairs if they were to be responsible citizens:

> We need a general goal upon which we can agree – one which is more explicit than simply 'peace'. For example, is our goal a co-operative international framework in which individual nations may develop politically, economically, culturally, as they see fit, provided their policies are peaceful? Is it our goal to strengthen the non-communist world against the possibility of conflict with the communist world? Is the second goal an alternative if the first fails? By having the second as an alternative do we make the failure of the first more likely?[16]

The LWV and other American women's organisations struggled to find answers to these vaguely rhetorical questions, and 'peace' remained a general aim for American women, rather than a concerted plan of action. This vacuum in meaning behind women's commitment to peace became a vulnerability when the US government identified a Soviet propaganda campaign to assure the people of the world that they wanted nothing more than world peace but were constantly thwarted by US warmongering. The Soviet 'peace offensive', as the US government called it, had a major effect on the relationship of American women's organisations to peace.

Underlying the fear that women would be particularly vulnerable to the vague appeal of 'peace' propaganda was a subtext regarding women's instability as political subjects, what Carol Patemen categorizes as the 'disorder of women'.[17] In his 1955 study *Are American Women Degenerating?*, the anonymous author colourfully illustrated the belief in the 'disorder of women':

> But ideals, to be practical, must be based on reason and judgement: Aristotle, Schopenhauer, Spencer, etc. have warned against the dangers to government of false ideas dominating politically influential but pathogenic emotional, hysterical women. In history their political record is a poor one. Such poorly adjusted personalities are subject to paroxysms of morbid sentimentality utterly uncontrolled by reason.[18]

Women were often feared to be particularly vulnerable to 'peace propaganda' that appealed to emotion and sentimentality, rather than rational political argument. Divorced from political context, women's emotional commitment to peace represented a dangerous vulnerability. Their well-intentioned response to peace issues lacked an understanding of wider political issues. Within the Cold War context this emotional response was potentially highly dangerous, leaving groups of women at the mercy of subversion by more politically astute actors. Jack Lotto, a columnist for the Hearst Press, charged that Women Strike for Peace (WSP) exhibited this feminine weakness, being exploited by external forces. Lotto claimed that although the organisation described themselves as 'a group of unsophisticated housewives and mothers who are loosely organized in a spontaneous movement for peace, there is nothing spontaneous about the way the pro-Reds have moved in on our mothers and are using them for their own purposes'.[19]

The US government has displayed a notable tendency to see peace campaigns as Soviet-inspired, duplicitous plots to undermine the American position. Their suspicion dates back to the World Congress of Cultural Activists in Defence of Peace, in Brotslav, Western Poland, in August 1948. Another meeting in March 1949 at the Waldorf-Astoria Hotel in New York City brought together over 800 prominent cultural figures including Lillian Hellman, Arthur Miller and Norman Mailer. The meeting called for peace, denouncing

'US warmongering'. Sidney Hook, one of the founders of the Congress for Cultural Freedom, an organisation that brought together intellectuals in defence of Western politics and culture, organised a spirited opposition to the Waldorf conference, including a rally and aggressive questioning of the Soviet delegates. Hook described the communist 'peace offensive' as a deliberate, orchestrated and meticulously planned campaign:

> In September 1947, at the 1st formal meeting of the Cominform in Poland under the leadership of Zhdanov, the directives and strategy of the world campaign against the democratic West were laid down. Soon in various countries of the West, committees approved resolutions, ostensibly in the defence of peace against the machinations of American imperialism, in actuality in furtherance of the aggressions of the Soviet Union. The distinctive feature of this round of 'non-partisan' peace front activities was the concentration of their appeals to the intellectuals of the West . . . to rally to the defense of peace and to the exposure of the 'American warmongers'.[20]

The meeting sparked an immediate response from the US government, with the State Department and the HUAC denouncing the Soviet 'peace offensive' as a propaganda trick.[21] Stalin's speeches calling for a Soviet–American 'peace pact' and the launching of the Stockholm peace petition at the meeting of the World Peace Council in Stockholm in March 1950 served as further evidence to the US government of a concerted propaganda campaign in the name of 'peace'. In July 1950 the HUAC responded, condemning the 'peace campaign and its manifestation in the form of petitions' which, they asserted, were designed to 'confuse and divide the American people'.[22]

The effect of the Soviet sponsored 'peace offensive' was to divided the world into 'camps', as the Soviet Union attempted to claim the moral high ground as the defenders of peace, castigating the US as warmongers. The Paris correspondent of *Pravda*, for example, wrote in praise of the Stockholm peace petition, asking his readers, 'Who are you with – the 500 million . . . or the handful of imperialists and their hired agents?'[23] Jeffrey Brooks has argued that the suspicion of the US government towards Soviet-sponsored peace campaigns resulted in their failure to come to a greater understanding with the Soviet Union following Stalin's death. He argues that Americans had, by 1953, come to see all Soviet expressions of peace as propaganda.[24] Calls for peace, rather than being read at face value, were immediately

assumed by the Americans to be a tactical move. As late as 1983, a CIA
review into possible Soviet responses to the US strategic defence initiative ('Star Wars') assumed that the Soviets' first move in blocking
ballistic missile defence (BMD) would be to 'mobilize existing
resources for a targeted peace offensive'. The report asserted that
'Moscow will make use of the peace movement'.[25] The context of the
US suspicion left little room for 'genuine' peace movements. As E. P.
Thompson asserts, 'Those who worked for Peace in the West were
suspected or exposed as pro-Soviet "fellow-travelers" or dupes of the
Kremlin'.[26] In her 1951 novel, *The Groves of Academe*, author Mary
McCarthy described the lengths to which identification with the cause
of 'peace' had come to be seen as dangerously un-American. The character Maynard Hoars, President of the fictional Jocelyn College,
'genially asserted' at a party 'that he could as soon in these times, as
president of a small, struggling college, appear at a "peace" rally as be
found playing strip poker on Sunday in a Whorehouse'.[27]

A clear example of this process occurred on 15 March 1951 when
a 'peace pilgrimage' from the American Peace Crusade (APC), including African-American entertainer and activist Paul Robeson, called on
Congress and was greeted by Francis Russell, Director of the Office of
Public Affairs in the State Department. At a time when preliminary
talks for a Foreign Ministers' meeting between the US, the Soviet
Union, the UK and France were under way in Paris, the APC urged
the State Department to co-operate with the Soviet Union to ensure
the success of the negotiations. In response, Russell attacked the APC,
reading from a letter from Secretary of State Dean Acheson that
asserted:

> From the membership of the group, and the general tenor of its pro
> nouncements, it is obvious that this 'American Peace Crusade' is
> merely a continuation or regrouping of the spurious Partisans of
> Peace movement, which, as you know, has been the most concen
> trated and far-flung propaganda effort of the International
> Communist Movement in the post-war period.[28]

Russell urged the APC to consider 'whether you are not allowing
yourselves to be exploited, if you are not, in fact, engaged in behalf of
a foreign totalitarian regime in exploiting honest differences of
opinion'.[29]

American women's organisations were not exempt from the
general suspicion of groups interested in peace or internationalism.

Despite letters in 1952 and 1955 from the HUAC verifying that the WILPF had not been cited as a 'Communist front' or a 'subversive' agency, WILPF was continually harassed by those, including the FBI, suspicious of their anti-war stance.[30] Inspiration for these attacks undoubtedly came in part from the WILPF's espousal of causes all too similar with those asserted in communist propaganda. The WILPF demanded:

> We must insist that because we are espousing a cause which the Communists are also working on, does not mean that we are communists, fellow travellers, communist infiltrated, etc. Our work must be judged by what we stand for, and the reasons for this stand. Not by who else is also working for a similar purpose.[31]

The WILPF, besieged by anti-communist paranoia at home, was undermined by the Soviet-sponsored 'peace offensive' abroad. Gertrude Bussey and Margaret Tims, historians of the WILPF, assert:

> It must be acknowledged as a matter of history that the activities of the [Soviet-backed] World Peace Council and its subsidiaries – Partisans for Peace and the Women's International Democratic Federation – often constituted as great a handicap to the established peace movement in the West as the Atlantic Pact. It was difficult, and sometimes painful, to cast doubts on expressions of solidarity in the cause of peace, freedom and democracy that claimed a mass following in the Eastern-bloc countries and sought to extend this following to the West.[32]

Bussey and Tims argue, 'The attempts of the Women's International Democratic Federation to use the older organization for its own partisan aims, even though unsuccessful, were a considerable embarrassment to WILPF national sections'.[33] As the Soviet-backed campaigns for peace became more vocal, the peace cause itself became, at least in the minds of many Americans, synonymous with communism. American peace activists found it increasingly difficult to assert their commitment to peace without risking accusations of being at best, duped fellow-travellers, and at worst, communist agents.

Historian E. P. Thompson has argued that during the Cold War, 'the causes of "peace" and "freedom" broke apart, with the Soviet Union claiming "peace" and the United States "freedom"'.[34] The division is overly simplistic. While it is true that Americans championed the cause of freedom, they did not entirely abandon the rallying cry of peace. Despite the US government's disparagement of peace movements as politically suspect, such appeals had an undeniable appeal both at home and abroad. The 1950 Stockholm Peace Pledge, for example, gained some 1,350,000 signatories in the USA and within five months of its launch had received 273,470,566 signatories worldwide.[35] A memorandum to Local State and League Presidents from Mrs John G. Lee of the LWV urged that women not be unwittingly drawn into support for what she called a 'misleading peace campaign' but recognised that such a campaign had a tremendous appeal: 'There is no reason to believe that League members themselves will subscribe to the Propaganda underlying the Peace petition, but the campaign for signatures may become active in your community and many people, sincerely wishing to do something personally to bring about peace, may sign or be drawn into the effort'.[36]

Outright rejection of the aim of 'peace' would leave Americans vulnerable to accusations or aggression or warmongering. The peace group Fellowship of Reconciliation (FOR) explained this dilemma neatly in a recruiting leaflet, 'But does that make PEACE a bad word? Because the communists misuse the word, are Americans going to agree that they prefer war?'[37] In recognition of the undeniable international appeal of 'peace', it would have been impossible for the US government simply to abandon the cause. Rather they sought to redefine 'peace' in such a way as to illustrate the difference between what the Soviet Union and the USA meant by 'peace'. *Newsweek* explained to its readers, '"Peace" was a fighting word. Everyone was for it, naturally, just as everyone was against the man-eating shark. The trouble was that it didn't mean the same thing in Russian that it did in English'.[38] United States officials therefore sought to offer an American definition of peace. Francis Russell wrote to Assistant Secretary of State Edward Barrett in February 1951: 'The Communist "Crusade for Peace" represents an opportunity for the State Department and for private citizens to point out the kind of peace for which we stand, i.e. a peace with freedom, liberty and justice'.[39]

The American insistence on retaining a claim to both the rhetoric and ideology of 'peace' is vividly illustrated in Eisenhower's 1953 announcement of 'Atoms for Peace'. Ostensibly a programme to share with the world peaceful and socially useful developments stemming from atomic power, the presentation of the USA as a peace-loving nation was an important propaganda coup. Gerald Clarfield and

William Wiecek, historians of American nuclear policy, explain: 'American policy-makers were also looking for some dramatic gesture to offset the Soviet achievement of developing nuclear weapons, particularly some accomplishment that would enhance America's sought-after reputation as a peace-loving nation facing an aggressive and militaristic U.S.S.R.'[40]

President Eisenhower's seeming obsession with defining 'peace' continued throughout his term in office and afterwards. A collection of his speeches is titled *Peace With Justice* and the second volume of his autobiography is *Waging Peace*. Eisenhower told the NCCW in November 1954, 'Preserving peace in the world, international peace, is not a static, is not a negative thing. It is a positive thing, of preparing the world, the conditions in the world, where people may live honourably and upright and at peace'.[41] Yet Eisenhower was quick to attach qualifications for the search for peace, asserting, 'Far better to risk a war of possible annihilation than grasp a peace which would be the certain extinction of free man's ideas and ideals'.[42]

This American conception of 'peace' was thus neatly conjoined with the expression of 'freedom'. In attaching preconditions to the achievement of peace, the USA sought to define a 'positive' rather than 'negative' peace. Peace theorists Robert Elias and Jennifer Turpin have described this difference, explaining, '[The] long standing notion of peace is "negative" peace – the absence of war and other direct violence. "Positive" peace includes the presence or promotion of social justice. Under this conception, a peaceful society or world requires the absence of war and other direct violence but also requires the protection of human rights'.[43]

American description of Soviet peace as 'negative' and their own peace as 'positive' was an important, if overlooked, manifestation of US Cold War policy in the early 1950s. American adoption of 'negative' peace, i.e., an end to the threat of violence with restrictions on military power, would have entailed an acceptance on their part of the Soviet sphere of influence in Eastern Europe. Charles Burton Marshall, a member of the Policy Planning Staff at the State Department, explained:

> Peace to the Soviet regime, as it would to anyone else means a legitimate order free of violence. Since in the Soviet view, however, legitimacy stands for whatever favors Communist interests and purposes, peace therefore stands for a non-violent situation

favourable to those interests and purposes, whatever tends otherwise is by definition deviant in the direction of war. Peace, then,
besides entailing an absence of war, means essentially a situation free
of impediment to Communist purposes. [44]

Acceptance of this type of peace depended upon the Soviet Union to
agree to abide by the same rules, a level of trust towards Moscow that
was conspicuously lacking in Washington.

To justify its rejection of the laudable-sounding calls for peace
emanating both from the Soviet Union and from seemingly innocuous, non-partisan, media-friendly groups of concerned world-citi-
zens, the US government needed to discredit both the Soviet
campaign and any independent call for peace which challenged the
American position of military preparedness. Rather than denigrate
'peace' itself, the American government and those Americans who
supported its agenda instead accused the Soviets of being insincere in
their use of the term, manipulating into a political weapon the
genuine desire of individuals for peace. As Robbie Lieberman has
commented, 'The way in which one defined peace had implications
for the way on which one worked to achieve it'.[45]

An example of the efforts of Americans to distance their definition of 'peace' from Soviet use of that word can be found in a speech
by Eleanor Roosevelt, broadcast on radio, in Paris on 14 April 1949.
Roosevelt asserted that people in Western Europe were in a difficult
position: 'They are faced with the choice of peace at any price, a peace
of compromise and appeasement, of submission to an aggressor who
believes in control of men's minds. On the other hand they think that
to preserve their freedom they must risk war.' She warned, however,
that the suffering of war should not mean that people were led to
believe that 'the value of freedom has lessened and that to obtain
peace we are willing to sacrifice freedom'. Waxing lyrical, she
described freedom as a 'fresh and running stream in which there is
refreshment for the soul', but 'peace without freedom is a stagnant
pool. It may look alluring at a distance, the lily pads may gleam white
in the sun, but underneath the water is foul'.[46]

Mainstream women's organisations participated in this wider
campaign to delineate and define an American peace. Mrs Theodore
Chapman, the President of the GFWC, began her 1954 address with
the standard praise of the voluntary association, announcing, 'There
is no clearer expression of the democratic process than the voluntary

organization. They are the free channels of communication and co-operation and are emotional safeguards in freedom'. Her speech committed the GFWC to the defence of a carefully constructed definition of 'peace':

> It is our collective responsibility, as the largest women's organization in the world, to raise our united voice in support of the forces at work for a lasting peace based upon justice and freedom for all mankind. And peace is more than the absence of war – it is the presence of creative forces – forces that will help us evolve some pattern of getting along together.[47]

American 'peace', linked to freedom, justice, and opportunity, was assertive, proactive, positive, and 'masculine'. Peace on Soviet terms, which was inactive, permissive of social injustice, and tolerant of repressive systems, was passive, negative and 'feminine'. Peace historian Robbie Lieberman is correct in her assumption that the US response to the Soviet Peace campaign was to view all peace movements, whatever their origin, as deeply suspicious and potentially communist.[48] However, women's peace campaigns, because of their alleged 'natural' predisposition to passivity and therefore 'negative' peace, were particularly suspect.[49]

This concern intensified as elements within the US government increasingly worried about the effect of communist propaganda, particularly accusations of germ warfare in Korea, upon women across the globe. Mary Cannon, Chief of the International Division of the Women's Bureau at the Department of Labor, wrote to Marion Sanders and Herbert McGushin of the State Department. She enclosed a copy of 'Korea we accuse', a report claiming to have uncovered the use of chemical weapons by the USA in Korea, 'The United States Women's Bureau is concerned that such a distorted picture of America's character is being circulated to women's organizations and leaders throughout the world . . . This kind of propaganda will probably be an effective weapon in gaining support among women for the Communist "peace offensive"'.[50]

Organisations identified by the US government as tools of the Soviet 'peace offensive' appealed to women in essentialist terms, citing their 'special interest' in peace. The report of the World Assembly for Peace, held in Helsinki in June 1955, pronounced:

> There is no doubt that mothers will everywhere prove among the most active workers for peace, with the object of changing the present

ruinous atmosphere of fear and uncertainty into an atmosphere of confidence and security; maternal love is undoubtedly one of the most powerful forces for peace represented at the Helsinki Assembly . . . Many women who have never before dared to take part in the fight for peace, who previously hid themselves behind the old argument that they did not wish to be political, today understand that they must act in order to protect their children from death and from all the physical and moral suffering which follows wars.[51]

Initially the US government's policy towards international peace organisations that targeted women was similar to their tactics for dealing with the rest of the 'peace offensive'. This included strategies such as denying individuals travelling to peace conferences permission to enter the USA. In March 1950, for example, the USA refused entry to twelve people, including Pablo Picasso and the Dean of Canterbury, acting for the World Congress of Partisans for World Peace. Similarly, the US occupation authorities in West Germany arrested Lily Waechter, a German woman who had been invited by the Women's International Democratic Women's Federation to speak at the World Peace Congress in London in 1951.[52] Waechter had been a representative on the WIDF Commission that had visited Korea and was scheduled to address the Congress on the topic. Her arrest was not a particularly astute move, sparking protests in Wuerttember-Baden.[53]

The obvious impact of these actions upon 'free speech' and 'freedom of movement' were not lost on critics of US policy. Even those who supported the government's hostility towards such 'peace' organisations were not enamoured of the strategy of exclusion. Government restrictions on women's rights to speak about the issue were particularly unpopular. Women's claim to a 'special' interest in peace was a hard one for men to challenge, since, as historian Harriet Hyman Alonso has argued, the 'maternal' claim gave 'women a unique position that men cannot share and therefore cannot really argue against'.[54] This was vividly illustrated in 1962, when the government's tactics of confrontation failed miserably. When the HUAC issued subpoenas to thirteen peace activists with the intention of discovering 'the extent of Communist Party infiltration into the Peace movement, in a manner and to a degree affecting national security', the WSP responded by invoking maternal constructions of womanhood.[55] The WSP defended their activities through women's interest in peace and, as Amy Swerdlow concludes, demolished HUAC along the way:

In their organizational response to the HUAC summons and in their testimony to the hearings, the women of the WSP were so effective and witty in evoking traditional assumptions regarding a woman's role that they succeeded in holding the committee up to public ridicule and damaging its image and reputation with the President, the Public and Congress.[56]

In the twelve years between HUAC's persecution of the CAW and its humiliation at the hands of the WSP, the US government's strategy was to delegate the problem of 'peace' and women to American women's organisations. These organisations therefore took a prominent role in presenting the international community with their brand of pacifism. The first collective example of this was the 1951 Memorial Day Statement. This statement, presented to the Honourable Warren Austin, the US representative to the UN, and broadcast to countries abroad by the Voice of America, was drawn up in the hope 'that this positive declaration may help to refute Soviet Propaganda against American Women and their organizations'.[57]

The Memorial Day Statement was a response to accusations from the WIDF, and the report, 'Korea, we accuse', which asserted that the US government was using germ warfare in Korea. In an open letter to Eleanor Roosevelt, the WIDF called on the former First Lady to raise awareness of the issue among American women and to rouse them to action to put an end to such atrocities. The germ warfare letter from Korea triggered a concerted effort by the leaders of American women's organisations, spearheaded by Rose Parsons of the NCW, to launch international opposition to the Soviet women's peace offensive. When the Memorial Day Statement did not initially receive widespread publicity,[58] the lack-lustre response convinced some American women that a more focused campaign against the Soviet peace offensive was necessary. The CofC, established as a direct result of the germ warfare accusations, served for fifteen years as a CIA-funded channel of propaganda, challenging Soviet assertions about American women's betrayal of their essentialist loyalty to the cause of peace.

Combating the Soviet 'peace campaign' internationally proved difficult. In 1962, after a decade of work by the CofC, Rose Parsons enlisted the help of her friend Eleanor Roosevelt. Parsons asserted:

The WIDF is trying to get women all over the world to combine for peace, love, etc. It is of course their way of infiltrating into international women's organizations. If they were voluntary organizations, the picture would be quite different as you well know, but so many do not realize that the whole communist machine is behind this and is making hay while we in the free world are still bickering over tiny differences. How can we get the gals in the free world to have a dynamic program and take the lead? You could do it![59]

Mrs Roosevelt agreed that 'the "serious" and "well-ordered" women's organisations must do something positive about peace and disarmament' and sympathised, 'It is of course terribly hard to think up exciting rabble rousing activities when they have to be realistic and possible and unemotional'. She was concerned that 'unclean' organisations (such as 'Women Strike for Peace and the Communists') 'are the ones arousing people to do things and catching those who are really anxious to do something for Peace'.[60] At a two-day conference entitled 'Peace Movements, National and International' in 1963, Parsons attempted to warn against these new movements, arguing that they could be used by communists. Parsons pointed out that the WSP had been mentioned many times in *Soviet Woman* and had received numerous telegrams of support form the WIDF. Parsons told her audience, 'We believe they [the WSP] have brought out a great many women for peace. They have stimulated women for peace. I have also shown you the dangers that happen when people do not have a very definite applied program in depth'.[61] The WSP were invited to join Women United for the United Nations (WUUN), but turned the offer down. Parsons explained, 'We asked if they would join other organizations that really were working for peace. They said that they are stodgy, too old. It took too long. We have to do this because our children will be there tomorrow sort of thing'.[62] Parsons saw the WSP, not as a communist organisation, but as an organisation that was being manipulated and used by communists:

> I think that they are being used by the communist women because they want to show how women in the United States really want peace. The government doesn't want it but women do. They use their babies as propaganda and their magazines, such as *Soviet Woman*. I don't think they [Communists] have taken them over at all. I think that many of the women in the WSP are completely non-Communist . . . I don't think they are fully aware that the Communists are using them in different ways.[63]

Mrs Marc Friedlander, the NCJW representative at the conference explained why the WSP was so successful, poignantly expressing the breakdown in the Cold War consensus, 'I think there must have been some of us right here who were impelled at moments to march in the United Nations Plaza, because it did represent a kind of direct action that so many of us feel we don't have an opportunity to express in our more responsible and effective groups'.[64]

Parsons' frustration is understandable. After more than a decade of efforts to limit and define closely the consequences of American women's commitment to peace, it was disconcerting to see newer groups seize the political moment and mount a successful campaign to challenge the aims and methods of their own government. Ironically, though, this pointed to the success of 'mainstream' groups throughout the 1950s in ensuring that they were the authoritative voice of American women. Organisations that did not share the approach of the US government were effectively silenced and denied access to the international stage. Typical of that 'silencing' was the undermining of journalist Dorothy Thompson's World Organization of Mothers of All Nations.

WSP
1960s

Notes

1   D. Riley, 'Am I that Name?' Feminism and the Category of 'Women' in History (Basingstoke: Macmillan, 1988), p. 1.
2   J. B. Elshtain, Women and War (New York: Basic Books, 1987), p. 4.
3   J. B. Elshtain, 'Reflections on war and political discourse: Realism, just war and feminism in a nuclear age', Political Theory, 13:1 (February 1985), p. 45.
4   H. H. Alonso offers a superb survey of the history of this connection in Peace as a Woman's Issue: A History of the U.S. Movement for World Peace and Women's Rights (Syracuse, NY: Syracuse University Press, 1993). See also B. A. Reardon, Women and Peace: Feminist Visions of Global Security (Albany, NY: State University of New York Press, 1993); R. R. Pierson (ed.), Women and Peace: Theoretical, Historical and Practical Perspectives (London: Croom Helm, 1987), especially the chapter by B. A. Carroll, 'Feminism and pacifism: historical and theoretical connections'; C. Enloe, 'Feminist thinking about war, militarism and peace', in B. Hess and M. M. Ferree (eds) Analyzing Gender (London: Sage, 1987). For an exploration of the link between women and peace from a psychological viewpoint, see J. Sayers, Sexual Contradictions: Psychology, Psychoanalysis and Feminism (London: Tavistock, 1986).
5   S. Ruddick, 'Maternal thinking', Feminist Studies, 6:2 (Summer 1980).
6   S. Ruddick, 'Preservative love and military destruction: Some reflections on mothering and peace', in J. Trebilcot (ed.), Mothering: Essays in Feminist Theory (Totowa, NJ: Rowman and Allanheld, 1984), p. 233.
7   Quoted in A. Swedlow, 'Female culture, pacifism and feminism: Women Strike for Peace', in A. Angerman, G. Binnema, A. Keunen, V. Poels and J. Zirkzee (eds), Current Issues in Women's History (Routledge: London, 1989), p. 109.

8   *Ibid.*
9   B. A. Carroll, 'Feminism and pacifism: historical and theoretical connections', in R. R. Pierson (ed.), *Women and Peace: Theoretical, Historical and Practical Perspectives* (London: Croom Helm, 1987), p. 2.
10   J. Vellacott, 'A place for pacifism and transnationalism in feminist theory: The early work of the Women's International League for Peace and Freedom', *Women's History Review*, 2:1 (1993), p. 24.
11   M. Miedzan, 'Real men, wimps and national security', in R. Elias and J. Turpin (eds), *Rethinking Peace* (Boulder, CO: Lynne Rienner, 1994). See also S. Tobias, 'Shifting heroisms: The uses of military service in politics', in J. B. Elshtain and S. Tobias (eds), *Women, Militarism and War: Essays in History, Politics and Social Theory* (Savage, MD: Rowman and Littlefield, 1990).
12   J. A. Tickner, 'Identity in international relations theory: Feminist perspectives', in Y. Lapid and F. Kratochwil (eds), *The Return of Culture and Identity in International Relations Theory* (Boulder, CO: Lynne Rienner, 1996), p. 155.
13   M. G. Dietz, 'Citizenship with a feminist face: The problem with maternal thinking', *Political Theory*, 13:1 (February 1985), p. 30.
14   M. Newcomber, 'A signpost towards international cooperation: Significance of Bretton Woods Conference', *Journal of the AAUW*, 38:1 (Autumn 1944), p. 20.
15   Editorial, *Independent Woman*, 27:4 (April 1948), p. 110.
16   'Wanted: adult citizens', *Action*, journal of the National League of Women Voters (May 1947), p. 25.
17   See C. Pateman, *The Disorder of Women: Democracy, Feminism and Political Theory* (Stanford, CA: Stanford University Press, 1989).
18   Anonymous, *Are American Women Degenerating?* (New York: Exposition Press, 1955), p. 6.
19   Quoted in A. Swerdlow, 'Ladies day at the capital: Women Strike for Peace versus HUAC', in J. B. Elshtain and S. Tobias (eds), *Women, Militarism and War: Essays in History, Politics and Social Theory* (Savage, MD: Rowman and Littlefield, 1990), p. 11.
20   S. Hook, 'The communist peace offensive', *Partisan Review*, 51 (1984), p. 696.
21   The Waldorf Conference, while the most notorious, was not the only peace conference. It was preceded by the World Congress of Intellectuals for Peace in Wroclaw, Poland, in August 1948 and was followed by the World Peace Congress in Paris in April 1949 and the Stockholm Peace Congress in March 1950.
22   G. Horne, *Black and Red: W.E.B. Dubois and the Afro-American Response to the Cold War 1944–1963* (New York: State University of New York Press, 1986), p. 132.
23   Quoted by J. Brook, 'When the Cold War did not end: The soviet peace offensive of 1953 and the American response', http://wwics.si.edu/kennan/papers/2000/brooks.pdf
24   *Ibid.*
25   'Possible Soviet responses to the US Strategic Defense Initiative', Interagency Intelligence Assessment, NIC M 83-10017, 12 September 1983, http://www.fas.org/spp/starwars/offdocs/m8310017.htm
26   E. P. Thompson, *Beyond the Cold War* (London: Merlin Press, 1982), p. 8. Robbie Lieberman has documented how a commitment to peace was liable to be interpreted as a commitment to communism. Lieberman cites the example of

the shelving of a planned movie by Monogram in 1950. The movie was to have been based on the life of Hiawatha, who had played an important role in ending the fighting among the Indians. It was cancelled, a spokesperson from Monogram claimed, because 'bringing out a movie praising a peace-maker would be playing into the hands of the communists since their propaganda was peace-centered'. R. Lieberman, '"Does that make peace a bad word?" American responses to the communist peace offensive 1949–50', *Peace and Change*, 17:2 (April 1992), p. 203.

27   M. McCarthy, *The Groves of Academe* (London: Weidenfeld and Nicolson, 1951), p. 13.

28   Franklin D. Roosevelt Presidential Library, Hyde Park, New York, Eleanor Roosevelt papers, box 3261, 'Transcript of remarks made at the visit of the "American Peace Crusade" to the State Department'.

29   *Ibid.*

30   See Alonso, *Peace as a Woman's Issue*. Alonso documents the infiltration of the Denver branch of the WILPF by the FBI.

31   *Ibid.*, p. 169.

32   G. Bussey and M. Tims, *The Women's International League for Peace and Freedom 1915–1965* (London: Allen and Unwin, 1965), p. 196. The WILPF was not new to the issue of communism. As Leila Rupp details in her account of international women's organisation, the WILPF had 'from the very beginning . . . steered a perilous course as a radical but nonsocialist group'. See L. Rupp, *Worlds of Women: The Making of an International Women's Movement* (Princeton, NJ: Princeton University Press, 1997), p. 31.

33   *Ibid.*, p. 169.

34   Thompson, *Beyond the Cold War*.

35   L. S. Wittner, *Rebels Against the War: The American Peace Movement 1941–60* (New York: Columbia University Press, 1969), pp. 204–5.

36   Library of Congress, Washington, DC, League of Women Voters papers, box 744, letter, Lee to Local and State League Presidents, undated.

37   As cited in Lieberman, 'Does that make peace a bad word?', p. 201.

38   *Newsweek*, 4 April 1949.

39   US National Archives, Records of the Department of State, Miscellaneous Records of the Bureau of Public Affairs 1944–62, box 126, letter, Russell to Barrett, 28 February 1951.

40   G. H. Clarfield and W. M. Wiecek, *Nuclear America: Military and Civilian Nuclear Power in the United States 1940–1980* (New York: Harper and Row, 1984), p. 182.

41   Eisenhower speech to the NCCW, 'The desire to be free', 8 November 1954 in Dwight D. Eisenhower, *Peace with Justice* (New York: Columbia University Press, 1961), p. 72.

42   Eisenhower address at Columbia University, 'World peace: A balance sheet', 23 March 1950 in Dwight D. Eisenhower, *Peace with Justice* (New York: Columbia University Press, 1961), p. 3. Reading this collection of speeches, no one could accuse Eisenhower of lacking a commitment to peace. The other speeches include 'Toward a golden age of peace', 'Peace begins with the individual', 'The art of peace', 'The ideal of peace', 'The force for peace' and 'First steps toward peace'.

43   R. Elias and J. Turpin, 'Introduction: Thinking about peace', in R. Elias and J. Turpin (eds), *Rethinking Peace* (Boulder, CO: Lynne Rienner, 1994), p. 4.

44   C. B. Marshall, 'The U.S. and the U.S.S.R. in the U.N', in J. Kirkpatrick (ed.), *The Strategy of Deception* (London, Robert Hale, 1964), p. 427.

45   R. Lieberman, 'Communism, peace activism and civil liberties: From the Waldorf conference to the Peekskill riot', *Journal of American Culture* 21:3 (1986).

46   Eleanor Roosevelt papers, box 3055, Roosevelt broadcast, 14 April 1949.

47   National Council of Negro Women papers, box 7, file 12, Chapman address to the Sixty-Third Annual Convention of the General Federation of Women's Clubs, 4 June 1954.

48   Lieberman, 'Does that make peace a bad word', p. 224.

49   Cynthia Enloe, explaining the unpopularity of peace as an area of critical study, has argued that this stems in part from, to use Elias and Turpin's phrase, the 'long standing notion of peace [as] negative/feminine'. Enloe argues, 'Peace has lacked adequate theoretical attention from patriarchal intellectuals because it has been defined in negative, often feminine terms. When war is seen as active, heroic, and masculine, then peace becomes merely the absence of all these stirring qualities'. C. Enloe, *The Morning After: Sexual Politics at the End of the Cold War* (Berkeley, CA: University of California Press, 1993), p. 64.

50   US National Archives, Records of the Women's Bureau, Office of the Director, General Correspondence File 1948–53, box 25, Cannon to Sanders and McGushin, 24 September 1951.

51   *The World Assembly for Peace, Helsinki, 22–29 June 1955* (Stockholm: Secretariat of the World Council of Peace, 1955).

52   Sophie Smith Collection, Smith College, MA, Ruth Woodsmall papers, box 52, file 6, Office of Land Commissioner for Wuerttemberg-Baden, Intelligence Division report, 7 September 1951.

53   Ruth Woodsmall papers, box 52, file 6, Office of Land Commissioner for Wuerttemberg-Baden, Intelligence Division report, 18 September 1951.

54   Alonso, *Peace as a Woman's Issue*, p. 12.

55   Quoted in Swerdlow 'Ladies day at the capital', p. 8. In addition to organizing the walk-out of an estimated 50,000 women from the workplace and the kitchen in a one-day peace strike on 1 November 1961, the WSP also sent telegrams to the White House and the Soviet Embassy urging Jacqueline Kennedy and Nina Khrushchev to appeal to their husbands to 'stop all nuclear tests'.

56   *Ibid.* Swerdlow credits the WSP for helping to change 'the image of the good mother from meek to militant, from private to public'. Swerdlow argues, 'By stressing global issues and international co-operation among women rather than private family issues, WSP challenged the key element of the feminine mystique: the domestication and privatisation of the middle-class white woman' (*ibid.*, p. 24) While I agree with Swerdlow's interpretation of the significance of the WSP's actions, I would argue that American women's associations had been using these tactics since 1945, albeit in a less confrontational manner. The WSP may have been effective in its ultimate aim: President Kennedy claimed the WSP affected his decision to negotiate an above-ground nuclear test ban with the Soviet Union. N. E. McGlen and M. R. Sarkees, *Women in Foreign Policy: The Insiders* (New York: Routledge, 1993), p. 3.

57   'Winning the peace: a statement from women's organizations', *Journal of the AAUW*, 44:4 (Summer 1951), pp. 253–4.

58 The Statement was recirculated in the following year, backed by a systematic and more successful public relations campaign. Its objective when it was rereleased, however, was less a general definition of peace and support of the UN. Instead it was specifically targeted at discrediting the claims of 'less reputable' American women's organisations to represent women's views on peace. See Chapter 7.

59 Eleanor Roosevelt papers, box 3612, Parsons to Roosevelt, undated [1962].

60 Eleanor Roosevelt papers, box 3612, Roosevelt to Parsons, 19 September 1962.

61 Records of the National Council of Women of the United States Inc. 1880–ca 1970, complied by L. K. O'Keefe (UMI, Ann Arbor, MI, 1988), fiche 746, notes on meeting, 'Peace movements national and international', 19–20 February 1963.

62 *Ibid.*

63 *Ibid.*

64 *Ibid.*

6

World Organization of Mothers of All Nations

A typical appeal to take account of women's essential interest in peace appeared in February 1946 in the *Ladies Home Journal*. The article was written by celebrated journalist Dorothy Thompson and entitled, 'A woman says you must come into the room of your mother unarmed'. Thompson claimed she 'came from Mary Doe' to address the 'Gentlemen of the United Nations Security Council'. As the universal woman, Thompson addressed statesmen by describing a vision of femininity through which women had served them:

> Housekeeper, homemaker, wife, mother. You, gentleman, have often called us the pillars and preservers of civilization. You have pinned golden stars upon our bosoms and laid Purple Hearts in our hands. You have asked us to give our sons, our children 'to save the world.' You have asked us to endure the crucifixion of our sons, that the sins of nations might be wiped out and all people everywhere live out their lives in freedom from want and fear. We have given you sons. Some are dead, and some are blind, and some gibber behind bars, and some walk without feet and work without hands, and each of those is as precious to us as all the world we gave them to you to save.[1]

Thompson warned the Security Council that women represented 'the greatest international in the world. We speak a common language from Chungking to Moscow, and from Berlin to New York'. She invoked images of maternal influence and authority to remind the statesmen, 'I am pushed forward by the host of the mothers, for whom you first groped in the dark'. This was a demand for peace: 'You must lay aside your guns. You cannot talk to the mothers with bombing planes and atomic bombs. You must come into the room of your mother unarmed'.[2]

Thompson's article was the beginning of a personal campaign to convert the supposed desire of mothers for peace into a political organisation to challenge the Cold War status quo. She posited the existence of an 'international' of women whose first loyalty was to a peaceful environment for their children and not to the interests of their respective nations. Yet Thompson's campaign and the World Organization of Mothers of All Nations (WOMAN) were not able to mobilise her constituency for a meaningful campaign. In part this failure can be ascribed to problems and rivalries that continually hampered the work of the organisation; however, even with the best management in the world, WOMAN would have faced overpowering opposition from both the government and American women's organisations. Dorothy Thompson's call, however genuine and heartfelt, immediately became part of the Cold War battle over the discourse of peace in which pacifist ideas were perceived as harmful to the American cause. The limitations placed upon WOMAN were not primarily achieved through the direct opposition of the US government. Instead, the repression of WOMAN was achieved through the efforts of the 'official' network of 'legitimate' American women's groups. The history of WOMAN is an important example of how voluntary organisations, rather than providing the dissenting voice for which theorists have lauded their existence, were so tied into government networks as to operate as semi-official agents of policy.

The World Organization of Mothers of All Nations was founded in September 1947 in response to the flood of letters that Dorothy Thompson received following the publication of her articles in the *Ladies Home Journal*.[3] 'You must come into the room of your mother unarmed' had been followed in July 1947 with 'If no-one else, we, the mothers'. Thompson claimed that she received approximately 2,700 letters from American women in response to 'You must come into the room of your mother unarmed' and 4,200 letters in response to 'If no-one else, we, the mothers'[4] Thompson was inspired to action by the depth of feeling shown in these letters. One response berated the journalist: 'You have no right to write as you do, to move us all as you do, unless you do more than write articles.'[5] Thompson responded to her correspondents with a form letter, telling them of her plans to establish WOMAN and assuring them:

> I cannot erase from my mind the conviction that in all countries, of whatever political and economic composition, the mothers – and the maternal instinct – are working, hitherto silently, for the total

abolition of war and violence as instruments for the furthering of national aims or theoretical ideas, and that among women there is an enormous and as yet untapped power, that can be released to dispel the present nightmare, which neither the political leaders, the theoretical ideologists, nor even the scientists have been able to do.[6]

Thompson launched the organisation with an article in the *Ladies Home Journal* in November 1947 entitled 'A woman's manifesto'. Setting out her belief in women's special interest in peace and drawing upon essentialist notions of womanhood, Thompson asserted, 'Despite our historically recent enfranchisement, and despite the opening for us of economic opportunities outside the home, we recognize our primary function, it is still our primary occupation, to be the reproduction and nurture of children to adulthood and the maintenance of the home, as the basic unit of all civilizations'.[7] Thompson contrasted the experience of human society as 'a perpetual state of naked or veiled war', with 'the condition of the home' that is 'peace [and] . . . harmony between all its members'. She then described how the separation of the home and the organisation of society were mirrored by women's separation from economic life:

> Men work for gain expressed in money, the convertible value. This gain goes in large part to the support of the family and the home. But the woman's contribution finds no recompense in, nor is it measurable by, such values . . . She, the homemaking, home-serving woman belongs in no organized body or category of workers or employers, operates under no recognized economic codes or laws, and falls into no economic class.[8]

Thompson's point was that a woman owed no loyalty to either systems of government or economic/class groupings, for 'she is bound less to organized class, and less to the force of state than her mate'. Instead women's loyalty was tied to something that had a primacy over these systems: the 'natural' and 'organic' life of the earth. Thompson wrote, 'As she first recognized the soul as the source of sustenance, so she is cosmically tied in other ways, her very reproductive system being part of the rhythm of seasons and tides responsive to nature'. The outcome of women's relationship to these 'natural processes' was, Thompson argued, a solidarity and commonality between women:

> There is on this earth, and would be wherever in this universe organic life exists, a solidarity which has hitherto been largely silent. It needs

no governments, nor unions, nor organized associations to bring it into being. It needs no flag to raise. No boundaries delineate it, whether they be boundaries of nation, or race, or class. It is the solidarity between women as mothers. It is the solidarity of a function and vocation transcending all ephemeral patterns of organized society – the function and vocation of protecting, through nurture, the human race.[9]

Ironically, given Thompson's insistence that women needed no organisation or association, the Woman's Manifesto sought to rally support for WOMAN. The Manifesto was shortened and simplified for distribution to established women's organisations and to individuals who had responded to Thompson's previous articles, along with a pamphlet entitled 'WOMAN's Demands' setting specific aims for the organisation. Katherine Kent, the first director of WOMAN, argued to Thompson, 'The solution is to have one very specific pamphlet [WOMAN's demands] for really intelligent people who won't join any vague movement, and to have a much vaguer and briefer set of demands for the average person who isn't willing to read anything difficult'.[10] The pamphlet listed three main requirements: the strengthening of the UN through the abolition of the power of veto, held by five countries including the US and the Soviet Union, control of the atomic threat, and the establishment of an effective World Police Force.[11] A supporting letter from Thompson asked that 'in garden clubs, political societies, peace organizations or home economics groups, wherever women are gathered for any purpose, allegiance to this statement of women's view could be secured'.[12]

Thompson had no history of involvement with women's organisations; instead it was her weekly column in the *Ladies Home Journal* that gave her tremendous influence with many American women. Her status as an 'expert' in international relations had been enhanced by her pre-war reports from Nazi Germany, which resulted in her expulsion from that country in July 1934. Through her role as a journalist she maintained an independence of thought and opinion outside the 'mainstream', illustrated by her support in the 1948 election of the socialist Norman Thomas.[13]

From the start, Dorothy Thompson was unenthusiastic about becoming involved in the day-to-day organization of WOMAN.[14] Thompson's personality and reputation, however, inevitably played a large role in the success or failure of the initiative. Because of her personal reputation, the appeals of WOMAN to American women's organisations met with some initial enthusiasm. Ruth Karr McKee, a member of the Federation of Women's Clubs in Washington State, wrote to Katherine Kent enthusiastically pledging to collect signatures for the 'Woman's Demands'. McKee added that a speech by Thompson at Spokane had been sold out but insisted, 'We are willing to make the trip if there seems to be any chance to meet Miss Thompson'.[15] Mrs Norman Whitehouse of the Women's Action Committee for Lasting Peace wrote to Thompson to commend the campaign, claiming her own organisation had failed because 'as our older workers retired, worn out, we failed to arouse the interest of younger women'.[16] There was also a positive response internationally. The President of National Federation of Women's Clubs of the Philippines sent $5.00 to join WOMAN, declaring, 'We hail this Crusade for Peace as a vital activity of the women today in a world fraught with political, economical and spiritual disturbances'.[17]

Not every response to WOMAN was so enthusiastic. Mrs Ruth Moffat wrote to Dorothy Thompson about her son and grandson, noting, 'Are there any more wholesome, un-neurotic reasons for woman to be peace-minded?' However, she then warned Thompson about the limited potential of WOMAN:

> I entertain few illusions as to womankind's destined role in bringing about a more creative, peaceful world. Teachers use the term 'Busy-work' for harmless, insignificant activities used to keep little fingers and minds out of mischief. From my viewpoint, Miss Thompson, much women's clubs activity is 'Adult Busy-work'. Meeting of thoughtful minds is practically non-existent.[18]

'Mainstream' women's organisations were even more suspicious about WOMAN. In February 1948 Eleanor Roosevelt enquired of Thompson, 'I have been asked about an organization called "Woman" which you are alleged to be starting. Will you be good enough to let me know about it if this is true?'[19] Thompson, unaware of Roosevelt's concerns, warmly told her about the history and aims of the organization and assured her:

> I welcomed your note as we would heartily welcome your help. I should have gone to you, had I not known how over-burdened you are and feared, also, that your connections with the United Nations might make it difficult for you to associate yourself with those who are certain that U.N. as presently constituted is far from enough.[20]

It its initial years WOMAN focused on enlisting membership and funds. By November 1948, WOMAN could boast 665 members, with

105 clubs with a membership of 46,744 offering their support.[21] Good intentions, however, lacked funds, plans and leadership. Jane Hayford, the new director of WOMAN, wrote despairingly to Thompson, 'For over a year, as a lone voice, I have battled for WOMAN and you as chairman using every moment of my time and every cent I could snatch from the budget of my family . . . I can go no further without an organization and funds'.[22] Her frustration continued throughout 1949, leading her to write in exasperation, 'We have everything – a definite plan – an irresistible appeal – and the women of all nations vitally interested – everything except organization and money'.[23] WOMAN drifted aimlessly for two years, issuing lofty pronunciations about the power of mothers but doing nothing to harness that power in a meaningful way.

In 1951 all this changed with WOMAN's proposal for a pilgrimage of women from every nation culminating in a Congress in Berlin. The planned trip coincided with personnel changes at WOMAN that would have significant effects on the smooth operation of the organisation. In April 1950 Jane Hayford had asked for Thompson's endorsement for the title 'American Mother of the Year'. Hayford had already been named the New Jersey Mother of the Year and felt that Thompson's endorsement would be vital in securing her the national title, especially since Thompson's 'great admirer, Mary E. Hughes, whom I met in your home, is the Director [of the sponsoring body]'.[24]

The American Mother of the Year was awarded by the American Mother's Committee, an organisation established in 1933 under the leadership of Mrs Sarah Delano Roosevelt, Franklin D. Roosevelt's mother. The ideology of the organisation in 1950, based on the views of Mary Hughes, was the celebration of motherhood and the potential force of mothers to foster peace. Hughes's letter to State Chairs in 1950 announced the award of 'Mothers of the Year' on a global basis:

> In view of the worldwide implications of the status of women in today's world, the American Mother's Committee recognizes an international responsibility. It was logical that this committee should evolve to help unite mothers of the world – certainly the mothers of the United Nations. Mothers want peace. United Motherhood will be invincible against the forces of destruction.[25]

Hughes's vision was not to be restricted to the selection and awarding of the title of 'Mother of the Year'. Seeking a more active role, Hughes wrote to Thompson:

There are 40 countries and others looking to us for a future program. They are evidently thrilled by the idea of a united motherhood in the interest of world peace. I might as well tell you this has been a 1 girl job. I have an international Association of Mothers on my hands and actually I don't know what to do with it – unless you and I could somehow join forces?[26]

Thompson was amenable to the coalition, and Mary Hughes joined WOMAN as an executive director.

Hayford, the permanent director, had become somewhat disappointed by the inactivity of WOMAN. She complained to Thompson, 'It is pitiful what has been accomplished with WOMAN and its wonderful program . . . unknown, no money, no staff. Yet about 3,000 Clubs with a supporting membership of over 600,000 . . . But what is that? A drop in the bucket, in the sea. I'm down to the last of my resources – not even literature to distribute'.[27]

To resuscitate the lagging fortunes of WOMAN, Hayford acted decisively. She took up a suggestion from Ilse Bentler, Chairman of the California State Division of WOMAN, that the UN recruit a volunteer army, 'This seems to me to be the moment we have been waiting for. Now, let us take the leadership in the International Crusade. Let us have our Convention in Berlin'.[28] At the same time Hayford received a statement from Vilma Monckeberg-Kollmar, Chair of WOMAN in Hamburg, encouraging the pilgrimage to Berlin.

Inspired by the ideas and 'frustrated by lack of funds and the feeling of impotence',[29] Hayford called a conference with Thompson and Hughes, who at this point was still representing the National Association of Mothers. Tentative plans for the pilgrimage were sketched. At Thompson's suggestion, it would involve playwright Carl Zuckmayer and a professional producer 'to put on this Congress with all the fanfare of parades, music, speeches'.[30] Hayford requested that Thompson write a letter to peace organisations explaining the objectives of the Berlin Congress and updating her Mary Doe article.[31] Hayford's plan was to enlist the support of top women, including Frances Perkins, Rose Parsons of the National Council of Women, Marian Anderson, Pearl Buck and Claire Boothe Luce, and to hold a meeting with them followed by a conference in September 1951. The next two weeks would then be dedicated to intense activity and planning for the pilgrimage to 'establish a "do or die" atmosphere'.[32]

Thompson's letter to the 'top women' invited them to join the

Board of Directors of WOMAN, 'at least for one momentous year'.[33]
She opened dramatically:

> It is my profound conviction that the present foreign policies of the
> great Powers, including the United States, are heading the peoples of
> the world, with or without a general war, toward a disaster unparal-
> leled since the dark age following the fall of Rome: that these policies
> – based ironically enough on universal appeals to Peace, Progress,
> Liberation and Democracy, and upheld, where they are upheld,
> largely through the appeal of such words – are totally unrepresenta-
> tive of the world's peoples, who are listening in despair for the voice
> that does not speak.[34]

Thompson argued that the voice had an obligation born of 'the function of nurturing and conserving human life'. She recognised the symbolic importance of Berlin as 'the spot where the two conflicting
powers met each other, in most dangerous tension – the ruined, battle-
scarred city of Berlin'. Inviting women from both sides of the Iron
Curtain to be present at the climax of the pilgrimage, Thompson
assured, 'I do not imagine anything loud, coarse, agitatory, or demon-
strative in the usual sense – for its purpose will be to create a new platform altogether, in a new atmosphere and mood'.[35]

Washington Post journalist Malvina Lindsay noted approvingly
that WOMAN was 'a group of American Women of intellectual standing and unquestioned patriotism'. Lindsay entertained high hopes
regarding the potential of WOMAN to rise above the 'red-tagging' of
peace activists, enthusing:

> Originating in the United States, it should help to counter the
> Communist chant about American warmongers. If, as planned, the
> world flight of its leaders ends in a Congress of Women in Berlin at
> which sincere and feasible disarmament proposals are made, a big
> step will be taken at a strategic spot towards grabbing the peace
> offensive.[36]

However, amid American anxieties regarding Soviet attempts to
target women, particularly with the 'peace campaign', Thompson's
plan aroused some scepticism. Not everyone shared Thompson's
optimism that an emotive demonstration would be able to distinguish
itself from Soviet-sponsored activities. A significant dissenting voice
was that of Thompson's personal friend, playwright Carl Zuckmayer.
Since Thompson had planned to make one of his plays central to the
pilgrimage, it was somewhat disheartening to discover that he was

less than enthusiastic. While Zuckmayer wrote in admiration of Thompson's 'imagination and honesty and deep appreciation for truth and right . . . [and] your passionate will to act and not only to talk for the good cause', he doubted the wisdom of the Berlin Scheme.[37] Zuckmayer feared that 'any group-statement in public would rather contribute and add to the general confusion in our world instead of light it up'. He warned Thompson, 'The policy of the East . . . is a cold icy-cold, calculated and enormously shrewd cunning, a way of turning everything to their advantage'. Recognising that a group of Americans criticising all governments could be represented as a group of Americans criticising their own government, Zuckmayer urged caution:

> You are certainly right when you say that there is no government in the world which really represents the people. But there are governments which represent it even less than the others altogether . . . I'm afraid we cannot deal with them by the true and honest means of 'going there and speaking it out' – without weakening our own position.

Zuckmayer suggested to Thompson that the best way for her to contribute her voice in opposition to the prospect of war and violence was as an individual, not as a member (or leader) of a group.

The plan for the Berlin Congress was especially alarming for the US government. Concern over the activities of WOMAN in Germany had surfaced as early as May 1949, when a paper investigating the organisation was sent to Ruth Woodsmall, Chief of the Woman's Affairs section of OMGUS, from two of her staff, Miss Joy Evans and Mrs Elizabeth G. Holt. The report recorded that WOMAN was functioning in several cities in the British zone and was particularly active in Hamburg. In the US zone, the activity centred on Frankfurt. Arguing that the rhetoric of the organisation was 'emotional and similar to the Frauenbewegung sponsored by the National Socialists', Evans and Holt criticized WOMAN on the basis that:

> the program puts little emphasis on civic education for women, for the necessity for women to assume thoughtful political responsibility, to correct social conditions in the community or to inform them of constructive social programs to improve conditions. It is unconstructive in that it draws the attention of women away from their role as responsible citizens with specific tasks in their community . . . Its principal danger is that it can become a peace movement which

through an emotional appeal leads women aside from the serious
task of being informed citizens.[38]

Evans and Holt recommended that Thompson be informed that 'the
organization in Germany is taking on its own character with aspects
foreign to the developments she envisaged when she founded it'.

Evans and Holt's fears that WOMAN in Germany was develop-
ing as a political pressure group were not without foundation. In April
1950, Vilma Monckeberg-Kollmar, Chair of the Hamburg branch of
WOMAN, wrote about her belief in the importance of a united
Germany and her role in the 'Society for Re-Uniting Germany' to
Thompson.[39] Monckeberg-Kollmar described her feelings about
Berlin:

> I now often have the chance to go to Berlin and I'm terribly upset to
> see what this unnatural separation leads to. Berlin is a smoldering
> volcano. Occidental mentality and mode of life in the east section is
> full of anxiety and fear, shy and ever hungry, the same as ourselves
> before the currency reform . . . They are anxious lest people in the
> western zone should drop them and leave them to the mercy of the
> Russians. For this reason we have started a big 'East Welfare
> Movement'. We members of WOMAN have made a proclamation
> asking people to take care of whole families in the East.[40]

Gabrielle Strecker, whose expenses-paid trip to the USA in 1946
under the Exchange of Persons programme was clearly paying rich
dividends, raised further concern about the intent and potential effect
of any women's demonstration in Berlin. Strecker wrote to Rose
Parsons in October 1951 with her concern about WOMAN. She
warned:

> It is exactly the least of all we need, it is exactly the unrealistic type
> of organization which we must get rid of. It will offer large possibil-
> ities for communist infiltration. The types of women who run
> WOMAN are apt to spoil sound activities of good organizations and
> will bring mischief and confusion in the German women's move-
> ment.[41]

Strecker's animosity towards WOMAN was not improved by a personal encounter with Monckeberg-Kollmar during a meeting of
women's organisations in Bavaria. Strecker and the wife of the US
High Commissioner, Mrs John McCloy, spoke about 'the communist
danger . . . [and] the big fallacy of peace slogans' but were interrupted
and angrily denounced by Monckeberg-Kollmar. Strecker reported

that she 'kept my sense of humour' but reflected, 'A mass of ignorant un-political women in the hands of such dangerous demagogues! It's terrible!'[42]

The State Department became increasingly concerned with the possible effects of the Congress. On 2 September 1951 Chester Williams, a member of the United States Delegation to the UN, wrote to the State Department with his comments on the plan. Williams explained Mary Hughes' background as Director of the International Committee of Mothers, 'whose main activity seemed to be the designation of "Mothers of the Year" in various countries and the convening of an international banquet in New York on the occasion of Mother's Day'.[43] He added that, even before her move to WOMAN, Hughes had been talking of 'her idea of taking a group of American mothers and some from other countries around the world'.

Williams was worried that '[Hughes] and Dorothy Thompson have now launched themselves upon an enterprise which could produce very disruptive and confusing results'. Furthermore, he indignantly reported, 'The State Department (especially the International Information and Educational Exchange of Persons Office) will be called upon to facilitate her plans'. Williams' personal assessment of Hughes was scathing:

> Miss Hughes is a voluble, energetic, optimistic, sentimental, presuming woman with very wide contacts among the elite in various countries. She has a greeting-card mind which, at least in her activities, avoids concern with political issues or controversial subjects. She has a flair for display and pageantry – an orchid approach with a touch of Whistler's Mother.[44]

Hughes's 'flair for display and pageantry' led her to describe the pilgrimage of mothers to Williams with 'many details in uninterrupted flow of enthusiastic, though disconnected, narrative'. She assured Williams that the world tour of 'flying mothers' would be greeted at each port of call by 'the most prominent people, kings and queens and prime ministers – already her Mother-of-the-Year in England assured her that the King and Queen and Churchill would receive the group'.

Williams concluded his report with the restrained comment that 'Miss Hughes is not an easy person to talk to on a practical basis'. He expressed concern that, while Hughes's plan did not have the backing of the leaders of 'the large women's organizations . . . she may have considerable influence with a coterie of prominent women who

appreciate being in the limelight of international society in the
company of queens and lady bountifuls'. Williams was also critical of
Dorothy Thompson, warning, 'It should be remembered that Dorothy
Thompson has a strong emotional antagonism towards the State
Department dating back to the Dumbarton Oaks days . . . She [has a]
vituperative attitude . . . dividing her invectives equally between the
State Department and the Kremlin'.

Williams believed that 'it would be impossible to guide this
group of women into safe and useful channels', but he was wary of
expressing outright opposition since 'it would be most difficult, if not
impossible, to discourage them from going ahead with their idea'. He
had a twofold solution. First he suggested that Doris Cochrane of the
Public Liaison Office of the State Department 'discuss the matter with
responsible women leaders' and find ways of 'bringing the influence
of the Non-Governmental Organizations to bear on WOMAN and
discourage the scheme'. Ultimately it would be this governmental
influence of the 'responsible' women's organisations that put a deci-
sive end to the 'Pilgrimage to Berlin'. Second, Williams recommended
that someone in the State Department 'categorically disabuse Miss
Hughes of the notion that the Department would facilitate such a
plan'. Williams also wanted to convince Mary Hughes that Dorothy
Thompson was dragging her into a dangerous political scheme.
Williams felt 'this might conceivably cause a controversy between the
two which would put the quiets on the whole affair'. Again, Williams
insisted that this strategy should be carried out by 'non-governmental people'.

Williams's strategy of 'divide and rule' within WOMAN was not
destined to be one of the labours of Hercules, given the suspicion and
distrust evident between Mary Hughes and Jane Hayford. Hayford,
who had enjoyed almost total control of the direction of WOMAN for
three years, quickly became unhappy with what she saw as Hughes's
intrusion into 'her' organisation. Not unnaturally Hayford resented
the fact that while she had subsidised WOMAN to the tune of $6,554,
Hughes was brought in (or, in Hayford's words, 'ensconced') as
Executive Vice-President with a salary of $100 a week.[45]

Hayford's indignation at the situation, and what she perceived as
Hughes's high-handed treatment of her, led her to contact Mrs
Milligan, Chairman of the American Mother's Committee. Milligan's
report, passed to Thompson via Hayford, was that Mary Hughes had
involved the Mother's Committee in a $50,000 lawsuit. Milligan

passed on the comment of the wife of the minister of Hughes's church that Hughes was 'a wild, dangerous woman – neurotic, irresponsible, selfish – [who] will finally destroy herself. The church has considered taking away from her the two children she adopted at the age of two weeks to protect them from her'.[46] Hayford informed Thompson that she would take care of the matter by terminating Hughes's employment.

Hughes's views of Hayford were no more flattering, as she inundated Thompson with letters describing the impossibility of working with Hayford, who was 'entirely too erratic, abrupt and lacking in diplomacy in dealing with people'.[47] Hughes concluded, 'I don't know what is wrong with Jane as I am not a psychiatrist'.[48] On 19 September 1951 matters came to a head when Hayford sacked Hughes and demanded she leave the office, threatening to change the locks on the doors. Hughes insisted on staying on until the Board meeting on 28 September. The irony of these events during the planning of the Berlin pilgrimage was noted by Hughes: 'We cannot hope to bring about better understanding and peace if in our personal lives there are unlovely qualities, discord, jealousy, greed, dishonesty.'[49] On 28 September Hughes resigned her position in WOMAN, citing Dorothy Thompson's distance as the cause of the problems of the organisation. Hughes advised Thompson, 'Because your time is so occupied with your writings and lecturing . . . you cannot give enough supervision to really be in control of the situation which you have termed "fraught with grave danger"'.[50]

Thompson demanded a complete rethink of the activities of WOMAN. Writing to Hayford, Thompson now criticised the focus on the pilgrimage. She questioned both the amateurish method of organisation and the ideological point of making an expedition at all. Thompson asked Hayford, 'One question is – *The* question is – is it possible to make a peace demonstration which will not play straight into the hands of the Russians and communists?'[51] Thompson had apparently begun to realise how much, haphazardly, was being done without her knowledge or approval. She was aghast at the women who had agreed to join the new Board of Directors, pointing out, 'Nine-tenths of the women . . . have no clear idea of what we are up to. I myself knew none of them personally, had no idea why they were selected, what groups they had behind them'. The composition of the new board was a consequence of the 'completely undiscriminating' nature of the list of women used as the basis for rallying women to the cause of WOMAN – a list which included women who 'by no stretch of the imagination' could be expected to support or even understand the aims and objectives of the organisation. Another unhelpful section of the list was those women who, as Thompson pointed out, were dead. Losing nothing of the original idealism of WOMAN, Hayford replied, 'In one generation the statesmen of the world have led us into two tragic wars and now we are careening toward a third an infinitely greater calamity'.[52] She acknowledged, 'There is some divergence of opinion on the Board . . . regarding the course of action which WOMAN should take'.

This confusion and lack of direction was exploited to the full by the 'private' allies of the US government. On 26 November 1951, Rose Parsons wrote to Gabrielle Strecker to explain what she and others were doing to obstruct WOMAN. Referring to WOMAN as a 'movement that has almost a psychopathic feeling about it', Parsons described Hayford as 'a very neurotic and excitable person . . . apt to go off the handle'.[53] Parsons also referred to the co-operation between herself and the State Department, describing a visit paid by Hayford, Parsons and another (unnamed) woman to the State Department. Parsons reported that the Department representative was 'of course . . . very disturbed about this pilgrimage to Berlin'. However, 'he felt it would be wrong for the State Department to discourage this cock-eyed plan, so he told [Hayford] the great expense it would be, and how it had to be planned down to every detail etc'. After the meeting the Department representative told Parsons that 'he thought it was up to the women's organizations to discourage this rather than the State Department'.[54]

The divisions between Hughes and Hayford were exacerbated by Thompson's disillusionment. In September 1950 Thompson, weary of the burden of involvement, tried to resign from WOMAN. Thompson outlined her fears to Hayford that involvement in an organisation was compromising her intellectual freedom and argued that 'WOMAN needs a chairman less apocalyptic than I'.[55] She explained that her position emerged from self-described 'mental sufferings . . . [that were] acute' and was mired in 'doubts, hesitations and questions'. It was a typical quandary for the Cold War liberal interested in the establishment of peace.

Thompson also complained of her need to function as a writer and a journalist independent of any organisation. She wrote to Ely Cuthbertson, her original co-worker on WOMAN, 'The dichotomy between independent writer and organization chairman is real. [It] seems irrelevant to debate the other issues of opinion and policy . . . I do not want to engage in argument, fearing that such argument would involve matters irrelevant to the real issue'.[56] Cuthbertson, a leading world expert on contract bridge and determined advocate of world federation, was not prepared to accept Thompson's polite excuses. Taking a 'brutally frank' tone, he warned Thompson that she was 'embarking on a road that can only lead you into a tragic blind-alley, equipped with fallacies and half-truths that are bound to wreak you as a public personality. In so doing you believe that you are being apocalyptic; actually you are apoplectic'. Cuthbertson accused Thompson of 'moral defeatism' and responded to Thompson's accusations of his belief in the necessity of a 'preventative war':

> My inner thought, and, I am convinced, that of the overwhelming majority of Americans, is to mobilize under a proper world authority the forces of peaceful nations, thereby making them irresistible. And having so mobilized them, confront the aggressor Russia with a choice: to renounce effectively designs for aggression and atomic armament for aggression, or to face the lawful punishment of the indignant world, meted out to gangsters in any community. If this be a preventative war, then the American people will bless it . . . It is a matter of survival that we meet the Communist aggressor now and in every part of the world, until he is either destroyed or militarily neutralized.[57]

Cuthbertson implied that Thompson's version of peace, accepting coexistence with the Soviet Union, lacked both the force and the logic of his vision:

> All thinking Americans know that any attempt for a negotiated peace with Soviet Russia on the basis of let's-kiss-and-forget reflects either Communist propaganda, or moral cowardice, and demagogically seeks to appeal to the lowest stratum of the American nation – the ignorant and selfish Moms and Pops who will buy peace at any price.[58]

Comparing Thompson's approach to that of '[Walter] Lippman and other pseudos', Cuthbertson concluded his letter 'affectionately'; 'patronizingly' might have been more accurate.

The response of non-government organisations to the publication of Thompson's Manifesto was to republish the Memorial Day Statement, the response to the claim of the WIDF that US women, through their tolerance of alleged germ warfare in Korea, demonstrated their lack of interest in issues of peace. The Statement was reissued after correspondence between Rose Parsons and Ruth Woodsmall about the 'confusion in the minds of German women' regarding WOMAN. Parsons reported Woodsmall's fears 'that German women were told that thousands of American women belonged to this organization, and therefore thought it must represent the most popular sentiment in the United States'. Thus Woodsmall was 'thrilled' with the idea of the republication of the Memorial Day Statement, 'It would be a great help to her if there could be more of this kind of thing from the representative U.S. Women's organizations. It would help her in the building of constructive and positive attitudes among German women'.[59]

Parsons enlisted the support of a further thirty American women's organisations, and the Statement was presented to Ambassador Gross, the acting chief of the US delegation to the UN, on 23 June 1952. After initial discouragement, with Parsons complaining, 'We left the publicity arrangement up to the State Department, which perhaps was a mistake because we got practically none', she asked Eleanor Roosevelt to publicise the Statement representing the views of 'at least 26,000,000 women'.

Parsons and Roosevelt not only organised maximum publicity for the re-released Statement but included a letter from the signatories to Eleanor Roosevelt and Anna Lord Strauss. The organisations explicitly offered the statement as both a response and an alternative to Thompson's manifesto:

> In view of the recent publication of a full-page advertisement in the New York Times and elsewhere of a 'Woman's Manifesto' under the auspices of Dorothy Thompson's group known as WOMAN . . . we believe it is appropriate to bring to your attention the carefully drafted statement in support of the United Nations, officially presented on Memorial Day 1951 to Ambassador Austin by ten of the most influential women's organisations in the United States.[60]

Boasting that the Statement 'expresses the realistic position of millions of American women who stand for collective security and insist upon linking peace with freedom and justice', the organisations asked if Roosevelt and Strauss could bring it to the attention of other members of the US delegation to the UN.

The Statement was vital in constructing an identity for American women that could claim a solidarity with women across the globe. However, it defined peace in specifically American terms:

> The women of the United States have long worked for peace. They know that peace, to endure, must be accompanied by freedom and justice and must be founded on law and order . . . Because it seems to us that peace, without justice and without freedom, is being promoted in an effort to undermine the unity of the free world, it seems wise at this moment for our organization to reaffirm our desire for a just and lasting peace, and for the preservation of human values everywhere.[61]

This was a statement on behalf of 'a combined membership of more than 26,000,000' who had 'co-operated with each other many times to support genuine efforts to bring the nations of the world together to secure peace and to promote freedom among all nations'. In implicit contrast to WOMAN, the organizations that signed the statement described themselves as democratic and representative, 'Each of our organizations arrives at its policies separately through democratic procedure. Each woman in her organization can have a part in electing the leaders . . . Each member can have a voice in influencing positions on questions of national and international policy'.[62]

Unsurprisingly, Roosevelt's reply to the signatories supported the Statement. In a strong allusion to WOMAN and its possible effect, Mrs Roosevelt warned:

> At a time when Soviet-inspired and directed 'peace-movements' are seeking to infiltrate and maneuver women's groups in various parts of the world, and especially in Germany, it is essential for all women's organizations to be on guard and to be precise in the positions they take in order to avoid being used in behalf of false peace propaganda[63]

Instead, peace had to be constructed to negate Soviet claims to that word:

> Support of aggression by the Soviets in Korea and in their imposition of Communist minority domination on Eastern Germany, the Baltic states, Poland, Czechoslovakia, Bulgaria, Hungary, Rumania and Albania should convince all of us that their use of the word 'peace' has nothing in common with our aspirations and struggles for a real peace with freedom and justice under the United Nations Charter.[64]

Roosevelt then turned to Thompson. While 'presuming' that Thompson had 'no intention of promoting Soviet objectives', Roosevelt nevertheless accused her of 'reflecting' the approach of communist-

front organizations. Roosevelt sternly rebuked, 'It shocks me to think
that any American women would bracket our country with the Soviet
Union in the light of their record'. In contrast, the former First Lady congratulated the organisations that were signatories of the Statement,
'which can reassure women in other parts of the world that this ill-con-
sidered expression of WOMAN is not really representative of any substantial group'.[65] It was these organizations, wrote Roosevelt, that bore
'a heavy responsibility to inform their sisters around the world on
where American women really stand in the common pursuit of peace'.[66]
Roosevelt's argument was that the ten organizations that signed the
Memorial Day Statement were the true voice of American women, representative bodies 'proven' by reference to their democratic methods.
On the other side, WOMAN, which was not organized along these lines,
could not claim to speak for a constituency. Anna Lord Strauss reiterated the point in her response to the Memorial Day Statement:

> One of the significant points made by the group of women's organi-
> sations in this statement is contained in the description of how these
> organizations truly represent large membership who participate in
> the formation of policy. This statement, unlike the 'Woman's
> Manifesto', was drafted by the responsible, elected heads of estab-
> lished women's organizations in consultation with each other, and
> reflects the official policies adopted in national conventions. These
> policies and opinions reflect discussion in local and state bodies in
> which the membership as a whole participates. They are not the mere
> literary expression of a small group of individual women, presuming
> to speak for a great body of American women ... The cause of Peace
> can be harmed by well-intentioned people who release statements
> with the intention of getting them accepted abroad as the considered
> expression of the great body of American women.[67]

Roosevelt sent Thompson the text of these letters and the
Memorial Day Statement, explaining, 'The representatives of a number
of important women's organizations who are here at the General
Assembly as observers have disowned the approach you are making
through WOMAN'.[68] The result was a bitter correspondence. In particular, Thompson resented Mrs Roosevelt's insinuation that Thompson's
actions risked confirming her as a misguided 'fellow-traveller':

> I deeply regret that in your reply to the memorandum apropos the
> Women's Manifesto, signed by ten American women's organiza-
> tions, in liaison with the U.N., you found it proper to 'presume' that
> 'Miss Thompson has no intention of promoting Soviet objectives'. I

think, Mrs Roosevelt, that you need not 'presume' it, but that you absolutely know it.[69]

Thompson expressed to Roosevelt the central dilemma posed to Americans advocating peace. She reasoned:

> If all popular peace demonstrations are to be confined to communist or communist-inspired groups, we are handing them the greatest weapon of psychological strategy that exists, and one which cannot be answered by the mere official accusation that they are 'fraudulent'. In all countries which I have recently visited, in Europe and the Middle East, I found many persons, positively anti-communist, who had signed the Stockholm Manifesto simply because they wanted to go on record for peace and no one else had offered them a chance.[70]

Thompson's analysis of the Memorial Day Statement was incisive. The linkage of 'peace' with other issues such as the 'Freedom and Justice' and 'Law and Order' proposed in the Statement was deeply problematic, as she noted:

> Philosophical considerations are involved – considerations of whose concepts of freedom, order and justice, and what moral and spiritual values. Even within the western world there is no unanimity regarding those, and the achievement of such objectives is inconceivable without the overthrow of the communist and many other regimes, which cannot be imagined without war.

Thompson's point that 'spiritual and moral values cannot be divorced from cultural and religious and historic experience' was the central criticism that could be made of American responses to the peace offensive. American propaganda had diluted the meaning of and commitment to peace until it was not only weakened but also actually inverted into a commitment to military preparedness.

Like Roosevelt, Thompson saw the role of the US in the Cold War as confronting the Soviet Union in a battle of ideals, 'The notion of a world with one concept of freedom, justice, order, law and spiritual and moral values is, in fact, the communist concept, nor do I anticipate success from trying to rival it with our own concept of the same values, but that we will do better to limit our aims and leave universal salvation to the millennium'.[71] Thompson's solution, through the founding of WOMAN, was not an attempt to end the Cold War hostility between the US and the Soviet Union. Such a détente was not realistic. Instead, Thompson attempted to separate support for peace and disarmament from any political position in the Cold War.

WOMAN merely urged disarmament so that the consequences of inevitable disputes would not be so devastating:

> Total disarmament would not remove communism from the world, nor even through total disarmament would a millennium of freedom, justice, law, order, and universal spiritual and moral values be established. Envy, hate, greed, and exploitation would not there-within be removed. There would still be disagreeable neighbors. The spirit of the Sermon on the Mount would not reign even by estab-lishing one prohibition of the decalogue. There would still be a strug-gle of classes and ideology. All that would be removed would be the possibility of governments launching vast organized masses of men and weapons at other vast organized masses of men and weapons, whether in the name of liberty or of equality, or for any other ideal.[72]

In a sense, Thompson's arguments against the Memorial Day Statement had become peripheral since she realised that the Berlin pil-grimage could not succeed. The organizational difficulties of WOMAN and opposition of the 'official' American women's organisations were insurmountable obstacles. In January 1952 Thompson wrote to Vilma Monckeberg-Kollmar, head of the Hamburg division of WOMAN:

> The attitude of the Occupation Authorities and women's groups rep-resented by Mrs Roosevelt makes it all but certain that our demon-stration would play into communist hands. For it could not escape being known that we held the demonstration counter to American policy and desire, without even benevolent neutrality, and this fact, by itself, would give the communist peace groups every opportunity to attack the U.S.A.[73]

Thompson's assessment of the women who had opposed her was not generous:

> These women . . . are not accustomed to independent thinking, along the lines of rigorous intellectual disciplines. They are women of more good will than hard thought. And women are not very courageous, as you know. Here, as in Germany, we have been subjected to hard pressures, most of them veiled. Women who have joined us with enthusiasm, and apparently after careful thought and long discus-sion, have afterward faded away and withdrawn their promised and greatly necessary funds.[74]

This, however, was a passing swipe. Thompson's most significant observation was her conclusion, 'There is therefore a clear connection between US policy . . . and these very powerful women's groups'.

The World Organization of Mothers of All Nations was in a shambles. Financially and administratively, the state of affairs was so bad that in January 1952 Jane Hayford invited Mary Hughes back into the office to 'straighten out' office affairs, and employed a secretary to help her.[75] Thompson was in despair, her disillusionment evident in the proposal that the Manifesto, 'together with whatever other assets we have', be handed over to the Women's League for Peace and Freedom.[76] Responding to Hughes' appeal to her to impose some order on WOMAN, Thompson complained plaintively, 'When I resigned two years ago from the Chairmanship of WOMAN, I did so on the grounds which are valid at this time, namely that I could not participate in organizational matters, not only because of lack of time but because of lack of talent. I am simply no good at it, and never have been'. This confusion was exacerbated by the fact that 'Jane [Hayford] has always wanted to spare me, but she has spared me to the extent that I have no idea what we have to go on'.[77]

Hughes's response to this opening was to tell Thompson that WOMAN had 'absolutely nothing . . . to go on – neither money nor responsible people'.[78] Hughes asserted that the 'constituents' of WOMAN were not 'very thinking or responsible persons. Many of the letters [from them] indicate illiteracy and most of them reveal grudges against society or the administration or the world in general'. Furthermore, those letters which were intelligent or even intelligible revealed a grave reservation about the Berlin Congress while those favouring the Manifesto's publication led Hughes to believe that the writers were 'definitely leftists, if not Communists. Most of these letters should be thrown into the waste-basket. They are tirades against our government, our military leaders, the United Nations, etc'. Hughes advised Thompson that her only option was the dissolution of WOMAN. Resignation alone would not suffice since 'as long as [WOMAN] exists, your name will be associated with it'. Hughes bluntly continued, 'Your best protection would be to dissolve the corporation and devote one of your syndicated columns to some statement of this sort so that you will be completely cleared of the stigma which has arisen and not necessarily through any fault of your own'.

In a last attempt to rally support for WOMAN, Thompson called a meeting of the representatives of the ten organizations who had signed the Memorial Day Statement. The move only encouraged those seeking to show Thompson the error of her ways. Following the meeting, Rose Parsons wrote to Thompson, pointing out the dangers inherent in the maternalistic view of peace offered by WOMAN. She warned of the activities of the Soviet-sponsored WIDF and the 'National Assembly of Women' called by the WIDF in London for 9 March 1952. The call to the Assembly was 'every woman in the world wants peace . . . An International Woman's Day – let us make our voice heard'. In this light, Parsons wrote to Thompson, 'You can see, I am sure, why the peace demonstration in Berlin would play directly into the Communist hands, as it is exactly their technique'.[79]

Parsons did concur with Thompson's main criticism of American responses to 'peace' campaigns: 'I agree with you that the Communists have left us far behind with their propaganda and their demonstrations. We appear to be completely impotent and apparently have no imagination in trying to speak up for the free democracies and for a united voice for Peace'. However, she insisted that WOMAN and the Woman's Manifesto were not the right way to take the initiative from the Soviets and informed Thompson, 'We would all be most grateful to you if you would consider dissolving WOMAN, Inc'. Thompson replied that she was going to Germany to see for herself the situation, leaving WOMAN in a 'state of suspended animation'.[80] Parsons, unsatisfied, wrote to Thompson again, 'You will be glad, I hope, to know that a few of us are now meeting together to lay a constructive plan – as to how we can publicise what the women of the western world are doing'.[81]

Parsons was undoubtedly referring to the establishment of the Committee of Correspondence, a CIA-funded organisation whose mission was to counter Soviet propaganda aimed at women. Of the founding members of the Committee, three (Rose Parsons, Mrs Arthur Forrest Anderson and Julie d'Estournelles) were present at the 25 February meeting with Thompson. A fourth, Anna Lord Strauss, was Eleanor Roosevelt's partner in the 'official' response to the Memorial Day Statement. The network of American women's organisations, having quashed the dangerous and 'irresponsible' voice of WOMAN, had begun to formulate their own response to Soviet 'Peace' propaganda.

There was one more chapter for WOMAN. Hayford's devotion to the cause was steadfast, and she remained unconvinced, felt no remorse and was hostile to Hughes:

WOMAN is a movement – a crusade. From the very beginning, Mary Hughes has attempted to destroy it as such – has wanted to make it another innocuous organization such as the American Mothers' Committee formed through her – and since they would no longer employ her she sought to destroy even what she had done there by taking their files and weaning their mothers away under her domination to WOMAN . . . She is strongly attached to the State Department.[82]

Hayford obtained Thompson's agreement to continue distribution of the Manifesto, if it could be done inexpensively. Thompson, however, was finished with her movement. On her return to the USA, she explained to Parsons that WOMAN was not being dissolved but seemed, in her absence, to have been taken over by Ely Cuthbertson's reassertion of leadership. Thompson assured Parsons that Cuthbertson's perspective was 'in closer harmony with those of the Citizen's Committee for United Nations reform . . . and will more closely approach your own views and those of most organised women's groups'.[83] Thompson was sure that the revised Manifesto would be one that she would be unable to 'conscientiously support'. Because of this, Thompson explained, she had tendered her resignation and would not return to WOMAN, 'This time [I] will not be re-persuaded, even assuming that the Executive wished to try to do so'.

In 1955 Dorothy Thompson wrote to General Douglas MacArthur to support a speech he had made. Detailing the fate of WOMAN, Thompson described how Eleanor Roosevelt had most of the women's organisations 'on the string' through their 'unofficial association with the U.N'.[84] This was far from paranoia. Throughout the history of WOMAN, 'official' American women's organisations and their influential leaders had, with the prompting of the US government, done their best to discredit and demolish WOMAN. Aided by the divisions and organisational chaos that marked much of WOMAN's history, the official network of American women's organisations ensured that its voice was the only one which would be heard overseas as the 'representative', 'responsible ' and 'official' outlet for American women. Eleanor Roosevelt's denial, expressed in an admonishing letter to Thompson, rang hollow, 'The fact that your advocacy so far has not won any substantial support from the organized American women, should not, however, be blamed upon the governmental authorities, who have, so far as I know, not restricted in the slightest your freedom of expression'.[85] Having collaborated to insure that no potentially confusing commitment to peace be issued internationally in the name of

American women, the leaders of American women's organisations
were now to turn their efforts to producing a more active promotion
of the American woman's position.

Notes

1   Syracuse University Library, Department of Special Collections, Dorothy
Thompson papers, series 5, box 4, manuscript, 'A woman says, "You must
come into the room of your mother unarmed"' (*Ladies Home Journal*, February
1946).
2   *Ibid.*
3   The exact date of the founding of the organisation appears variously as
August or September 1947.
4   Dorothy Thompson papers, series 1, box 31.
5   *Citizen's Committee for United Nations Reform Bulletin*, 1:4 (November 1947),
Dorothy Thompson Papers, series 1, box 31.
6   Dorothy Thompson papers, series 1, box 31, form letter from Dorothy
Thompson.
7   Dorothy Thompson papers, series 5, box 4, manuscript, 'A woman's manifesto' (*Ladies Home Journal*, November 1947).
8   *Ibid.*
9   *Ibid.*
10 Dorothy Thompson papers, series 1, box 31, letter, Kent to Thompson, 3
November 1947.
11 Dorothy Thompson papers, series 1, box 31, pamphlet, 'WOMAN's
Demands'.
12 Dorothy Thompson papers, series 1, box 31, form letter from Dorothy
Thompson.
13 L. S. Wittner, *Rebels Against War: The American Peace Movement 1941–1960*
(New York: Columbia University Press, 1969), p. 194.
14 Jane Hayford, a successful businesswoman, quickly replaced WOMAN's first
director, Katherine McElroy Kent, a one-time professor at Wellesley College
and President of Pierce College. Thompson saw her role as a spiritual and
intellectual leader, who would inspire the movement rather than direct it.
Initially WOMAN was conceived as a sister organisation to the Citizens
Committee for United Nation's Reform (CCUNR), which was run by
Thompson's friends Ely and Dorothy Cuthbertson. The aims of the organisation were the reformation of the UN as an elected congress established along
federal principles.
15 Dorothy Thompson papers, series 1, box 31, letter, McKee to Kent, 14 January
1948.
16 Dorothy Thompson papers, series 1, box 31, letter, Whitehouse to Thompson,
20 May 1949.
17 Dorothy Thompson papers, series 1, box 31, letter, Legarda to Thompson, 31
January 1950.
18 Dorothy Thompson papers, series 1, box 31, letter, Moffat to Thompson, 19
February 1950.
19 Dorothy Thompson papers, series 1, box 25, letter, Eleanor Roosevelt to
Thompson, 16 February 1948.

20 Dorothy Thompson papers, series 2, box 3, letter, Thompson to Eleanor Roosevelt, 8 March 1948.

21 Dorothy Thompson papers, series 1, box 31, Statistics on WOMAN, 30 November 1948.

22 Dorothy Thompson papers, series 1, box 31, letter, Hayford to Thompson (Not Dated).

23 Dorothy Thompson papers, series 1, box 31, letter, Hayford to Thompson, 30 July 1949.

24 Dorothy Thompson papers, Series 1, box 31, letter, Hayford to Thompson, 23 April 1950.

25 Dorothy Thompson papers, series 1, box 31, letter, Hughes to State Chairmen, 1950.

26 Dorothy Thompson papers, series 1, box 31, letter, Hughes to Thompson, 1 June 1950.

27 Dorothy Thompson papers, series 1, box 31, letter, Hayford to Thompson (undated).

28 Dorothy Thompson papers, series I, box 31, letter, Bentler to Hayford, 15 March 1951.

29 Dorothy Thompson papers, series 1, box 31, letter, Hayford to Monckeberg-Kollmar, 29 May 1951.

30 *Ibid.*

31 Dorothy Thompson papers, series 1, box 31, letter, Hayford to Thompson, 29 May 1951.

32 Dorothy Thompson papers, series 1, box 31, letter, Hayford to Thompson, 29 June 1951.

33 Dorothy Thompson papers, series 1, box 31, form letter from Dorothy Thompson, undated [1951].

34 Schlesinger Library, Radcliffe Institute, Harvard University, Women United for the United Nations papers, file 22, letter, Thompson to Parsons *et al.*, 9 July 1951.

35 *Ibid.*

36 M. Lindsay, 'Dramatizing peace aims', *Washington Post*, 10 June 1951.

37 Dorothy Thompson papers, series 1, box 31, letter, Zuckmayer to Thompson, 10 August 1951.

38 Dorothy Thompson papers, series 1, box 31, memo, Evans and Holt to Woodsmall, 26 May 1949.

39 Dorothy Thompson papers, series 1, box 31, letter, Monckeberg-Kollmar to Thompson, 8 April 1950. Vilma Monckeberg-Kollmar was very much a leading influence upon WOMAN in Germany. Her personal commitment to the cause can be explained by the death of her husband in the First World War and of her son in the Second World War.

40 *Ibid.*

41 Women United for the United Nations papers, file 22, letter, Strecker to Parsons, 16 October 1951.

42 *Ibid.*

43 US National Archives, Records of the Department of State, Miscellaneous Records of the Bureau of Public Affairs, 1944–67, box 118, letter, Williams to Underhill, 12 September 1951.

44 *Ibid.*

45 Dorothy Thompson papers, series 1, box 31, letter, Hayford to Thompson, undated [1951].

46 *Ibid.*
47 Dorothy Thompson papers, series 1, box 31, Hughes to Thompson, 20 September 1951.
48 Dorothy Thompson papers, series 1, box 31, letter, Hughes to Thompson, 21 September 1951.
49 Dorothy Thompson papers, series 1, box 31, letter, Hughes to Thompson, 4 October 1951.
50 Dorothy Thompson papers, series 1, box 31, letter, Hughes to Thompson, 28 September 1951.
51 Dorothy Thompson papers, series 2, box 4, letter, Thompson to Hayford, 30 September 1951.
52 Dorothy Thompson papers, series 1, box 31, form letter from Jane Hayford to Board Members, 4 October 1951.
53 Women United for United Nations papers, file 22, letter, Parsons to Strecker, 26 November 1951.
54 *Ibid.*
55 Dorothy Thompson papers, series 2, box 3, letter, Thompson to Hayford, 30 August 1950.
56 Dorothy Thompson papers, series 1, box 31, letter, Thompson to Cuthbertson, undated.
57 Dorothy Thompson papers, series 1, box 31, letter, Cuthbertson to Thompson, 26 September 1950.
58 *Ibid.*
59 Dorothy Thompson papers, series 1, box 31, text of communications regarding 'Women's Manifesto', 21 December 1951.
60 Dorothy Thompson papers, series 1, box 31, Memorial Day Statement, 1951.
61 *Ibid.*
62 Dorothy Thompson papers, series 1, box 31, Eleanor Roosevelt's reply to 'Women's Manifesto', 21 December 1951.
63 *Ibid.*
64 *Ibid.*
65 *Ibid.*
66 *Ibid.*
67 Dorothy Thompson papers, series 1, box 31, Anna Lord Strauss's reply to 'Women's Manifesto', 17 December 1951.
68 Dorothy Thompson papers, series 1, box 25, letter, Eleanor Roosevelt to Thompson, 21 December 1951.
69 Dorothy Thompson papers, series 2, box 1, letter, Thompson to Eleanor Roosevelt, 7 January 1952. In her study of Dorothy Thompson, Susan Ware explains, 'Eleanor Roosevelt warned her that WOMAN was being used as a propaganda tool by the communists and by 1952 Thompson withdrew her support'. In fact, Thompson was far less receptive to Roosevelt's advice. S. Ware, *Letter to the World: Seven Women Who Shaped the American Century* (New York and London: W. W. Norton, 1998), p. 86.
70 Dorothy Thompson papers, series 2, box 1, letter, Thompson to Eleanor Roosevelt, 7 January 1952.
71 *Ibid.*
72 *Ibid.*
73 Dorothy Thompson papers, series 2, box 4, letter, Thompson to Monckeberg-Kollmar, 7 January 1952.

74   *Ibid.*
75   Dorothy Thompson papers, series 1, box 32, letter, Hughes to Thompson, 29 January 1952.
76   Dorothy Thompson papers, series 2, box 4, letter, Thompson to Hughes, 30 January 1952.
77   *Ibid.*
78   Dorothy Thompson papers, series 2, box 32, letter, Hughes to Thompson, 12 February 1952.
79   Dorothy Thompson papers, series 1, box 32, letter, Parsons to Thompson, 4 March 1952.
80   Dorothy Thompson papers, series 2, box 4, letter, Thompson to Parsons, 10 March 1952.
81   Dorothy Thompson papers, series 1, box 32, letter, Parsons to Thompson, not dated.
82   Dorothy Thompson papers, series 1, box 32, letter, Hayford to Thompson, 3 March 1952.
83   Dorothy Thompson papers, series 2, box 4, letter, Thompson to Parsons, 9 August 1952.
84   Dorothy Thompson papers, series 1, box 32, Thompson to Hayford, 3 March 1952.
85   Dorothy Thompson papers, series 1, box 25, letter, Eleanor Roosevelt to Thompson, 23 January 1953.

7

The Committee of Correspondence

In January 1967, the left-wing periodical *Ramparts* published an exposé of the CIA funding of the National Student Association. The allegations were quickly taken up by the mainstream press and provoked a widespread outcry about the covert activities of the CIA. *Ramparts* proclaimed its exposé was a 'case study in CIA corruption'.[1] The *New York Times* concurred that the revelations of covert funding had not only been hugely damaging to America's reputation abroad, but threatened the very essence of American democracy: 'Faith in American institutions has been besmirched in a way that would have evaded the reach of any foreign enemy'.[2]

In the general rush to both expose and condemn the level of the CIA's covert and sinister behaviour, one group escaped the intense media scrutiny. In February 1967 the *New York Times* announced, 'A fourth fund with apparent CIA connections, the J. Frederick Brown Foundation of Boston, Mass. has been making contributions to a New York based women's group called the Committee of Correspondence'.[3] Indicative of the lack of real concern produced by the *Times* article was a letter written by the Metropolitan Editor of the *Times* to the Committee of Correspondence. Requesting the home telephone numbers of the members of the Committee, the letter, addressed 'dear Gentlemen', met with no response.[4]

The CofC was established as a direct response to the Soviet peace campaign and the activities of the WIDF, notably their charges about US militarism and the use of chemical weapons in Korea. A report by the NCW entitled 'Information on the communist dominated WIDF' asserted that that organisation 'directs its appeal to women by championing Child Welfare, Peace and Women's Rights. The implication is that the USSR and other communist countries are the originators and sole supporters of these causes, which in fact have long been the active concern of the free world'.[5] *McCall's* magazine publicised these fears in an article, 'The Soviet attack on women's minds':

> The Communists have carefully calculated the influence of women on the next generation as well as on this one and have devoted an immense proportion of their world war to capturing the hearts and minds of women all over the world. Moscow regards women second only to youth as the most highly sought after ally in the struggle for communism.[6]

The calling of a 'World Congress of Women' in Copenhagen for June 1953 raised US concerns over the Soviet propaganda attack through women's organisations further. Against this backdrop of Soviet-backed propaganda, some way had to be found of informing women in other nations of the peaceful nature of American women. Doris Cochrane of the Division of Public Liaison in the State Department wrote to Mr Fierst, head of the United Nations Association:

> Do you think it would be helpful for some women's organizations to issue comments on the WIDF report? It is possible that one or more of the other organizations which has consultative status with Economic and Social Commission might be interested in preparing statements on the WIDF report – or that the American Secretary of one of these international organizations might take the initiative.[7]

Fierst's contacts with international women's organizations, or at least their US representatives, was through the Women United for the United Nations. The WUUN had been set up in 1947 after an informal meeting at the Women's City Club in New York called by Rose Parsons. Parsons had served as an American Regional Director of the Red Cross during the Second World War and had become involved in the NCW following the war.[8] The purpose of the meeting at the Women's City Club was to find out what each of the women's groups was doing in disseminating material to their members about the UN. Concluding that it would be best to have a clearing-house for this activity, the meeting set up the WUUN in May. Within two years, thirty American women's organisations were involved with the WUUN, which had enlisted the support of Eleanor Roosevelt, a personal friend of Rose Parsons, after a meeting between the two women.[9]

So it was that on 16 April 1952, Rose Parsons called a meeting in her New York apartment of leaders of prominent women's voluntary associations. Parsons presented a report, 'What steps should be taken to rally the women of the free world to counteract communist propaganda'. She described the 'intensive propaganda campaign which is being waged by communists', pointing out 'that women of the free world are for the most part unaware of these tactics'. She identified the Cold War battlefield in which communist organisations were assaulting women's voluntary associations, '[The communists were] holding large conferences, organizing letter-writing campaigns, and using other mass communications media which in many cases appeared above reproach on the surface, yet were really only clever disguises for their communist aims'.[10]

The Committee, which took the temporary title the 'Anonymous Committee', agreed that it was vital that women around the world be alerted both to the techniques of the communist women and to the true nature of American women. By the time of the second meeting of the Committee on 20 May, all connections had been severed with the Liaison Committee of the UN and with the various organisations to which the members of the Anonymous Committee belonged. The Committee members were now acting as individuals in order, in Parsons' words, to 'get along faster'.[11]

Anne Hester, a member of the Committee, reported on the implications of the WIDF's letter on germ warfare. Hester claimed that the picture the rest of the world received of the USA through Soviet propaganda was one of:

> . . . a depraved, immoral country, where the few rich imperialistic warmongers are preparing a new war to exterminate women and little children and that they are deliberately corrupting the poor, hungry masses of Americans by means of brutal comic books, gangster films and pornographic literature to soften them up for cannon fodder. Our God is the dollar.[12]

Therefore, the purpose of the Anonymous Committee should be to 'assume the role of a catalytic agent. We should be a kind of planning committee where ideas originate and be put into effect through many different channels'. Suggestions for action included requesting information about the WIDF through the CIA, persuading the *Saturday Evening Post* to publish an article on Soviet propaganda and supporting a more extensive information service by the US government. Julie d'Estournelles, member of the Committee and an executive director of the Woodrow Wilson Foundation, then drafted a response to the WIDF's letter vehemently denying the use of germ warfare by US troops. The response claimed it was impossible that this could be happening without the knowledge of American women since 'in our country every citizen can express his views through newspapers, organisation and government, and thereby, assert his influence in public affairs. Therefore, no official act such as germ warfare could take place without its becoming known'.[13] The women of America, the Committee's response asserted, 'want peace and are working for peace in every possible way. We resent this spreading of false accusations because it creates hate and does not help towards a peaceful solution'.

Following the advice of the State Department, the letter was signed by Eleanor Roosevelt, Anna Lord Strauss of the LWV, and Edith Sampson, the first African-American woman to serve on the US Delegation to the UN.[14] It was well publicised, with reports in the *New York Times*, the *New York Herald Tribune* and the *Washington Post*. Two hundred copies were distributed to US information services abroad, through the State Department, and it was broadcast to South East Asia on Radio Free Asia and to Eastern Europe on Radio Free Europe. Parsons sent a further seventy-five copies to the heads of various women's organisations.[15]

The initial campaign of the CofC focused on direct opposition to the 'peace offensive' and its attack on women. The second letter produced by the Committee attacked the Peace Congress in Vienna in December 1952. Counter-measures included a plan to send a letter to the six American women who had just gone to Germany at the expense of the German government, suggesting that they might stress in their press interviews the 'constructive work that women are doing in the U.S. on Peace and Child Welfare'.[16] It was further suggested that Dorothy Thompson might be encouraged to write to the leaders of the German organisation of WOMAN 'warning them off the Vienna Conference'. However, this suggestion met with a conspicuous lack of enthusiasm, since 'a great deal of skepticism was expressed on what she [Thompson] might write'.[17] The Committee contented itself with writing its own letter about Vienna to prominent women in other countries.

This letter was typical of American women's counter-offensive in the campaign over 'peace'. Opening with the traditional linkage of 'peace' with other values, the letter stated, 'No woman believes that peace can be gained where hate is encouraged, whether it be in a family or in a nation, and it is for this reason that we are addressing this letter to you'.[18] The letter defined the Soviet campaign as one of hate, rather than peace, arguing that 'if [Vienna] follows the same pattern as the last four of the so-called peace conferences, we can expect the same theme of violence and hate for the United States and the Free World'. The letter informed its readers of the many ways in which American women were making genuine efforts for peace, including education about the UN, celebration of UN Day, and the contribution by the USA and its private agencies of $80,750,000 to the United Nations International Children's Emergency Fund (UNICEF), some 70 per cent of the total contributions to that organisation. The letter then pointed an accusing finger at the Soviet Union:

> In contrast to our efforts to create understanding and to give tangible aid, there was the theme of 'hate' for the United States in particular and the free world in general expressed at the conference on 'Defence of Children' held in Vienna in April 1952 and sponsored by the Communist-controlled Women's International Democratic Federation. If the Communist Controlled countries are so interested in the welfare of children, we would ask why they are not participating in the great co-operative work being done by the United Nations. They have not contributed a penny to UNICEF.[19]

Advertising the commitment of American women to peace, the letter informed its readers:

> Women's organizations in the United States with a combined membership of over twenty-six million have re-affirmed their belief in the work of the United Nations and their Specialized Agencies and are working to achieve peace. We can, and will, send you specific details of the vigorous and practical programs in the United States and the Free World to promote Peace and advance the welfare of children, if you so request. Find out the facts and join with us in protesting the spread of false accusations all in the name of Peace and the Welfare of children.[20]

The aims of the Committee were not limited to the issue of peace. In a memorandum for members in December 1952, Parsons consolidated the ideas and motivations behind the foundation of the Committee. Its purpose was to strengthen the women of the free world against communism by 'stating affirmatively, persistently and widely the principles and practices of democracy'.[21] Parsons explained:

> The policy of the Committee will be to emphasize the favourable position of women in the free world, insofar as it effects their political, economic, social religious and domestic life. Further, it proposes

to exchange constructive information on women's efforts to attain peace and their efforts to support the United Nations and to child welfare and health service. When it is deemed advisable, it will answer directly the charges so recklessly made by Communist groups.[22]

While many women's organisations were prepared to launch their own 'private' campaigns to counter Soviet propaganda, the Anonymous Committee would become a small but effective agent of the US government. Rose Parsons had complained in a letter to Eleanor Roosevelt of the drawbacks of self-financing women's organisations:

> This whole problem of finances is very bothersome to me because we, in the voluntary agencies in this country, especially the women's organizations spend at least half our time trying to raise money, whereas the communist women have only to put out their hand and money is poured in from the government. This, of course, is why they can so easily do such a terrific propaganda job.[23]

In the case of the Committee, Parsons sidestepped this problem by simply not bothering to attempt to secure private funds and relying instead on government money. At the first meeting of the Committee, it was suggested that 'maybe the Government could subsidize the enterprise (though this would have to be done secretly to achieve the desired results)'.[24] On the surface, all mention of government funding was quickly dropped after an anonymous grant of $25,000 allowed the aptly titled 'Anonymous Committee' to operate as a private, non-governmental organisation. The gift, however, coincided with an interest in the initiative by individuals connected with the US government.

The key link between the state and 'private' spheres was the freelance journalist Dorothy Bauman. Bauman, following a tour of Europe sponsored by the State Department, had drafted a plan for the CIA to counter communist propaganda aimed at women. In Bauman's words, the plan envisaged 'a group of very competent women who would form a nucleus and then start doing some constructive work with women'.[25] Bauman then met with her friend, Rose Parsons, who told her about the Anonymous Committee. Bauman recalled, 'She thought it was a fine idea so I went back to the government and said that she was willing to get this small group of women together and start this thing with me'. At this stage the

Anonymous Committee had met only informally and was, in Bauman's words, 'just a committee that had met once or twice to see what they could do in answering these attacks'.[26] She first attended a meeting of the Committee in August 1952 when the situation had changed and the newly titled Committee of Correspondence was operating.[27] Within six months the committee was corresponding with 1200 women in seventy-three different countries.[28]

The original focus of the Committee was countering communist propaganda through a combination of personal letters and a newsletter to individual contacts of the Committee's members. This list quickly grew and split into two sections – personal friends (A category) and 'friends of friends' (B category). Initially the tone of the letters was anti-communist in the extreme, such as a circular letter from Parsons, Bauman and Mrs Burnett Mahon which vilified 'the present Hate campaign of the Soviet Union against the Free World and the U.S. in particular'.[29] In December 1952, the plan for the Committee outlined the need for a campaign to strengthen the position of women in the 'free world' as 'protagonists of the principles of the free world and against the onslaught of communism':

> Communist proselytising and infiltration of women's organisations is not new, but their expansion of activities and their use of every available means to press their attack on the United States is an emphasis which was not so obvious a few years ago. Therefore it seems reasonable that the answers to these attacks, as well as constructive information about women's efforts, should be provided by American women leaders.[30]

The newsletters produced by the Committee were strident in their response. The bulletin for 15 April 1953, for example, criticised the Soviet government for paying lip-service to the ideals of family life, while at the same time putting into practice a 'clever device . . . to disrupt family life', namely 'forcing the mother to work outside the home'.[31] This, argued the Committee, resulted in the removal of the mother's influence over her children, a deliberate tactic to 'give the Communists absolute control over the child with the opportunity to mould him into the pattern of well-disciplined little robots'. The Soviet approach was contrasted with the findings of the International Study Conference on Child Welfare, held in Bombay in December 1952. The conference had concluded by calling upon all countries 'to do everything you can to preserve and strengthen family life, since a happy home life is essential to the greatest growth and development of every child'.

The tone of these communications was a little too vehement for the non-American market to swallow. Bauman complained that 'Europeans think we are . . . too hysterical on the subject of Communism'.[32] Parsons' visit to Belgium and Holland resulted in similar conclusions: 'I felt at once a certain distrust and resentment of our communications. The criticisms were too much U.S. Propaganda, too obvious a campaign against the USSR'.[33] So in August 1953 Anne Hester, the Executive Director of the Committee, recommended a new approach. Hester argued that the Committee had begun its work with the assumption that 'mis-understanding of the U.S., hostility towards us, was primarily caused by Communist propaganda. The Committee itself felt that combating Communist propaganda would help correct the situation'. After six months, however, the time had come to reappraise the situation 'in the light of cold realism and realize that every great foreign power, especially when it has only recently achieved such power, is bound to arouse envy, hatred, resentment and misunderstanding'. Hester's analysis of the situation focused on the 'rising tide of Neutralism and anti-Americanism throughout the world':

> Europe is afraid the U.S. is going to push her into a war against the USSR. She resents us. There are many other causes for resentment, including the natural psychological reaction against the donor of financial help on the part of the recipient. Resentment in Asia, South America and the Middle East likewise result from U.S. foreign policy – economic, social or political.

Hester concluded, 'The Committee has a great deal more to do than counteract communist propaganda. It must try to contribute to the restoration of confidence in the U.S., the leader of the free world'.[34]

The bulletin began to concentrate on a positive image of the USA rather than attacks upon the Soviet Union. Issues were published on topics such as 'The Negro in the U.S.' and 'Atomic power for peaceful purposes'. Bulletin 18 was devoted to showing 'Typical days in the lives of five American women' to 'counteract Hollywood publicity and anti-American propaganda which depicts American women as selfish idlers'.[35] Other changes in emphasis reflected an increasingly sophisticated recognition of the appeals of communist propaganda to a shared gendered identity. Henry Loomis, Director of the Office of Research and Intelligence at the US Information Agency, stressed to a meeting organised by Parsons in April 1957, 'The mutual interest of women is being increasingly exploited by the Communists to serve their own ends and this latent energy is being turned into hatred of the West'.[36] Actions such as the celebration of 'International Women's Day' in Iron Curtain countries emphasised the idea of commonality of identity among women.

The Committee did not limit itself to correspondence.[37] Eight conferences were organised from 1956 to 1963, starting with 'The responsibility of freedom' for thirteen correspondents from South and South East Asia. The effect of the workshop on participants was, in one instance at least, beneficial to American policy. Mrs Le-thi-An, a participant of this first conference, was inspired to act when she returned to Vietnam. She reported back that she had founded the Association of Children's Friends that took care of working people's children 'with the purpose of preventing the spread of Communist propaganda'.[38] She also joined the National Revolutionary Committee of South Vietnam, becoming President of the women's section of the party. Le-thi-An was responsible for a programme to train and send out hundreds of female 'cadres to work among the people to prevent communist propaganda'.[39] Other conferences covered topic such as 'The contribution of women through voluntary work' and 'The role of the women in the community and home'. The Committee also published a great deal of educational material such as the 'Community Action Series' to help voluntary organisations. This material was designed to guide women in other countries in the principles of voluntary organisations. Titles included, 'What is leadership?', 'How to run a Buzz Session' and ' The Constitution and By-Laws of an Organization'. The series was published in four languages and sent to 5,000 correspondents in 139 countries. Fieldworkers were sent to Africa and South America to encourage women's participation in public life.

These praiseworthy efforts were almost entirely bankrolled by the CIA from the first Anonymous Grant of $25,000 in 1953 until the revelations about funding in 1967. The first grant of money to the Committee in January 1953 was made through Dorothy Bauman on behalf of a 'donor, representing a group of people, [who] prefers to remain anonymous'.[40] Jean Picker claimed that the source of the money was Parsons' friend, CIA director Allen Dulles.[41] By the next year funding became a more complicated affair. From 1954 to 1958 the Committee was supported almost entirely through grants from the

Dearborn Foundation. Unusually for a charitable foundation, Dearborn wrote to the CofC on 23 February 1954, soliciting an application from them for funds. Subsequently the foundation made a grant for 1954 of $25,000. In 1955 this grant increased to $34,000, as the foundation wrote to the Committee asking them to consider making a bigger application next year for the purpose of 'non-administrative activities'. A special grant of $17,750 was made in 1956 to cover the expenses of the Conference for South East Asia. In all, the Dearborn Foundation contributed $587,500 between 1954 and 1966. While not named in the 1967 allegations, the Dearborn Foundation was undoubtedly a CIA front. Oral histories confirm that the CIA supported the Committee from the start and Dearborn was the only contributor to the Committee from 1954 to 1957, remaining their chief contributor until 1965.[42] The foundation is not listed in the Foundation Directory and has no tax records.

As the activities, and therefore the budget, of the Committee of Correspondence grew, the CIA developed an increasingly complex method of channelling funds. The Agency established fronts that would make grants to foundations, which would then fund the Committee of Correspondence. The McGregor Educational Institutions Endowment Fund, for example, described its purpose in the third edition of the *Foundation Directory* as 'endowment grants for higher educational institutions, including technical schools, located exclusively in Vigo County (Indiana)'. In 1964 it made grants of $8,051. Of this sum, $8,000 was a grant to the CofC, which had never expressed a particular interest in Vigo County, Indiana. The Florence Foundation served a similar purpose, receiving $15,000 in gifts in 1964 and making a grant of exactly $15,000 that year to the CofC. The Hobby Foundation also channelled $20,000 into the Committee. On being named as a recipient of CIA money, trustee William Hobby admitted to channelling 'substantial amounts' and declared, 'I'm glad to have co-operated with the CIA'.[43]

This complicated system of funding made it impossible, when news of the funding scandal broke, to assess the extent of the subsidy.[44] A February 1967 memo from the then Executive Director of the Committee, Anne Crolius, considered the allegations made in the press regarding CIA funding. Crolius pointed out that the Brown Foundation, which had been accused of being a CIA front and which had given the CofC a total of $25,000, had also made grants to organisations such as 'Notre Dame Law School, Urban League and the New

York Zoological Society'.[45] The implication is that a foundation, which gave money to the harmless New York Zoological Society, could not be a CIA front but had to be a legitimate organisation. In fact, it was probably both.

The confusion over the source of funding, however, allowed the 'witting' members of the Committee (those who were aware of the CIA's involvement) to hide their complicity in CIA support from the other members of the Committee. Executive Secretary Anne Crolius insisted, 'Regardless of whether the foundations mentioned did receive CIA funds and pass these same funds on to us, the Committee of Correspondence was not aware of any connection of these foundations with the CIA'. The press statement reluctantly released by the Committee argued with some plausibility, at least for the 'unwitting' members:

> We, with other educational organizations, have evidently been caught up in a situation of which we were not aware. Our policy has always been to seek funds for our program from private sources. The Committee of Correspondence have never sought or received direct support from the CIA, nor has it knowingly received CIA support indirectly. [46]

The statement was prefaced with a note to Committee members, 'This is a statement only to be used when needed. It is still our understanding that the less attention we bring to ourselves, the better'.

As the Committee faced increasing disarray, witting members were forced to acknowledge their complicity in the funding to unwitting colleagues. A meeting of the witting members of the group on 3 April 1967 acknowledged that the lack of funding was likely to lead to difficult questions from the unwitting participants. Since legitimate foundations would know of the CIA funding, they would not believe denials by the Committee's staff and would be unlikely to make grants to a group that was dishonest with them. The minutes of the meeting summed up the dilemma of the witting members: 'If the knowing members acknowledge to a foundation our past connections, we run the risk of this information reaching our unknowing members as well as others in the U.S. and abroad; if we do not acknowledge, we will get no money'.[47]

In an emotionally charged special meeting on 24 July 1967, Spencer Arnold, introduced coyly as 'a representative of our past donors', came from Washington to speak to the Committee. Arnold was at pains to assure the women that they had not been the front of a propaganda campaign, like that of the Soviets, but rather a policy of 'orderly development, avoiding the Soviet approach . . . and at the same time building to insure that in the future these countries would not be susceptible to propaganda'. The work of the Committee was genuinely important and constructive and 'the propaganda was icing on the cake if and when it came'. Arnold emphasised the idea that the CIA and the Committee had had common interests, 'In working with groups like the Committee of Correspondence, it came down to the fact that we had the same goals, methods, techniques, and experience to do the same thing that the government wanted to see done for long-range United States policy'.[48] Arnold attempted to soothe the feelings of the unwitting members of the Committee, explaining, 'You keep the circle of knowledgability as small as you can as long as you can'.

Members argued whether the Committee would be able to carry on and if it would be ethical to do so. In fact, without CIA support, funds quickly dried up. Committee member Jean Picker made an emergency donation of $5,000 in 1967. Its purpose was more to avoid the embarrassment of folding immediately after the revelations rather than to ensure the long-term future of the Committee. In February 1969 the Committee sent its last correspondence. Since many of the readers were still unaware of the CIA funding, the letter made no reference to the agency and instead attributed the Committee's retirement to the huge growth in the number of concerned women and the variety and range of their interests. This, the letter argued, made it impossible for the Committee to continue in its practice of person-to-person relationships.[49]

The last months of the Committee were fraught with tension and recriminations. The minutes of the July special meeting recorded, 'Someone said that some of the members of the Committee let the rest of them stick their neck out'. Rosemary Harris complained, 'We have set ourselves up as an example of what an organization that is private can do. We couldn't have done it without government help'. A statement in the files of the Committee went further in its disapproval of the way in which the unwitting members had been used. Its signatories, Eleanor Coit, Elizabeth Jackson and Alice Clark, wrote 'It is not in keeping with our philosophy to have CIA funds used for an organization with a goal such as that of the Committee of Correspondence which was to strengthen the free world by encouraging citizen responsibility and democracy'.[50]

The differences in outlook between the witting and unwitting members of the Committee mirror the important contradictions in the relationship between private groups and the public sector in Cold War America. While many of the unwitting members of the Committee felt that, if they were to retain any significance, the distinctions between private and public must be maintained, the witting members did not recognize any boundaries between the sectors. Amid the confusion of the funding revelations in 1967, many commentators argued from the moral high ground that the blurring of distinctions between the private sphere and the realm of government was unacceptable and had caused irreparable damage to the American ideal of voluntarism. Covert CIA funding destroyed the strength of American voluntary organizations, which was according to the *New York Times* 'their freedom from government domination'.

Such distinctions were not always as clear-cut to members of the Committee, since it was impossible to separate their public and private roles. The Committee worked through a combination of their own private contacts and liaison on various levels with the government. Its first Annual Report established that members travelled extensively overseas on behalf of their own organisations. The report continued, 'On these trips, they have created new contacts and had the opportunity to sound out "correspondents" on their reaction to the work of the Committee'.[51] For example, Parsons had travelled to France, Germany and Italy in her role as the Chairwoman of the American branch of the International Council of Women, as well as touring in Japan, South East Asia, and the Middle East. On both occasions, Parsons provided the Committee of Correspondence with detailed reports on the conditions in the countries, the strength of communism and opportunities for the Committee. Other members of the Committee travelled not as direct representatives of their organisations but at government expense as a result of their affiliations. For example, Anna Lord Strauss visited Japan, Burma, Indonesia and the Philippines under the auspices of the State Department's Leader Exchange programme.

Liaison with various government agencies was common. All material produced by the Committee was made available to USIA, who awarded the Committee a Certificate of Merit in 1954 in recognition of its help in developing 'world understanding of American concepts and purposes'.[52] The United States Information Agency Public Affairs Officers co-operated closely with the Committee, twenty-six of them sending in 'carefully selected' lists of women in their communities whom the Committee should add to its mailing lists.[53] Minutes of a Committee meeting on 9 December 1958 recorded a discussion 'concerning sharing confidential information received from our correspondents with the U.S. Department of State. There was a general agreement that this would be done'.[54]

To the witting members of the Committee, attempts to make distinction between their roles as private citizens and public servants were meaningless. Experience of voluntary work during the Second World War and the crisis atmosphere of the Cold War made redundant the distinction between the individual as private citizen and as government employee. Working for America was the important thing, not squabbles over funding. The CIA's Donald Jameson explained in a television interview:

> It's hard, I think, for people, particularly of a younger generation, to understand the degree to which the Government and its activities had the confidence of its people. It was almost nobody that I couldn't go to in those days and say I'm from the CIA and I'd like to ask you about so-and-so and at the very least get a respectful reception and a discussion.[55]

Amid the bitter debates that ended the Committee, Rose Parsons felt the need to rescue this motivation from the more squalid arguments and recriminations. Not without pathos, she reminded members, 'It was important to remember that when this started it was a real emergency and there was a great need for this kind of program. We knew it would be impossible to raise money. We tend to forget now that it was a patriotic thing'.[56]

As experts, the leaders of women's organisations were frequently called upon to lend their expertise to the US government. The 'private' contacts of these women through their work in international women's organisations were invaluable, as few government officials had any knowledge of international women's organisations. Arguably, few cared. Dorothy Bauman complained, 'It was amazing to me how little interest and how little knowledge our government had about women's effectiveness and certainly not abroad'.[57] It was probably a relief for these officials to hand much of the responsibility for propaganda aimed at women to a competent, enthusiastic outside group. Thus the relationship was based on shared goals and an understanding on the part of the government that the members of the

Committee were the experts in the field. A letter from the Dearborn Foundation stated:

> We believe the Committee has the stature and competence to propose and develop means by which American women can make a responsible, co-ordinated contribution to non-communist Women's organizations . . . We want to assist you in your program but feel you have the specialized and detailed knowledge not available to us, to provide the necessary leadership.[58]

It is clear that the members of the Committee who were aware of the source of their funding thought it unimportant. Connie Anderson, for example, argued there was little pressure from the CIA, 'Just a little bit, not very much . . . they told us some people to see and some people not to see in other lands. But that really amounted to very little. It was mostly our own selves'.[59] In this view, Anderson was joined by the official historian of the Committee of Correspondence, Jacqueline Van Voris, who interjected in her interview with Ezzat Aghevi, an Iranian correspondent of the committee:

> I don't think it made any difference in the work they did. People like Susan McKeever and Jean Picker and the rest were sincerely working hard and knew later, but not all the time. I'm not sure who knew when and I don't think it made any difference because the work they did was done with s genuine feeling of helpfulness and working together and learning from their correspondents.[60]

Van Voris considered the matter of funding to be important only in that it was 'something that comes up and was responsible for the final dissolution'. She argued that the outrage of the unwitting members of the Committee on learning of the funding was due to indignation at being 'out of the loop'; they were upset 'just because they hadn't been told, but on the other hand it didn't really matter'.[61]

Van Voris's interviewee, Aghevli, felt differently about the funding, asserting, 'I think it would have made a lot of difference for the people who were participating . . . I didn't know then. It would have made a difference'. Aghevli elaborated:

> I didn't know what the expectation of the CIA was then. It would have made the difference for me. I think just the idea they were funded by the CIA would make their job much more difficult because they would lose their credibility with a lot of people because everybody would think, 'Why does the CIA fund it? They want some sort

of information. So where are all these things we are sending going? How are they going to be used?'[62]

The witting members of the Committee did not share this view on the inevitability of the principle that he who pays the piper calls the tune. They rejected the argument that inevitably direction and control came hand in hand with financial assistance. They were not the only CIA-funded organisation to protest their independence. In his examination of the CIA-backed Congress for Cultural Freedom, Christopher Lasch points to the continued insistence of the Congress that they had been 'independent'. Lasch argues:

> To point to their independence from overt official control did not nec-
> essarily prove their independence from the official point of view . . .
> Even when subsequent disclosures had made their complicity, in the
> larger sense, quite clear, they continued to protest their innocence, as
> if innocence in the narrow and technical sense were the real issue in
> the matter.[63]

Evidence of the CIA's intervention in the running of the Committee is rare, although this may be because of the destruction of such evidence or of the failure to commit directions to paper. Thomas Braden, who supervised the cultural activities of the CIA, admitted that one of the editors of *Encounter*, the magazine of the CCF, was a CIA agent. This meant that the other editors, ignorant of his connections, would remain unaware of any direct intervention by the CIA.[64] It is not inconceivable that a similar method of operation was in place at the CofC, leaving many members of the Committee unaware of the real extent of CIA involvement. For Braden the usefulness of agents was that they 'could not only propose anti-communist programs to the official leaders of the organization but they could also suggest ways and means to solve the inevitable budgetary problems. Why not see if the needed money could be obtained from "American Foundations"?'[65] It is interesting to note that this was a function remarkably similar to that performed by Dorothy Bauman.[66]

Further evidence of the confusion between the 'public' and 'private' sphere in the Cold War was the fact that direction (or advice) when it occurred was as likely to come from unofficial sources as from the state. In January 1952, for example, Paul Hoffman wrote to Anna Lord Strauss with a list of countries which he, 'off the record', considered to be 'most likely to break through into being economically pliable in the next ten years'. Strauss endorsed the list to the

Committee, 'It seemed to me that in our various activities with women it would be wise to work in these countries so that the women developed along with the other facets of society'.[67] Hoffman was a private businessman, President of the Studebaker Automobile Company. He had worked in government as head of the European Recovery Programme.

If advice and direction from non-governmental contacts was informal, so were any directives issued by the CIA or other government agencies. Connie Anderson asserted that review of the Committee's work was exercised through personal meetings between her and two men who would visit her apartment once a month and 'talk about things, and what we should do and so on'. She insisted, however, that the control was of a limited nature, 'It was a simple thing, there was never any direction, there was just hearing about what we were doing rather than any direction on their part'.[68] Anne Crolius concurred, 'It was a good program and as far as I know there was no hanky-panky, no underhanded influence on the committee to do anything other than what it intended to do'.[69]

To a certain extent, direction or control was a moot point, since the members of the Committee did not see themselves as opponents to their government but as accessories and 'helpers'. In December 1966 Anna Lord Strauss reported to the Committee on a trip she made to Vietnam at the request of the President and in the company of Ambassador Ellswoth Bunker and Eugenie Anderson.[70] When asked by another member of the Committee what the President wanted her to do now, Miss Strauss replied, 'The President hasn't said what he wants us to do now. He took a chance on what our reactions would be'. Jean Picker's response is perhaps indicative of the kind of 'chance' the President had taken. Somewhat predictably, rather than call for an end to the war, Picker suggested, 'An interview of Miss Strauss might be a good Bulletin Article ... We have to be careful because of the war, but on the citizen level, what Anna Lord Strauss saw would be most valuable'.

Some allowance must be made for the willing suspension of reality on the part of these committee members with their assertions of independence; no one likes to think he or she is being used as a puppet. It is important to recognise, however, that the issue of funding is important in and of itself regardless of the level of control the CIA actually exercised. The very fact that the CIA funded the dissemination of information through the efforts of a 'private' group, rather than operating on their own, demonstrated the importance they placed upon the attachment of the 'private' tag on information. By masquerading as a private organisation, the Committee was able to present itself as living proof of the vitality of the voluntary organisation in American life. As Committee member Louise Backus pointed out, the Committee wound up exploiting this ideal, 'We say we are an example and this is a democracy. You can have enough voluntary interests to carry the load. In other countries it is truly impossible for organizations to exist without government help. Now we discover that individual organizations [in the US] just don't seem to be able to exist without government help'.[71]

If it was, as Bauman, Anderson, Picker and others argued, unimportant that the money came from the CIA, why go to the trouble to hide it? Bauman claimed in her article 'Right or wrong?', 'From my observation, it would have made little difference to most participants had it been said that government funds were involved, for they were accustomed to having their own governments control most delegates to international meetings and provide transportation'.[72] In an oral history, however, Bauman was more realistic about the importance of being private. Jacqueline Van Voris asked her, 'Why did you not want to be identified with the government? Were you more effective?' Bauman readily admitted, 'Oh much, yes . . . The moment you put the government's label on it that would have caused suspicion and resentment . . . I think it was the only way they could do things and it was so obvious that the communists controlled organizations, they were all underwritten by their government'.[73]

By presenting itself as a 'private' group, the Committee was able to influence people who would have been hostile to governmental, 'public' propaganda. The Committee had quickly found how hostile many of its correspondents were to any suggestion of state influence. Rose Parsons, in her report to the Committee on a trip to Japan in 1954, wrote of the Japanese people's fear of propaganda. She described how the Committee for Free Asia (CFA) had offered Japanese women a free room for their meetings, 'which they had enjoyed very much and were most grateful for until they found that CFA propaganda was so exaggerated in favor of the U.S. and against the USSR that they refused to meet there any more'.[74] Parsons noted, 'They [the Japanese women] agreed with our European friends that U.S. propaganda was just as abhorrent to them as Communist propaganda and they hope our bulletins will be free from it'.

Committee bulletins were at pains to point out that the Communist women's organisations were funded by their government and therefore were mere mouthpieces of the Soviet system. Referring to the WIDF's call for the Congress of Women in Copenhagen in June 1953, Parsons declared in a letter to correspondents: 'The Committee of Correspondence feels very strongly that when a Congress is called in the name of all women in the world, women should be able to obtain accurate information as to the sponsorship, aims and purposes of that Congress'. Since, according to a WIDF bulletin, 'expenses for the delegates' visits to Copenhagen are being provided', Parsons worried that 'many women, unaware of the Communist sponsorship of the "World Congress of Women" and of the tactics used to attract them there, will no doubt be tempted to avail themselves of this opportunity to travel'.[75] The difference between this situation and the CofC's convening of a Conference of Women's Non-Governmental Organizations in 1962, where delegates were paid travel and living expenses, lay entirely in the Committee's assumption of a double standard.

If the Committee symbolised the infiltration of the public world into the private sphere, it was also an important example in the willingness of private groups to co-operate with the government. By the time the revelations of CIA funding were made in 1967, public hostility and suspicion towards government involvement in private groups were rife. CIA involvement could only be a bad thing, a threat to the 'free society'. Thus the editorial in *Ramparts* proclaimed moralistically, 'The spectre of CIA infiltration of domestic institutions – and the covert creation of co-ordinated leadership among them – must horrify those who regard unfettered debate as vital to representative democracy'.[76]

However, in their attempt to vilify the shady agents of the CIA as instruments of corruption, such accounts failed to take into account the willingness of the private sector to be 'corrupted'. In her account of the activities of the Committee, 'Right or wrong?', Bauman clearly implies that the acceptance of CIA funding was 'right', 'With today's questioning of all of CIA's activities, it seems to me only fair to tell of one operation that was highly constructive and successful and where no overt pressure from the CIA was ever used on a group of competent, individualistic women'.[77] Bauman's argument is that, rather than being a corrupting influence in their private organization, the CIA merely facilitated what the group would have done anyway, given sufficient funds. Bethke Papanek, who had worked harder than any other member to secure private funding, told the Committee that 'she couldn't understand why the exposure of the fact in *Ramparts* has made the CIA evil. We were asked to do a job we were considered fit for'.[78] Members' perception of the relationship of their organization to the government may best be understood through the description the Committee wrote for the 1962 conference of Women's International Non-Governmental Organizations. The Committee explained:

> Although traditionally voluntary organizations have prided them-selves on their independence of government 'control' of 'interfer-ence', changing conditions have modified this attitude to some degree. The emergence, since 1945, of many new independent coun-tries and the enormous sudden increase in demands and desires of their people for rapid social, educational and economic progress have resulted in necessary changes in earlier methods of handling organization programs. It has been discovered that voluntary orga-nizations can co-operate with governments and still maintain their independence; equally, governments have discovered that they can co-operate with private groups in mutual trust without assuming full responsibility for the activities of the group. Support from and co-operation with governments enables voluntary organizations to undertake specific projects which they would otherwise be unable to do.[79]

One-dimensional interpretations of the covert funding of private organizations which cast the CIA as the Machiavellian puppet-masters of simple-minded, if well-intentioned, citizens overlook the willingness of these 'private citizens' to accept funding. As Richard J. Barnet has commented on the CIA funding of the CCF, 'There may have been CIA money even at the outset, but the intellectuals were not pawns of the government; they were enthusiastic volunteers in the ideological war'.[80] The frustration of people such as Rose Parsons at the difficulties in opposing Soviet state-funded organizations with the meagre resources of the private sector was genuine. However, protests of an 'uneven playing field' in terms of funding were disin-genuous. Elizabeth Wadsworth, an unwitting member of the Committee, commented:

> There were those on the Committee who thought that, if we got any government money, it would be impossible for us to continue our job because too many women we were writing to out there wouldn't approve. And perhaps they were right. If so, then the worst thing we

could do was to take government money and lie about it because that put the lie to the whole integrity which was supposed to underlie the organization . . . You cannot do everything to give the impression that you don't take government money and take it. If it's important that you not take government money, then you don't take it. If it's not important that you not take government money, then take it. That's the point. It's not a question of whether you take government money or not. It's whether you make an issue of it. We did make an issue of it and then we took it. Dumb.[81]

The oft-repeated assertions by the CofC that they were private served an important purpose in advertising their detachment and independence from 'official' American policy and allowing the Committee to represent itself as an example of the disinterested altruism of the American people. Connie Anderson's report on her trip to Asia in 1960 noted this effect in commenting, 'Our efforts received as proof of the concern of American women and so of the United States, but we demonstrate the uniqueness of our country in caring to carry out a program of this sort without any ulterior motives'.[82] When the truth was painfully exposed, the effect on the genuinely private sector was devastating. The *New York Times* editorialised:

The disastrous effects of the systematic penetration of American educational, cultural and labor organizations by the Central Intelligence Agency daily becomes more apparent. The strength of these organizations, both in the structure of American Society and in their relations with their opposite numbers in other nations, always has been their freedom from government domination. Now, through the deviousness of C.I.A. operations, thousands of scholars, students, unionists and professional leaders discover long after the fact that they have performed unwitting and undesired duty as secret agents. The integrity of pro-American positions, honestly taken by groups and individuals in the worldwide battle of ideas, has been undermined. The independence of America's private foundations has been brought into question. In short, faith in American institutions has been besmirched in a way that would have evaded the reach of any foreign enemy.[83]

Members of the Committee were not the unthinking lackeys of the US government. The original motivation behind the Committee was a response by concerned, informed citizens to a perceived problem rather than an initiative by scheming government officials. Many of the members of the Committee, far from working at the direction of the CIA, contributed their voluntary effort completely unaware of the source of their funding. In the end, however, covert government funding of the organizations was a direct contradiction of the Committee's message of what voluntary, concerned women's organisations could achieve. The notion of an independent private sector in the US campaign against the Soviet Union was an illusion.

Notes

1   *Ramparts* (March 1967), p. 38.
2   *New York Times*, 20 February 1967, p. 36.
3   *New York Times*, 16 February 1967, p. 26.
4   Sophia Smith Collection, Smith College, Massachusetts, Committee of Correspondence papers, Financial file, unnumbered box, letter, Metropolitan Editor, *New York Times*, to Committee of Correspondence, 17 February 1967.
5   Records of the National Council of Women, L. K. O'Keefe (ed.) (Ann Arbor, MI: University of Michigan Press), fiche 695, National Council of Women report, 'Information on the Communist dominated WIDF', undated.
6   'The Soviet attack on women's minds', *McCalls* (August 1953).
7   US National Archives, Washington, DC, Records of the Department of State, Miscellaneous Records of the Bureau of Public Affairs 1944–62, box 118, letter, Cochrane to Fierst, July 1951.
8   The NCW had grown out of the National Women's Suffrage Association.
9   For details of the history of the WUUN, see Records of the National Council of Women, series 7, fiche 965.
10 Schlesinger Library, Radcliffe University Institute, Harvard University, Lena M. Phillips papers, box 7, report of first meeting of Anonymous Committee, 16 April 1952.
11 Lena M. Phillips papers, box 7, letter, Parsons to Phillips, 8 May 1952. The members of the Committee saw the lack of affiliated branches as an advantage to their work. Connie Anderson noted in a report on her trip to Asia, 'The Committee of Correspondence as a "committee of fifteen United States women", with no branches or affiliates is in a unique position in that it is not furthering new organizations of local units and is in truth only seeking to help women do a better job in the organization of which they are already members or in which they may serve' (Schlesinger Library, Radcliffe University Institute, Harvard University, Anna Lord Strauss papers, box 13, file 275, Anderson memorandum, 'General Report on Asian Trip', January–February 1960). Until December 1955, the Committee remained in a loose affiliation with the NCW, which allowed them to use NCW office space and channel funds through NCW accounts. However, on 21 December 1955, Julie d'Estournelles wrote to Mrs Leydon at the NCW, telling her that the Committee wished to become autonomous and suggesting, 'Would it also be easier for the Council if our funds came directly to us instead of through your account?' (Records of the National Council of Women, series 7, fiche 411, letter, d'Estournelles to Leydon, 21 December 1955).
12 Lena M. Phillips papers, box 7, comments and suggestions by Anne Hester (undated).

13 Lena M. Phillips papers, box 7, draft reply to WIDF, read at second Meeting of Anonymous Committee, 20 May 1952.
14 See H. Laville and S. Lucas, 'The American way: Edith Sampson, the NAACP and African-American identity in the Cold War', *Diplomatic History*, 20:4 (Autumn 1996).
15 Lena M. Phillips papers, box 7, Parsons report at meeting of the Anonymous Committee, 22 August 1952.
16 Lena M. Phillips papers, box 7, minutes of Committee of Correspondence meeting, 24 October 1952.
17 *Ibid.*
18 Lena M. Phillips papers, box 7, form letter from Parsons, Mahon, and Bauman, 24 November 1952.
19 *Ibid.*
20 *Ibid.*
21 Lena M. Phillips papers, box 7, Parsons memorandum to members of the Committee of Correspondence, 19 December 1952.
22 *Ibid.*
23 Records of the National Council of Women, fiche 707, letter, Parsons to Eleanor Roosevelt, 19 June 1958.
24 Lena M. Phillips papers, box 7, report of first meeting of the Anonymous Committee, 16 April 1952.
25 Committee of Correspondence papers, box 54, file 888, Dorothy Bauman oral history.
26 *Ibid.*
27 The Committee was named after the committees established by individuals such as Thomas Jefferson and Samuel Adams in the early American colonies. Other names that the Committee of Correspondence considered in its first year included Committee on Constructive Action, Blank Committee, and, referring to its work in countering Communist propaganda, the Wreckers Committee.
28 Lena M. Phillips papers, box 7, personal views and recommendations of the Executive Director for the program and activities of the Committee of Correspondence.
29 Lena M. Phillips papers, box 7, form letter from Parsons, Mahon, and Bauman, 24 November 1952.
30 *Ibid.*
31 Lena M. Phillips papers, box 7, Committee of Correspondence Bulletin, 15 April 1953.
32 Lena M. Phillips papers, box 7, letter, Hester to Phillips, undated.
33 Lena M. Phillips papers, box 7, report of the Committee of Correspondence, 13 August 1953.
34 Lena M. Phillips papers, box 7, personal views and recommendations of the Executive Director for the program and activities of the Committee of Correspondence, 27 August 1953.
35 Committee of Correspondence papers, box 2, file 20, Committee of Correspondence Bulletin, February 1955.
36 Records of the National Council of Women, fiche 700, 'Remarks of Henry Loomis', 3 April 1957.
37 For greater detail on the programmes of the Committee see J. Van Voris, *The Committee of Correspondence: Women with a World Vision* (Northampton, MA: Interchange, 1989).

38 Schlesinger Library, Radcliffe Institute, Harvard University, Louise Backus papers, box 1, file 3, Le-thi-An to the Committee of Correspondence, 6 May 1956.
39 *Ibid*.
40 Quoted in Van Voris, *The Committee of Correspondence*, p. 26.
41 Committee of Correspondence papers, box 54, file 901, Jean Picker and Harvey Picker oral history.
42 Committee of Correspondence papers, financial file, Foundations which have supported the Committee of Correspondence, 1 March 1967.
43 *New York Times*, 21 February 1967.
44 Susan McKeever claimed that in the years 1953–68 the Committee spent more than a million dollars. It is impossible to assess how much of this came from the CIA. Louise Backus papers, box 11, file 241, Minutes of meeting, 21 October 1968.
45 Committee of Correspondence papers, box 4, file 32, letter, Crolius to Picker, 27 February 1967.
46 Committee of Correspondence papers, box 1, file 8, statement drawn up by Jean Picker.
47 Committee of Correspondence papers, financial file, minutes of meeting, 3 April 1967.
48 Committee of Correspondence papers, financial file, notes on special board meeting, 24 July 1967.
49 Committee of Correspondence papers, box 1, file 3, letter to be sent to correspondents, February 1969.
50 Committee of Correspondence papers, box 19, file 9, Statement by Coit, Jackson, and Clark, December 1970.
51 Lena M. Phillips papers, box 4, Committee of Correspondence annual report, 1 March 1953–1 April 1954.
52 Lena M. Phillips papers, box 4, letter, Streibert to Parsons, 16 April 1954.
53 Lena M. Phillips papers, box 4, Hester to Members of the Committee, 12 August 1954.
54 Committee of Correspondence papers, box 2, file 2, minutes of meeting, 9 December 1958.
55 Donald Jameson interview in Channel 4 Television, *Hidden Hands: A Different History of Modernism*, 1995.
56 Committee of Correspondence papers, financial file, notes on special board meeting, 24 July 1967.
57 Committee of Correspondence papers, box 54, file 888, Dorothy Bauman oral history.
58 Lena M. Phillips papers, box 7, letter, Dearborn Foundation to Parsons, 7 March 1955.
59 Committee of Correspondence papers, box 54, file 887, Connie Anderson oral history.
60 Committee of Correspondence papers, box 54, file 886, Ezzat Aghevli oral history. Van Voris's sympathy to the witting members of the Committee is perhaps explained by the fact she was commissioned to write the history of the Committee by Interchange, a publishing company owned by Jean and Harvey Picker. Her book is dedicated to the Pickers (Van Voris, *The Committee of Correspondence*). Van Voris's angle on the story of the Committee is explained in her musing to Anne Crolius, 'How do you tell a story about something that

happened 30 years ago that was an interesting experiment in international goodwill and understanding and towards education and peace and all those good things?' (Committee of Correspondence papers, box 54, file 892, Anne Crolius oral history) Director, Alison Raymond Lanier, shared the belief in the peevishness and jealousy of the unwitting members of the Committee as the motivation for their concern regarding the source of the funding. When Van Voris told her, 'I just don't think it's so horrendous [the funding] and I didn't know why everybody reacted as they did', Lanier agreed, 'It's only horrendous because they felt cheated . . . and jealous too, why wasn't I one? All those reasons. It wasn't because it was C.I.A. so much as because they'd been made a fool of, or they thought they had'. Lanier noted that if Eleanor Coit had been told of the funding, she 'would have had a fit'. (Alison Raymond Lanier oral history, Committee of Correspondence papers, box 54, file 895).

61 Committee of Correspondence papers, box 54, file 886, Ezzat Aghevli oral history.

62 *Ibid*.

63 C. Lasch, 'The cultural Cold War: A short history of the Congress for Cultural Freedom', in B. Bernstein (ed.), *Towards a New Past* (New York: Pantheon Books, 1968), p. 332.

64 *Ibid*., p. 350.

65 *Ibid*., p. 349.

66 It is also interesting to note the speed at which Anne Crolius left the country following the disclosure of CIA connections with some US organisations. In June 1966 Crolius left for Vietnam, travel expenses being paid by the Agency for International Development but 'acting solely on the behalf of the Committee of Correspondence'. Louise Backus papers, box 11, file 19 minutes of meeting, 28 June 1966.

67 Anna Lord Strauss papers, box 13, file 275, letter, Strauss to the Committee of Correspondence, 22 January 1960. The countries Hoffman listed were: Mexico, El Salvador, Columbia, Ecuador, Peru, Chile, Argentina, Venezuela, India, Burma, Ceylon, Ghana, Nigeria, Liberia, Iran and Turkey.

68 Committee of Correspondence papers, box 54, file 887, Connie Anderson oral history.

69 Committee of Correspondence papers, box 54, file 892, Anne Crolius oral history.

70 Anna Lord Strauss papers, box 13, file 264, Strauss remarks at Board Meeting, 11 December 1967.

71 Committee of Correspondence papers, financial file, notes on special board meeting, 24 July 1967.

72 Committee of Correspondence papers, box 54, file 890, Dorothy S. Bauman, 'Right or wrong?'.

73 Committee of Correspondence papers, box 54, file 888, Dorothy Bauman oral history.

74 Lena M. Phillips papers, box 7, Parsons report, 28 August–6 November 1953. This pro-American bias is perhaps explained by the fact that the CIA also supported the Committee for Free Asia.

75 Lena M. Phillips papers, box 4, letter from Parsons, 6 May 1953.

76 *Ramparts* (March 1967), p. 38.

77 Committee of Correspondence papers, box 54, file 890, Dorothy Bauman, 'Right or wrong?', October 1974.

78   Notes on Special Board Meeting, 24 July 1967, Committee of Correspondence papers, Financial file. The unwitting Bethke Papanek's search for funding was described in sympathetic terms by director Alison Raymond Lanier: 'Bethke was the treasurer and . . . she worked like a dog to raise money and then we would tell her, "Write this foundation" or "write that Foundation". Then she would get some money and she was absolutely thrilled and everyone congratulated her. It was such a farce, it was a terrible thing to do to anybody'. Committee of Correspondence papers, box 54, file 895 Alison Raymond Lanier oral history

79   Committee of Correspondence papers, box 19, file 196, Report of the Conference of Women's International Non-Governmental Organizations, 3–16 March 1962. Ironically the report went on to note, 'Although the participants took a positive attitude towards possibilities of voluntary organizations cooperating with government on specific projects and activities, they recognized that circumstances could arise in this relationship which would jeopardize the independent and voluntary character of the private groups. This situation could arise in any of several ways such as government decree of law requiring inspection of organization administration, apathy of the organization or the public towards government interference, too great a reliance on government funds'.

80   R. J. Barnet, *By the Rockets' Red Glare: War, Politics and the American Presidency* (New York: Simon and Schuster, 1990), p. 307.

81   Committee of Correspondence papers, box 54, file 902, Elizabeth Wadsworth oral history.

82   Anna Lord Strauss papers, box 13, file 275, Anderson memorandum, 'General Report on Asian Trip', January–February 1960.

83   *New York Times*, 20 February 1967, p. 36.

Conclusion

The so-called 'kitchen debate' which has come to dominate accounts of the visit of Vice-President Nixon to the Soviet Union in 1959 has been used by many historians to demonstrate the way in which women were incorporated into Cold War discourse. The meeting encapsulated the relationship between the feminine, domestic, private sphere and the masculine, international, public realm. Within these accounts women are passive symbols of American capitalism, content in their kitchens, surrounded by the marvels of domestic technology.

A less well-known account of the trip to Moscow is that of Nixon's wife, Patricia. The journal of the NFBPWC, the *National Business Woman*, reported on her view of the trip in an article entitled 'Mrs Nixon: Ambassadress on her own'. The journal reported that, while the men talked of 'the big difficult problems of the world – the political and economic and diplomatic ideas which divide us', Mrs Nixon talked to the Soviet women about 'strengthening the simpler and possibly more fundamental ideas which we share'.[1] Mrs Nixon reported to American women, 'They want peace . . . They have seen war and they want peace. That is what women spoke to me so much about. I said to them, "We women will have to find a way to get the men to bring about peace", and they liked that'.[2]

Without even mentioning the Kitchen Debate, the article in the *National Business Woman* conveyed a quite different understanding of the function of gender in international politics than that of Richard Nixon or Elaine Tyler May. Mrs Nixon told the journal:

> She and the wives of the three top Russian officials had sat in silence for six hours at Mr Khrushchev's dacha while Mr Nixon and their host debated the issues of the Cold War. 'We women did not say a word the whole time. Neither did anyone else', she recalled, 'It was

just the two men talking'. At the end of the lengthy discussion, Mrs Nixon continued 'I said jokingly to the women, "They ought to let the women settle this". Mrs Kozlov (the wife of Russia's Deputy Premier) agreed with me. Quite earnestly she said, "Yes. They should let the women do it"'.[3]

Patricia Nixon's conversation with her Soviet counterparts illustrates an important conception of gender, absent from the standard portrayal of an international relations dominated by discussions between men. Instead of a competition between two opposing nationalities with women serving as the symbolic markers of achievement, the Soviet women and Mrs Nixon agreed on a set of shared priorities and values stemming not from their national identity, but from their gender. The article asserted that, 'Besides her gracious friendliness, her widespread invitation to "come and see us", the Vice-President's wife again and again suggested that peace was the universal desire of *women* in all parts of the world'.[4] The *National Business Woman* concluded, 'Perhaps the visit to Russia and Poland of the Second Lady of our land will tip the balance a bit further and the seeds of friendship planted with "small talk" between women will bear fruit in the homes of the men who will meet around conference tables'.[5]

It is not the intention of this book to make any argument for Patricia Nixon as a hitherto unknown behind-the-scenes activist. There is no evidence that after her interview with the *National Business Women*, Mrs Nixon acted on her meeting with the Soviet women. However, her accounts, together with the historical account of her husband's more famous meeting with his Soviet counterparts demonstrate two very different approaches to women and international relations. In Vice-President Nixon's version women are passive representatives of nation, in his wife's story women are active agents of internationalism. In reality neither of these accounts represent the reality of the activities and experiences of American women in the Cold War. American women did not serve simply as symbols of their national identity. They were active participants in the projection of American values to the world, and took seriously their role in constructing and representing their version of American womanhood to the world. They vigorously fought against accounts of their lives that restricted them to the kitchen, and sought to disseminate a picture of American womanhood centered on their political activism, mediated through their voluntary associations. In their efforts to educate the women of the world in citizenship and democracy, American women may have been overly confident, dogmatic and arrogant, but they were certainly not passive symbols.

However, if leaders of American women were not merely trophies of national identity, neither were they the committed internationalists of Patricia Nixon's account. Like Mrs Nixon, leaders of American women's organisations made frequent reference to their gender-based identity in their international work but they made little effort to understand the implications of this identity. While never actually challenging or repudiating the idea of women's greater commitment to peace, American women's associations nevertheless managed to qualify this commitment in such a way as to allow them to embrace the cold war imperatives of their government.

One example serves to demonstrate the conditional and ambivalent approach of American women to internationalism. Following the death of Carrie Chapman Catt, who had been a founding and active participant in the international women's movement, the LWV chose to honour their former president by establishing a fund dedicated to international work. The Carrie Chapman Catt Memorial Fund was established in 1947, one year after Catt's death. But the CCCMF was not a part of any international organization and was from the beginning deeply imbued with national purpose. Its statement of purpose was stark in its certainty about the need for American leadership, pledging itself to the task of 'acquainting the women of other countries, especially those newly enfranchised with democratic methods of stimulating more effective citizen participation in government'.[6] From its early years the fund served American aims, co-operating with the Civil Administration Division of OMGUS to sponsor visits of German women to America. In 1952 the fund applied to the Ford Foundation for a grant, explaining their work as an important part of the Cold War effort:

> Who knows where time is running out fastest, what chances there are that the cold war will turn hot, where the infiltration process is likely to extend the Iron Curtain? . . . The Vice-president of a French women's group begs for help in reaching the farm women whose only newspaper bringing the welcome recipes, household hints etc., is poisoned with vicious lies about the U.S. and the U.N.[7]

The CCCMF operated as the overseas aid and education branch of the LWV and was renamed the Overseas Education Fund in 1961. Anna Lord Strauss explained that the change in name reflected linguistic confusion, explaining, 'So often on the telephone people would say "Catt Fund?" and they figured it was "Cats" instead of "Catt". So we decided that we should really change the name and make it sound a little closer to the League'.[8] The change in title was more than appropriate, however. The fund had less to do with the pioneering internationalism of Carrie Chapman Catt and more to do with the zeal of the League for 'educating' women in other nations.

While the CCCMF and later the OEF co-ordinated the efforts of the LWV to preach their model to women across the globe, the League itself maintained a determined distance from international entanglements. At a meeting in 1946 between representatives of women's associations and representatives of the State Department, leaders of American women's associations were asked to report back to their government on the attitude of international women's associations, with particular reference to the UN. Anna Lord Strauss reported back from the meeting of the IAW she had attended in Interlaken in August. She told the meeting that 'the group would have liked the U.S. to take leadership and responsibility. Neither Miss Strauss or Miss Kenyon, the U.S. delegate, felt free to undertake the international presidency, but noted the sincerity of the Europeans in asking a U.S. candidate'.[9] Both Strauss and Kenyon proved to be too busy with international work directed by their national organisations and their government to commit themselves to a leadership role in their international affiliated organisations. Not only was the League unwilling to take a leadership role in the IAW; by 1950, they were unwilling to take any role at all, withdrawing from their membership in the IAW. The then president of the League, Mrs Charles Heming explained, 'LWV members do not like to be committed to statements, programs and activities over which they really have no control'.[10] American women were prepared to be active on the international stage on their terms only and consistently refused any position on internationalism that would necessitate the compromise of their views.

Other American women's organisations were slightly less unwilling to co-operate on an international level. The AAUW and the NFBPWC maintained relationships with their international bodies, sending participants to their international conferences and reporting enthusiastically on their debates there. Lena Phillips, former president of the NFBPWC also served as the international president of the IFBPWC. However, the majority of the international work of the

AAUW and the NFBPWC was mediated, not through their membership in trans-national organisations, but through their co-operation with their Department of State. While the AAUW co-operated with the IFUW in the matter of international scholarships and sponsorships, this effort was dwarfed by their co-operation with their government in programmes such as the exchange of persons programme in West Germany.

The failure of the leaders of the US women's organisations to accept closer ties with their international affiliates is illustrative of the conditional, ambivalent approach of many Americans to internationalism. Edward Luck's study of the US approach to international organisations demonstrates this ambivalence. Luck shows that what passes for American internationalism could often more accurately be described as the attempt to make Americanism international. Luck explains, 'Most Americans believe in international organizations, but as a way of propagating American values, not compromising them in order to get along with the majority'.[11] As a result of their confidence in their national values, Luck asserts, Americans frequently displayed 'the tendency to see within global bodies unfriendly and irresponsible factions that could use these organizations to milk America's wealth and power or to challenge its values'.[12]

Despite their growing reluctance to tie themselves to international women's organisations, American women made repeated reference to their commitment to an international sisterhood, based on a vision of understanding and commonality among women across the globe. Pleasant as this vision of sisterhood among women of all nations may have been, it must be understood as a rhetorical and discursive strategy rather than a real goal or plan of action. International relations theorist J. Ann Tickner has warned, 'The creation of global identities necessary for building conflict-reducing universal structures must be approached with caution'.[13] She notes, 'When women create trans-national alliances, non-western women complain that they are required to accept models based on Western understandings of feminism and Western ways of doing things'.[14] This caution should not be limited to relations between Western and non-Western women. In all of their international relations, women's actions are inextricably tied to national assumptions and agenda. In the case of American women's associations, their sense of superiority was based upon both their belief in the national superiority and their confidence in their organisations as the model for women's political participation.

In part the withdrawal of American women's' associations form their international affiliations is accounted for by their national context. Most Americans in the post-war world were crusaders for Americanization, rather than participants in internationalism. Furthermore, the division of the international women's movements into Cold War camps, precipitated by the founding of the WIDF in 1945, reinforced American women's suspicions that female internationalism could all too easily be subverted into sympathy for peace campaigns and communism. American women's associations' loyalty to national rather than international claims owed much to this Cold War context.

However, even without the Cold War, the strength of gendered internationalism as a political base rather than as a rhetorical ideal must be questioned. Even from the earliest days of international organising, some women were dubious as to the possibility of uniting women across the globe in a meaningful way. The founding years of the ICW are an example. The Council elected Millicent Garrett Fawcett, the British suffragette, as its first president. Mrs Fawcett, however, declined the honour. When May Wright Sewell, chief organiser for the ICW, travelled to London to attempt to change her mind, she met with failure. Mrs Fawcett explained firmly that she believed, 'It was quite impossible that English and American women should have anything in common, the conditions of their lives and societies being so different'. 'An utter disappointment', Mrs Sewell reported back.[15] Fifty-six years later, Lena Phillips expressed a similar scepticism towards women's internationalism on a radio show, *Woman of Tomorrow*. Phillips was asked by her interviewer, 'I've always maintained that until women unite on this, we're going to have wars . . . but do you think women would ever join in a world-wide movement of this kind?' Phillips responded, 'No, I doubt if women of the world will ever be able to form a substantial block. At least, they will work at first as men and women together . . . our political parties illustrate what I mean . . . men and women join forces on national questions'.[16]

Feminist scholars have begun to challenge visions of feminist or feminine internationalism that reject, ignore or play down the importance of national identity. Valerie Amos and Pratibha Parmer, for example, have rejected white women's claims to a lack of culpability in imperialism on the basis of their lack of obvious power and influence within their own nations, pointing to the extent to which they were complicit in the imperialist project of their nations.[17] Feminist theorist Anne Marie Goetz has similarly critiqued the relationship between women of the developed and developing world. Goetz has argued that, while basing their actions on an expression of shared interests and experience, 'the claim to know', Western feminists nevertheless quickly assert a 'claim to know better'.[18] Work such as this points to the conclusion that, however earnestly women may believe their rhetoric of international sisterhood, in practice national identity cannot be easily suppressed.

These identity debates have serious consequences for the study of women in international relations. Shared gender identity often becomes a mask to disguise conscious and unconscious national allegiances and agendas. In her study of the internationalism of the British Vera Brittain and German Edith Stein, historian Joyce Avech Berkman has shown how disappointingly fragile the concept of women's internationalism can be. As soon as national interests were threatened, Berkman concludes, 'They elevated their national identity above their gender and European identity without a second thought'.[19] Leila Rupp, in her study of three transnational women's organisations, has similarly problematised the idea of women's internationalism, asserting that 'internationally minded women did not all agree on the significance of their collective consciousness for individual national identities. For some, internationalism coexisted with a strong national loyalty, unless the two came into conflict, in which case nationalism took precedence'.[20] Similarly, the work of American women's associations in the Cold War demonstrates the weakness of women's internationalism in the face of national loyalties. Leaders of American women's associations co-operated enthusiastically with their government, sharing their national assumptions and agenda. In their international work, American women abandoned the ideals of gendered internationalism in favour of a role in the national Cold War effort.

Notes

1 'Mrs Nixon: Ambassadress on her own', *National Business Woman*, 38:9 (September 1959), p. 4.
2 *Ibid.*
3 *Ibid.*
4 *Ibid.*
5 *Ibid.*
6 Schlesinger Library, Radcliffe Institute, Harvard University, Lucile Koshland Papers, box 1, file 9, CCCMF Statement of Activities, 1948.

7   Lucille Koshland Papers, file 15, box 1, Request for a grant from the CCCMF to the Ford Foundation, June 1954.

8   The reminiscences of Miss Anna Lord Strauss, p. 382.

9   Mary McLeod Bethune Memorial Museum, Washington, DC, National Council of Negro Women Papers, box 35, file 9, US Department of Labor, Women's Bureau, Report on meeting of Women's organisations.

10 Library if Congress, Washington, DC, League of Women Voters papers, box 1725, letter, Mrs Charles E. Heming, President, League of Women Voters, to Lorna Warfield, 22 April 1952.

11 E. C. Luck, *Mixed Messages: American Politics and International Organization 1919–1999*. (Washington, DC: Brooking Institution Press, 1999), p. 7.

12 *Ibid.*, p. 76.

13 J. A. Tickner, 'Identity in international relations theory: Feminist perspectives', in Y. Lapid and F. Kratochwil (eds), *The Return of Culture and Identity in International Relations Theory* (Boulder, CO: Lynne Rienner, 1996), p. 158.

14 *Ibid.*, p. 159.

15 Schlesinger Library, Radcliffe Institute, Harvard University, Lena M. Phillips papers, box 6, *In the Nineties: Ishbel Aberdeen and the I.C.W.* (London: The Caxton Press, 1947).

16 Lena Phillips Papers, Box 6, script, 'Woman of Tomorrow', April 6th 1944.

17 V. Amos and P. Parmar, 'Challenging imperial feminism', *Feminist Review*, 17 (1984). For an account of debate following this article, see A. Burton, 'Some trajectories of 'feminism' and 'imperialism'', *Gender and History*, 10:3 (November 1998).

18 A. M. Goetz, 'Feminism and the limits of the "claim to know": Contradictions in the feminist approach to women in development', *Millennium: A Journal of International Studies*, 17:3 (Winter 1988).

19 J. A. Berkman, '"I am myself it": Comparative national identity formation in the lives of Vera Brittain and Edith Stein', *Women's History Review*, 6:1 (1997), p. 57.

20 L. J. Rupp, 'Constructing internationalism: The case of transnational women's organizations 1888–1945', *American Historical Review*, 99:5 (December 1994), p. 1587.

Select bibliography

Archives

Dwight D. Eisenhower Presidential Library, Abilene, Kansas
Papers of Dwight D. Eisenhower
Papers of Katherine G. Howard

Franklin D. Roosevelt Presidential Library, Hyde Park, New York
Papers of Eleanor Roosevelt

Harry S. Truman Presidential Library, Independence, Missouri
Papers of Clarence Decker
Papers of India Edwards
Oral History Collection, India Edwards, conducted by Patricia Zelman
Papers of Harry S. Truman

Mary McLeod Bethune Memorial Museum, Washington, DC
National Council of Negro Women Papers

Sophia Smith Collection, Smith College, Massachussetts
Papers of the Committee of Correspondence
Papers of Eleanor Coit
Papers of Ruth Woodsmall

National Archives, Washington, DC
Records of the Women's Bureau of the U.S. Department of Labor

Library of Congress, Washington, DC
Records of the League of Women Voters

Schlesinger Library, Radcliffe Institute, Harvard University, Cambridge, Massachusetts
Papers of Louise Backus
Papers of Eleanor Gwinnell Coit

Papers of Katherine Graham Howard
Papers of Mary S. Ingraham
Papers of Emily Kneubuhl
Papers of Lucille Koshland
Papers of Esther Peterson
Papers of Lena M. Phillips
Papers of Frieda Segelke Miller
Papers of Edith Spurlock Sampson
Papers of Anna Lord Strauss
Papers of Dorothy Zeiger
Records of the Young Women's Christian Association of Boston
Women United for the United Nations papers
The Black Women Oral History Project, vol. 5, 1991, Dorothy Height, conducted by
    Polly Cowan

Syracuse University Library, Department of Special Collections
Papers of Dorothy Thompson

Oral History Research Office, Columbia University
Katherine Howard
Esther Peterson
Anna Lord Strauss

Records on microfilm

National Council of Women Records, ed. L. K. O'Keefe (Ann Arbor, MI: University
    of Michigan Press, 1988)
Records of the American Association of University Women (Microfilming
    Corporation of America)
Records of the Women's Bureau of the US Department of Labor 1918–1965, ed. D.
    Grinder (Frederick, MD: University Publications of America)

Official publications

Foreign Relations of the United States, 1954, vol. 1 (Washington, DC: Government
    Printing Office, 1983)
The United Nations and the Advancement of Women 1945–1995 (New York: UN
    Department of Public Information, 1995)
The World Assembly for Peace, Helsinki, 22–29 June 1955 (Stockholm: Secretariat of the
    World Council of Peace)

Newspapers and journals

Action, journal of the National League of Women Voters
General Federation Clubwoman, January 1952–May 1954
Independent Woman, journal of the Nation Federation of Business and Professional
    Women, January 1948–November 1959

International Woman's News, journal of the International Association of Women
Journal of the AAUW, Autumn 1944–January 1955
Life, January 1945–January 1955
National Business Woman, journal of the National Federation of Business and
Professional Women's Clubs
The National Voter, journal of the League of Women Voters
Ramparts
Woman's Day, April 1946–November 1959
Women of the Whole World, journal of the Women's International Democratic
Federation

Books and monographs

Alonso, H. H., *Peace as a Woman's Issue: A History of the U.S. Movement for World Peace and Women's Rights* (Syracuse, NY: Syracuse University Press, 1993)
Anderson, E., *Guide to Women's Organizations: A Handbook about National and International Groups* (Washington, DC: Public Affairs Press, 1950)
Angerman, A., Binnema, G., Keunen, A., Poels, V. and Zirkzee, J. (eds), *Current Issues in Women's History* (London: Routledge, 1989)
Anonymous, *Are American Women Degenerating?* (New York: Exposition Press, 1955)
Balakrishnan, G. (ed.), *Mapping the Nation* (London: Verso, 1996)
Barnet, R. J., *The Rocket's Red Glare: War, Politics and the American Presidency* (New York: Simon and Schuster, 1990)
Batho, E., *A Lamp of Friendship, 1918–1968: A Short History of the International Federation of University Women* (Eastbourne: Sumfield and Day, 1968)
Bell, D., *The End of Ideology: On the Exhaustion of Political Ideas in the Fifties* (London: The Free Press, 1960)
Bell, D. (ed.), *The Radical Right: The New American Right* (New York: Doubleday, 1964)
Bernard, J., *The Female World from a Global Perspective* (Bloomington, IN: Indiana University Press, 1987)
Bernstein, B. J. (ed.), *Towards a New Past* (New York: Pantheon, 1968)
Blair, K. J., *The Clubwoman as Feminist: True Womanhood Redefined 1888–1914* (New York: Holmest Meier, 1980)
Blair, K. J., *A History of American Women's Voluntary Organizations 1810–1960* (Boston, MA: G. K. Hall, 1989)
Bock, G. and James, S. (eds), *Beyond Equality and Difference* (London: Routledge, 1992).
Boulding, E., *The Underside of History: A View of Women through Time*, vol. 2 (London: Sage, 1992)
Brenner, R. and Reichard, G. W. (eds), *Reshaping America: Societies and Institutions 1945–1960* (Columbus, OH: Ohio State University Press, 1982)
Bridenthal, R. and Koonz, C. (eds), *Becoming Visible: Women in European History* (Boston, MA: Houghton Mifflin, 1977)
Bussey, G. and Tims, M., *The Women's International League for Peace and Freedom 1915–1965* (London: Allen and Unwin, 1965)
Butler, J., *Gender Trouble. Feminism and the Subversion of Identity* (New York: Routledge, 1990)

Butler, J. and Scott, J. (eds), *Feminists Theorize the Political* (New York: Routledge, 1992)

Chafe, W. H., *The Paradox of Change: American Women in the Twentieth Century* (New York: Oxford University Press, 1991)

Chatfield, C. and Van Den Dugen, P. (eds), *Peace Movements and Political Culture* (Knoxville, TN: University of Tennessee Press, 1988)

Chodorow, N., *The Reproduction of Mothering: Psychoanalysis and the Sociology of Gender* (Berkeley, CA: University of California Press, 1978)

Clarfield, G. H. and Wiecek, W. M., *Nuclear America: Military and Civilian Nuclear Power in the United States 1940–1980* (New York: Harper and Row, 1984)

Clay, L., *Decision in Germany* (Westport, CT: Greenwood Press, 1950)

Cook, B. W., *The Declassified Eisenhower* (New York, Penguin, 1981)

Davidson, E., *The Life and Death of Germany: An Account of American Occupation* (London: Jonathan Cape, 1959)

Decker, M. B., *The World We Saw with Town Hall* (New York: Richard R. Smith, 1950)

Divine, R., *Second Chance: The Triumph of Internationalism in America during World War II* (New York: Atheneum, 1971)

Donaldson, L., *Decolonizing Feminisms: Race, Gender and Empire-Building* (London: Routledge, 1993)

Duberman, M. B., *Paul Robeson* (New York: Alfred A. Knopf, 1988)

Duke, L. L., *Women in Politics: Outsiders or Insiders?* (Englewood Cliffs, NJ: Prentice-Hall, 1993)

Duverger, M., *The Political Role of Women* (Paris: United Nations Educational, Scientific and Cultural Organization, 1955)

Edwards, I., *Pulling No Punches: Memoirs of a Woman in Politics* (New York: G. P. Putman and Sons, 1977)

Eisenhower, D. D., *Peace with Justice* (New York: Columbia University Press, 1961)

Eisenstein, H. and Jardine, A. (eds), *The Future of Difference* (New Brunswick, NJ: Rutgers University Press, 1985)

Elias, R. and Turpin, J. (eds), *Rethinking Peace* (Boulder, CO: Lynne Rienner, 1994)

Ellis, S. J. and Noyes, K. H., *By the People: A History of Americans as Volunteers* (Philadelphia, PA: Energize, 1978)

Elshtain, J. B., *Public Man, Private Woman: Women in Social and Political Thought* (Princeton, NJ: Princeton University Press, 1981)

Elshtain, J. B., *Women and War* (New York: Basic Books, 1987)

Elshtain, J. B. and Tobias, S. (eds), *Women, Militarism and War: Essays in History, Politics and Social Theory* (Savage, MD: Rowman and Littlefield, 1990)

Enloe, C., *Does Khaki Become You? The Militarization of Women's Lives* (London: Pandora Press, 1988)

Enloe, Cynthia, *Bananas, Beaches and Bases: Making Feminist Sense of International Politics* (London: Pandora Press, 1989)

Enloe, Cynthia, *The Morning After: Sexual Politics at the End of the Cold War* (Berkeley, CA: University of California Press, 1993)

Epstein, C. F. and Coser, R. L. (eds), *Access to Power: Cross National Studies of Woman and Elites* (London: Allen and Unwin, 1981)

Evans, R. J., *Comrades and Sisters: Feminism, Socialism and Pacifism in Europe 1870–1945* (New York: Wheatsheaf Books, 1987)

Evans, S., *Personal Politics: The Roots of Women's Liberation in the Civil Rights Movement and the New Left* (New York: Vintage Books, 1979)

Fitzgerald, T. A., *The National Council of Negro Women and the Feminist Movement* (Washington, DC: Georgetown University Press, 1985)

Fraser, A., *Looking to the Future: Equal Partnership between Women and Men in the 21st Century* (Minneapolis, MN: Hubert Humphrey, 1985)

Friedan, B., *The Feminine Mystique* (New York: Dell, 1963)

Friedan, B., *It Changed My Life: Writings on the Women's Movement* (New York: Random House, 1979)

Giddings, P., *When and When I Enter: The Impact of Black Women on Race and Sex in America* (New York: William Morrow, 1984)

Gimbel, J., *The American Occupation of Germany* (Stanford, CA: Stanford University Press, 1968)

Glenn, E. N., Chang, G. and Forcey, L. R. (eds), *Mothering: Ideology, Experience and Agency* (New York: Routledge, 1994)

Gluck, S. B., *Rosie the Riveter Revisited: Women, the War and Social Change* (Boston, MA: Twayne, 1987)

Grant, R. and Newland, K. (eds), *Gender and International Relations* (Milton Keynes: Open University Press, 1991)

Groom, A. J. R. and Light, M., *Contemporary International Relations: A Guide to Theory* (London: Pinter, 1994)

Haas, E., *Beyond the Nation-State: Functionalism and International Organization* (Stanford, CA: Stanford University Press, 1964)

Halle, L. J., *The Society of Man* (London: Chatto and Windus, 1965)

Handlin, O. and Handlin, M., *The Dimensions of Liberty* (Cambridge, MA: The Belknap Press, 1961)

Harris, A. and King, Y. (eds), *Rocking the Ship of State: Towards a Feminist Peace Politics* (Boulder, CO: Westview Press, 1995)

Hartmann, S. M., *The Homefront and Beyond: American Women in the 1940s* (Boston, MA: Twayne, 1982)

Herz, J. H., *International Politics in the Atomic Age* (New York: Columbia University Press, 1959)

Hess, B. and Ferree, M. M. (ed.), *Analyzing Gender* (London: Sage, 1987)

hooks, bell, *Aint I a Woman? Black Women and Feminism* (Boston, MA: South End Press, 1981)

Horne, G., *Black and Red: W.E.B. DuBois and the African-American Response to the Cold War 1944–1963* (New York: State University of New York Press, 1986)

Howard, K., *With My Shoes Off* (New York: Vanatge Press, 1977)

Janeway, E., *Man's World, Woman's Place: A Study in Social Mythology* (Harmondsworth: Penguin, 1977)

Jeffreys-Jones, R., *The CIA in American Democracy* (New Haven, CT: Yale University Press, 1989)

Jeffreys-Jones, R., *Changing Differences: Women and the Shaping of American Foreign Policy 1917–1994* (New Brunswick, NJ: Rutgers University Press, 1995)

Joel, J. and Erikson, G. M., *Anti-communism: The Politics of Manipulation* (Minneapolis, MN: Marxist Educational Press, 1987)

Jones, K. and Jonascdottir, A. (eds), *The Political Interests of Gender. Developing Theory and Research with a Feminist Face* (London: Sage, 1988)

Kaledin, E., *American Women in the 1950s: Mothers and More* (Boston, MA: G. K. Hall, 1984)

Kaplan, M. A., *System and Process in International Politics* (New York: John Wiley, 1957)

Kellerman, H., *The Educational Exchange Program between the United States and Germany 1945–1954* (Washington, DC: Bureau of Educational and Cultural Affairs, Department of State, 1978)

Kerber, L., *No Constitutional Right to be Ladies: Women and the Obligations of Citzenship* (New York: Hill and Wang, 1998)

Kerber, L., Kessler-Harris, A. and Sklar, K. K. (eds), *U.S. History as Women's History: New Feminist Essays* (Chapel Hill, NC: University of North Carolina Press, 1995)

Kirkpatrick, C., *Women in Nazi Germany* (London: Jarrods, 1939)

Kirkpatrick, J. (ed.), *The Strategy of Deception* (London: Robert Hale, 1964)

Koonz, C., *Mothers in the Fatherland: Women, the Family and Nazi Politics* (London: Methuen, 1988)

Kraditor, A. (ed.), *Up from the Pedestal* (New York: Quadrangle, 1968)

Kristeva, J., *Nations without Nationalism*, trans. L. S. Roudiez (New York: Columbia University Press, 1993)

Lapid, Y. and Kratochwil, F. (eds), *The Return of Culture and Identity in International Relations Theory* (Boulder, CO: Lynne Rienner, 1996)

Lefever, E.W., *Ethics and United States Foreign Policy* (Cleveland, OH: Meridian Books, 1957)

Le Veness, F. P. and Sweeny, J. P., *Women Leaders in Contemporary U.S. Politics* (Boulder, CO: Lynne Rienner, 1987)

Levering, R., *The Public and American Foreign Policy 1918–1978* (New York: William Morrow, 1978)

Lewis, M. O. (ed), *The Foundation Directory* (New York: Russell Sage Foundation, 1967)

Lifton, R. J. (ed.), *The Woman in America* (Boston, MA: Houghton Mifflin, 1965)

Lorde, A., *Sister Outsider: Essays and Speeches* (Freedom, CA: The Crossing Press, 1984)

Lorence, J. (ed.), *Enduring Voices*, vol. 2 (Lexington, MA: D. C. Heath, 1996)

Lucas, S., *Freedom's War: The U.S. Crusade against the Soviet Union 1945–56* (Manchester: Manchester University Press, 1999)

Luck, E. C., *Mixed Messages: American Politics and International Organization 1919–1999* (Washington, DC: Brooking Institution Press, 1999)

Lynn, S., *Progressive Women in Conservative Times: Radical Justice, Peace and Feminism 1945 to the 1960s* (New Brunswick, NJ: Rutgers University Press, 1992)

McAllister, P. (ed.), *Re-weaving the Web of Life: Feminism and Non-Violence* (Philadelphia, PA: New Society, 1982)

McClintock, A., *Imperial Leather: Race, Gender and Sexuality in the Colonial Contest* (London: Routledge, 1995)

McDowell, L. and Pringle, R. (ed.), *Defining Women: Social Institutions and Gender Divisions* (Cambridge: Polity Press, 1992)

McEnaney, L., *Civil Defense Begins at Home: Militarization Meets Everyday Life in the Fifties* (Princeton, NJ, and Oxford: Princeton University Press, 2000)

McGlen, N. E. and Sarkees, M. R., *Women in Foreign Policy: The Insiders* (New York: Routledge, 1993)

May, E. T., *Homeward Bound: American Families in the Cold War Era* (New York: Basic Books, 1988)

May, E. T., *Pushing the Limits: American Women 1941–1961* (Oxford: Oxford University Press, 1994)

Marling, K. A., *As Seen on T.V.: The Visual Culture of Everyday Life* (Cambridge, MA: Harvard University Press, 1994)

Mercer, P., *'Peace' of the Dead* (London: Policy Research Publications, 1986)

Merritt, R. L., *Democracy Imposed: U.S. Occupation Policy and the German Public 1945–1949* (New Haven, CT: Yale University Press, 1995)

Meyerowitz, J. (ed.), *Not June Cleaver: Women and Gender in Post-War America 1945–1960* (Philadelphia, PA: Temple University Press, 1994)

Mills, C. W., *The Power Elite* (New York: Oxford University Press, 1956)

Moghadam, V. (ed.), *Gender and National Identity* (London: Zed Books, 1994)

Moghadam, V. (ed.), *Identity Politics and Women: Cultural Reassertions and Feminisms in International Perspective* (Boulder, CO: Westview Press, 1994)

Moi, T. (ed.), *The Kristeva Reader* (Oxford: Blackwell, 1986)

Mouffe, C. (ed), *Dimensions of Radical Democracy: Pluralism, Citizenship, Community* (London: Verso, 1992)

Mouffe, C., *The Return of the Political* (New York: Verso, 1993)

Ninkovich, F. A., *The Diplomacy of Ideas: U.S Foreign Policy and Cultural Relations 1938–1950* (Cambridge: Cambridge University Press, 1981)

Oshinsky, D., *A Conspiracy So Immense: The World of Joe McCarthy* (New York: The Free Press, 1983)

Pateman, C., *The Disorder of Women: Democracy, Feminism and Political Theory* (Stanford, CA: Stanford University Press, 1989)

Pateman, C. and Gross, E. (eds), *Feminist Challenges: Social and Political Theory* (Boston, MA: Northeastern University Press, 1986)

Pells, R., *The Liberal Mind in a Conservative Age: American Intellectuals in the 1940s and 1950s* (New York: Harper and Row, 1985)

Pennock, J. R. and Chapman, J. W. (eds), *Voluntary Associations* (New York: Pantheon Press, 1969)

Pierson, R. R. (ed.), *Women and Peace: Theoretical, Historical and Practical Perspectives* (London: Croom Helm, 1987)

Preston, Jr, W., Herman, E. S. and Schiller, H. I., *Hope and Folly: The United States and Unesco 1945–1985* (Minneapolis, MN: University of Minnesota Press, 1985)

Ranelagh, J., *The Agency: The Rise and Decline of the CIA* (New York: Simon and Schuster, 1986)

Reardon, B. A., *Women and Peace. Feminist Visions of Global Security* (Albany, NY: State University of New York Press, 1993)

Reichard, G., *Politics as Usual: The Age of Truman and Eisenhower* (Arlington Heights, IL: Harlan Davidson, 1988)

Ridd, R. and Callaway, H. (eds), *Caught Up in Conflict: Women's Responses to Political Strife* (Basingstoke: Macmillan Education in association with the Oxford University Women's Studies Committee, 1986)

Riley, D., *'Am I that Name?': Feminism and the Category of 'Women' in History* (Basingstoke: Macmillan, 1988)

Rosaldo, M. Z. and Lamphere, L. (eds), *Women, Culture and Society* (Stanford, CA: Stanford University Press, 1974)

Rose, A. M., *Political Process in America* (New York: Oxford University Press, 1967)

Rosenberg, E., *Spreading the American Dream: American Economic and Cultural Expansion 1890–1945* (New York: Hill and Wang, 1982)

Roszak, B. and Roszak, T. (eds), *Masculine/Feminine Readings in Sexual Mythology and the Liberation of Women* (New York: Harper and Row, 1969)

Rowbotham, S., *Women in Movement: Feminism and Social Action* (New York: Routledge, 1992)

Rupp, L. J., *Worlds of Women: The Making of an International Women's Movement* (Princeton, NJ: Princeton University Press, 1997)

Rupp, L. J. and Taylor, V., *Survival in the Doldrums: The American Women's Rights Movement 1945 to the 1960s* (New York: Oxford University Press, 1987)

Sayers, J., *Sexual Contradictions: Psychology, Psychoanalysis and Feminism* (London: Tavistock, 1986)

Sicherman, B. and Green, C. H. (eds), *Notable American Women: The Modern Period* (Cambridge, MA: The Belknap Press, 1980)

Scmitt, H. A. (ed.), *U.S. Occupation in Europe after World War II* (Lawrence, KS: The Regents Press of Kansas, 1978)

Scott, J. W., *Gender and the Politics of History* (New York: Columbia University Press, 1988)

Shils, E., *Political Developments in the New States* (The Netherlands: Moulon, 1962)

Siltanen, J. and Stanworth, M. (eds), *Women and the Public Sphere: A Critique of Sociology and Politics* (London: Hutchinson, 1984)

Spelman, E., *Inessential Woman: Problems in Exclusion in Feminist Thought* (London: The Woman's Press, 1990)

Smith, C. and Freedman, A., *Voluntary Associations: Perspectives on the Literature* (Cambridge, MA: Harvard University Press, 1972)

Tent, J. F., *Mission on the Rhine: Reeducation and Denazification* (Chicago: University of Chicago Press, 1982)

Terrell, M. C., *A Colored Woman in a White World* (New York: Arno Press, 1940)

Thompson, E. P., *Beyond the Cold War* (London: Merlin Press, 1982)

Tickner, J. A., *Gender and International Relations: Feminist Perspectives on Achieving Global Security* (New York: Columbia University Press, 1992)

Tilly, L. and Gurin, P. (eds), *Women, Politics and Change* (New York: Russell Sage Foundation, 1990)

Trebilcot, J. (ed.), *Mothering: Essays in Feminist Theory* (Totowa, NJ: Rowman and Allenheld, 1984)

Trommber, F. and McVeigh, J. (eds), *America and the Germans: An Assessment of a Three-Hundred Year History*, vol. 2 (Philadelphia, PA: University of Pennsylvania Press, 1985)

Van Voris, J., *The Committee of Correspondence: Women with a World Vision* (Northampton, MA: Interchange, 1989)

Vogel, U. and Moran, M. (eds), *The Frontiers of Citizenship* (London: Macmillan, 1991)

Ware, S., *Letter to the World: Seven Women Who Shaped the American Century* (New York and London: W. W. Norton, 1998)

Weed, E. (ed.), *Coming to Terms: Feminism, Theory, Politics* (New York: Routledge, 1989)

Wesley, C. H., *A History of the National Association of Colored Women's Clubs: A Legacy of Service* (Washington, DC: Mercury, 1984)

White, L. C., *International Non-governmental Organizations: Their Purposes, Methods and Accomplishments* (New Brunswick, NJ: Rutgers University Press, 1951)

Whittick, A., *Woman into Citizen* (London: Athenaeum with Frederick Muller, 1979)

Willetts, P., *'The Conscience of the World': The Influence of the Non-Governmental Organizations in the UN System* (London: Hurst, 1996)

Wittner, L. S., *Rebels Against War: The American Peace Movement 1941–60* (New York: Columbia University Press, 1969)

Woolf, V., *Three Guineas* (London: Hogarth, 1938)

Wynn, N. A., *From Progressivism to Prosperity: World War I and American Society* (New York: Holmes and Meier, 1986)

Yurval-Davis, N., *Gender and Nation* (London: Sage, 1997)

Yuval-Davis, N. and Anthias, F. (eds), *Woman-Nation-State* (London: Macmillan, 1989)
Yergin, D., *Shattered Peace* (Boston, MA: Houghton Mifflin, 1977)
Zink, H., *The United States in Germany 1944–1955* (Westport, CT: Greenwood Press, 1957)
Zinn, H., *Postwar America 1945–1971* (Indianapolis, IN: Bobbs-Merrill, 1973)

Articles

Alonso, H. H., 'Gender and peace politics in the First World War', *International History Review*, 19:1 (February 1997)
Baker, P., 'The domestication of politics: Women and American political society 1780–1920', *American Historical Review*, 89:3 (June 1984)
Berkman, J. A., '"I am myself it": Comparative national identity formation in the lives of Vera Brittain and Edith Stein', *Women's History Review*, 6:1 (1997)
Bosch, M., 'Internationalism and theory in women's history', *Gender and History*, 3:2 (Summer 1991)
Bowlby, R., '"The problem with no name": Rereading *The Feminine Mystique*', *Feminist Review*, 27 (September 1987)
Brown, S., 'Feminism, international theory, and international relations of gender inequality', *Millenium: A Journal of International Studies*, 17:3 (1988)
Burton, A., 'Some trajectories of "feminism" and "imperialism"', *Gender and History*, 10:3 (November 1998)
Chatfield, C., 'Concepts of peace in history', *Peace and Change*, 11:2 (Spring 1986)
Christiansen-Ruffman, L., 'Participation theory and the methodological construction of invisible women: Feminism's call for an appropriate methodology', *Journal of Voluntary Action Research*, 14:3 (April 1985)
Collins, C. J. L., 'Women as hidden casualties of the Cold War', *Ms.* (November–December 1992)
Cox, R. W., 'The crisis of world order and the pattern of international organizations', *International Journal*, 35:2 (1980)
Dietz, M., 'Citizenship with a feminist face: the problem with maternal thinking', *Political Theory*, 13:1 (February 1985)
Eagly, A. and Kite, M. (eds), 'Are stereotypes of nationalities applied to both men and women?', *Journal of Personality and Social Psychology*, 53:3 (1987)
Elshtain, J. B., 'Reflections on war and political discourse. Realism, just war and feminism in a nuclear age', *Political Theory*, 13:1 (February 1985)
Freedman, E., 'Separatism as strategy: Female institution building and American feminism 1870–1930', *Feminist Studies*, 5:3 (Autumn 1979)
Goedde, P., 'From villains to victims: Fraternization and the feminization of Germany 1945–1947', *Diplomatic History*, 23:1 (Winter 1996)
Goetz, A. M., 'Feminism and the limits of the claim to know: Contradictions in the feminist approach to women in development', *Millennium: A Journal of International Studies*, 17:3 (Winter 1988)
Habermas, J., 'Citizenship and national identity: Some reflections on the future of Europe', *Praxis International*, 12:1 (April 1992)
Harsch, D., 'Public continuity and private change? Women's consciousness and activity in Frankfurt 1945–1955', *Journal of Social History*, 27:1 (Autumn 1993)
Heineman, E., 'The hour of the women: Memories of Germany's "crisis years" and West German national identity', *American Historical Review*, 101:2 (April 1996)

Hook, S., 'The Communist peace offensive', *Partisan Review*, 51:2 (1984)

Horne, G., '"Myth" and the making of "Malcolm X"', *American Historical Review*, 98:2 (April 1993)

Horowitz, D., 'Rethinking Betty Friedan and *The Feminine Mystique*: Labor union radicalism and feminism in Cold War America', *American Quarterly*, 48:1 (March 1996)

Kandiyoti, D., 'Identity and its discontents: women and the nation', *Millennium: A Journal of International Studies*, 20:3 (1991)

Kuhn, A., 'Power and powerlessness: Women after 1945 or the continuity of the ideology of femininity', *German History*, 7:1 (April 1989)

Laville, H. and Lucas, S., 'The American way: Edith Sampson, the NAACP and African-American identity in the Cold War', *Diplomatic History*, 20:4 (Autumn 1996)

Lewis, J., 'The lessons of the "Peace Offensive"', *Encounter*, 65:2 (July–August 1985)

Lieberman, R., 'Communism, peace activism and civil liberties: From the Waldorf Conference to the Peekskill Riots', *Journal of American Culture*, 28:3 (1986)

Lieberman, R., '"Does that make peace a bad word?": American responses to the communist peace offensive 1949–50', *Peace and Change*, 17:2 (April 1992)

Lynn, S., 'Gender and post World War II progressive politics: A bridge to social activism in the 1960s USA', *Gender and History*, 4:2 (Summer 1992)

Mechling, E. W. and Mechling, J., 'Hot pacifism and Cold War: The American Friends Service Committee's witness for peace in 1950s America', *Quarterly Journal of Speech*, 78:2 (1992)

Meyerowitz, J., 'Beyond *The Feminine Mystique*: A reassessment of postwar mass culture, 1946–1958', *Journal of American History*, 79:4 (March 1993)

Miller, F., 'Feminisms and transnationalism', *Gender and History*, 10:3 (November 1998)

Mitrany, D., 'The functional approach to world organizations', *International Affairs*, 24:3 (July 1948)

Mosowitz, E., '"It's Good to blow your top": Women's magazines and a discourse of discontent 1945–1965', *Journal of Women's History*, 8:3 (Autumn 1996)

Peterson, V. S., 'The politics of identity in international relations', Fletcher Forum of World Affairs, 17 (1993)

Rosenberg, E., ' "Foreign affairs" after World War II', *Diplomatic History*, 18:1 (Winter 1994)

Ruddick, S., 'Maternal thinking', *Feminist Studies*, 6:2 (Summer 1980)

Ruddick, S., 'Pacifying the forces: Drafting women in the interests of peace', *Signs: Journal of Women in Culture and Society*, 8:3 (1983)

Runyan, A. S. and Peterson, V. S., 'The radical future of realism: Feminist subversions of IR theory', *Alternatives*, 16 (1991)

Rupp, L. J., 'Constructing internationalism: The case of transnational women's organizations 1888–1945', *American Historical Review*, 99:5 (December 1994)

Schlesinger, Sr, A. M., 'Biography of a nation of joiners', *American Historical Review*, 50:1 (October 1944)

Snitow, A., 'Feminism and motherhood: An American reading', *Feminist Review*, 40:3 (Spring 1992)

Vellacott, J., 'A place for pacifism and transnationalism in feminist theory: The early work of the Women's International League for Peace and Freedom', *Women's History Review*, 2:1 (1993)

Young, I. M., 'Gender as seriality: Thinking about women as a social collective', *Signs: Journal of Women in Culture and Society*, 19:3 (Spring 1994)

Young, L., 'Women's place in American politics: The historical perspective', *Journal of Politics*, 38 (August 1976)

Zarlengo, K., 'Civilian threat, the suburban citadel and atomic age: American women', *Signs: Journal of Women in Culture and Society*, 24:4 (Summer 1999)

Zeiger, S., 'Finding a cure for war', *Journal of Social History*, 24:3 (1990)

Dissertations

Harrison, C. E., 'Prelude to feminism: women's organizations, the federal government, and the rise of the women's movement 1942–1968', PhD dissertation, Columbia University, 1982

McEnaney, L., 'Civil defense begins at home: domestic political culture in the making of the Cold War', PhD dissertation, University of Wisconsin, Madison, 1996

Whitworth, S., 'Feminism and international relations: gender in the International Planned Parenthood Federation and the International Labor Organization', PhD dissertation, Carleton University, Ottawa, Ontario, 1991

Published conference proceedings

Adams, M., 'The world we live in, the world we want', Records of the International Assembly of Women, South Korkright, New York, October 1946 (Hartford, Connecticut: Stone Book Press, 1947)

'As one! For equality, for happiness, for peace', World Congress of Women, Copenhagen, 5–10 June 1953 (Berlin: Women's International Democratic Federation, 1953)

Index